GETTING INTO MEDICAL SCHOOL

Eleventh Edition

The Premedical Student's Guidebook

By Sanford J. Brown, M.D.

Director, Mendocino Foundation for Health Education
and Premedical Advising
Family Practice and Preventive Medicine, Fort Bragg, California
Fellow, American Academy of Family Physicians

All inquiries should be addressed to:
Barron's Educational Series, Inc.
250 Wireless Boulevard
Hauppauge, New York 11788
www.barronseduc.com

Library of Congress Catalog Card No. 2010037656

ISBN-13: 978-0-7641-4597-1

Library of Congress Cataloging-in-Publication Data
Brown, Sanford Jay, 1946–
    Getting into medical school : the premedical student's guidebook /
Sanford J. Brown.—11th ed.
        p. cm.
    Includes bibliographical references and index.
    ISBN-13: 978-0-7641-4597-1 (alk. paper)
    1. Medical colleges—United States—Admission. 2. Medical colleges—
United States—Entrance requirements. 3. Premedical education—United States.
I. Title.
    R838.4.B76 2011
    610.71′173—dc22   2010037656

PRINTED IN THE UNITED STATES OF AMERICA

9 8 7 6 5 4 3 2 1

Dedication

For Sue, Margot, Gabe, Kristin, Barbara, and Dudley

Acknowledgments

For help with the eleventh edition of my book, I have members of U.C. Berkeley's premed honor society to thank. Daniel Yang spearheaded the project and revised and updated Chapter 6, Rejection and Your Alternatives. Chapter 3, the Medical College Admission Test (MCAT), was ably handled by Preeya Desai. Eric Lu updated the Survival Bibliography and Michael Chang did the same for Summer Programs for the Premed. Arman Zaman undertook revising Chapter 4, Applying to a Medical School—When, Where, and How. All students did a fine job and finished their work on time. I owe you all a debt of gratitude and wish you all success in your medical careers.

I want to thank my editor at Barron's, David Rodman, for his guidance and for assuming responsibility for updating the information on individual medical schools.

I want to thank the AAMC for much of the hard data included in this edition. Also, an acknowledgment to *The New Physician* magazine for permission to use the piece, "Patients' Education," and to the now defunct *Western Journal of Medicine* for the essay, "From 'Doctor' to Physician."

Finally, I want to thank my readers for keeping *Getting Into Medical School* in print for many years. I know from your correspondence that many of you have been successful in your quests to become physicians, in small part from this book, and I find that extremely gratifying. May you all find happiness in your healing art.

Contents

PREFACE   vii

INTRODUCTION   xi

1 Choosing a College, Choosing a Major   1

It's Not Where You Go to School or What You Study, 1 The Myth of the Premedical Major, 2 Getting A's in the Sciences, 3 The Physician As a Scientist, 4 Abraham Flexner and His Flexner Report, 5 Emphasis on the Sciences, 6 What Kind of Doctor Do You Want to Become? 7 Avoid the Extra Science Courses, 9

2 The Premed Syndrome   11

The Premedical Mind, 11 The Premedical Society and the Premedical Adviser, 12 Does Your Adviser Attend the Meetings? 13 Get Acquainted...See What They Write About You, 15 The Premedical Student, 17 The Premedical Syndrome, 19 Failure Is Always a Possibility, 20

3 The Medical College Admission Test (MCAT)   21

The Most Important Criterion, 21 MCAT—a Means for Comparison, 22 The Test, 24 Registering for MCAT and Test Day, 24 Future Changes to the MCAT, 26 How Is It Scored? 26 Preparing for the MCAT, 27 Preparatory Courses, 28

4 Applying to a Medical School—When, Where, and How   33

Where to Apply? 33 How Many Schools to Apply To? 34 When to Apply? 36 How to Apply? 37 Early Assurance Programs, 39 Early Decision, 40 Combined MD/PhD Programs, 41 Cost of Applying, 42 Meeting the Costs, 42 Minority Students, 46 Staying In Can Be Harder Than Getting In, 48 Women, 48 Special Interest Groups, 49 What Makes You Different? 50 Recommendations, 55 AMCAS Letter Service, 58 The Interview, 60 Sample Personal Statements, 65

5 How Medical School Admissions Committees Evaluate Applicants 71

Can the Applicant Make It? 71 Determining the Motivation, 73

6 Rejection and Your Alternatives 77

Rejection and Reapplication, 77 Consider Reapplying, 78 The Post-baccalaureate, 85 Osteopathy, 88 Attending an International Medical School, 90

7 Amazing Success Stories 97

8 The Future of Medicine 119

Appendixes

Appendix I: Internet Advising: Sara's Story   126
Appendix II: Summer Programs for the Premed   169
Appendix III: Directory of American Medical
                Schools   188
Appendix IV: Directory of U.S. Schools of
                Osteopathic Medicine   324
Appendix V: Survival Bibliography   355

Index to U.S. Medical Schools 366

Index to U.S. Osteopathic Schools 370

Preface

It's hard for me to believe that *Getting into Medical School* was first published thirty-seven years ago. When I wrote it, as a senior medical student in 1972–73, I had the motivation of wanting to tell my story—that of an atypical premed who had somehow made it into medical school—to other unusual applicants and aspirants. I remember writing the original manuscript almost nonstop in three weeks—in longhand! (This was before the era of word processing.) It was purely anecdotal. During the next year I added meat to the bones in the form of statistics, quotations, and other relevant data. In 1974, the first edition of *GIMS* was published. Now, I'm delighted to be writing yet another preface—this time for the eleventh edition. Remaining in print for all these years makes me hope that not a few discouraged premeds have taken heart from my writing, persevered, and succeeded in their quests. I know that many have.

Traditionally, I have used the preface to bring my readers up to date on my professional activities and my attitudes and thoughts about medicine, and have usually ended with a heartening statement about what makes a good physician. To some extent, I still like what I have said. To quote the first edition: "A professor of mine once said, 'What this country needs is fewer MDs and more physicians.' I believe what he meant was that we need more people to take care of the *whole* patient and not just his or her pathology. By that criterion, you don't have to be a great scientist to be a good physician. All you have to be is a good human being." And to quote the sixth: "Let each of you recognize the limits of health, the limits of your skill, and use creativity to find satisfaction in your healing art." Those sentiments still ring true for me; I find no need to change them.

What has changed, however, is the medical profession, and in some ways the change has been dramatic. In 1989, in the preface to the seventh edition, I had this to say: "In the past fifteen years, from when I first began to practice, we have seen a doctor shortage turn into, in some areas, a doctor glut. Malpractice premiums have risen precipitously and forced some practitioners either out of practice or into a different type of practice. There is much less physician autonomy as the solo practitioner is replaced by HMOs, PPOs, and IPAs, as well as forms of group practice. And, on the other side of the equation, the applicant pool to medical schools has been declining for the past seven years. This has a lot of medical school deans and premedical advisers worried, as they fear that the caliber of the entering medical student may be declining. I, for one, do not share this concern.

"Medicine has always attracted people with varied interests. Primarily, there is the desire to serve, to be useful, to make people better through our ministrations. But there is also the need for autonomy, for financial security, for continual busyness, and for mobility. For some people these needs are primary, and these are the people, I believe, who are now making alternative career choices, thereby reducing the applicant pool. What's left is still the stuff fine physicians are made of. Letters I've been receiving from discouraged premeds over the years convince me of it.

"Since *GIMS* was first published, I've received hundreds of letters from my readers. Several years ago, I chose the best of them for a new book, *You Can Get into Medical School: Letters from Premeds.* Some represent fresh inquiries; others are follow-ups from earlier correspondences in which the aspirant either did or did not matriculate into a medical school. The successes and failures, as well as the personal and intimate premedical concerns expressed by readers of *GIMS,* formed a natural sequel to this book. *You Can Get into Medical School* is available from the Mendocino Foundation for $14.99 postpaid.

"Since writing the preface for the sixth edition, my work focus has changed. Always giving lip service to preventive medicine, 1 was finally able to actualize my concept of it through a program called *HealthTrends.* In it, we computer track the changes in our patients' health over time and alert them when they become at risk for a disease. The idea is to suggest lifestyle changes to reverse abnormal trends, thus obviating a future need for medicine. The patient receives a full physical as well as multiple computer printouts on his or her health. All of this information is incorporated into a chart that is the patient's to keep and bring back yearly for updating. In time we hope to accumulate enough of a database on each patient to show him or her graphic depictions of changing health patterns. *HealthTrends* gives substance to the ritual of the yearly physical and has been personally satisfying to me as well. Patients become more than a series of episodic diagnoses; they are seen as total individuals, and a clear picture of how their lifestyles influence their health emerges.

"The computer will become, I predict, as important to the practice of medicine as the automobile and telephone. Not just an instrument for billing and sending timely reminders, the computer will revolutionize the way we practice. Artificial intelligence, databasing, and interactive video are already making inroads into physicians' consciousness. Premeds need to become computer literate. Fluency in Spanish won't hurt either. (Besides not learning how to play the piano, taking six years of high school and college French is the only other thing I rue.)

"Despite the vagaries of economics, there will always be patients and there will always be physicians and other health-care workers to care for them. And no matter how much medicine changes, it will always offer its practitioners challenge, reward, and a sense of purposefulness. I continue to encourage altruistic and inquisitive spirits to choose a medical career. It remains a great profession."

I look at these words, twenty-one years later, and marvel at my prescience while I remain somewhat embarrassed by my optimism. The corporatization of American medicine is now nearly complete. The MBAs are now riding herd over the MDs, and we live in a world of managed care and capitated lives. Physicians no longer work for themselves; indeed, it is virtually impossible to hang out a shingle in many places in America and earn a living. We work in large groups, are paid a salary, and our performance is monitored in myriad ways, with careful attention to the bottom line of costs and profits. Allegiances are now to stockholders, not to doctors or patients. Many of the motivating factors that stimulated bright young men and women to choose medicine in the past—autonomy, high pay commensurate with hard work, and specialty and living area choice—are no longer operant. And yet, astoundingly, there are more applicants to medical school than ever before. Since the tough years of the mid-to-late 1980s, when there were fewer than two applicants for every place in medical schools, there are now nearly three. These numbers are still rising, whereas first-year places in medical schools are static. I remain confounded by these phenomena.

It has never been my intent to convince my readers to opt for medicine. That's a personal choice. Once committed, it has been my intent to provide you with the best possible advice. That is what this book is all about. It has been my custom to bring you up to date about my own medical practice and offer some predictions for the future. This year I am not so sanguine.

I continue to be a solo practitioner providing fee-for-service medicine in a rural area. But now I feel like a dinosaur rather than a maverick. I am a preferred provider for many insurers, which simply means that I have agreed to accept their fee schedules to retain my patients. I still consider myself self-employed, as I have to pay my own overhead, but have organizations willing to purchase my practice and render me an employee. It's tempting, but it's not why I went into medicine.

I have now been in practice for thirty-eight years, time enough to see several generations of patients. *Continuity of care* is not just a phrase; it's real and it's rewarding. My patients consider me not only their doctor but their friend, and it's given me great pleasure to age along with them while being afforded the privilege of knowing them and their families so well. I fear for the doctor-patient relationship in the way medicine is now being practiced.

My wellness program, *HealthTrends,* has entered its twenty-third year and continues to delight. I have watched many of my patients make positive changes in their health because of the information they have been fed back, both in their charts and on screen, year after year. They have stopped smoking, started exercising, and lost weight. They have reduced their stressors. Many drive less, drink less, and consume less salt, cholesterol, and fat. Seeing graphic depictions of their changing health patterns has been a great motivator. As a result, I have fewer sick or chronically ill patients and more time to do the things that I enjoy, like dirt-bike riding, bicycling, playing racquetball, and making firewood. Preventive medicine is good for the doctor as well as for the patient.

I now have an almost exclusively office-based practice. It's always been gratifying for me to have the variety of practice that rural medicine affords. I became a generalist because I was unwilling to waste any of my medical education; living in a small town has let me use most of it.

I again encourage comments and questions from my readers. I am now offering a comprehensive premedical advisory service. Inquiries may be made by letter (P.O. Box 1377, Mendocino, CA 95460) or through e-mail (sbrown@mcn.org). I am primarily interested in you nontraditional, atypical, not-straight-arrow students, but will also consider advising 4.0 science majors with 45 MCAT scores who wind up rejected by medical schools. As the Ann Landers of the premedical world, I welcome all queries. Go ahead and drop me a line!

Introduction

Again this year, almost three times as many premed students will apply to medical school as will be accepted. Even though the number of places in U.S. medical schools has risen steadily from 8,298 in 1960–61 to 13,697 in 1972–73 to 16,686 in 1987–88 where it leveled off, there has been an increase in applicants of more than 500 percent for the same time period. This year it is anticipated that more than 42,000 applicants and reapplicants will apply for fewer than 19,000 places. In 1967–68, 52 percent of applicants were admitted; in 1981–82, 47 percent were admitted; in 1987–88, 59 percent were admitted. This year, fewer than 50 percent will be admitted. These figures show that there simply are not enough places in the medical schools for all who have completed the premedical curriculum and are eager to become MDs.

In the main, I'm not going to use this book to discuss the unfolding transformation of American medicine, although I do feel that I owe my readers a projection for the future. Premedical and medical education is a long tunnel, sometimes lasting over fifteen years, and I would be remiss in not offering some thoughts about what awaits you. I have added a final chapter with that in mind. Primarily, though, I am going to use this book to get you, the premedical student, *out* of the conventional and often erroneous ways of thinking about how to get into a medical school and *into* a more informed and advantageous position. After all, we haven't all had the same advantages, so this book will attempt to be an equalizer.

I am talking also to the premed dropout and the unsuccessful applicant: students from minority groups, borderline nonminority students, those with financial problems, women, students from colleges where there is no premedical adviser, and, generally, students who, for one reason or another, have been discouraged from continuing in the premed curriculum. This book is a survival kit, if you like, for the committed. It is a step-by-step guide that anyone who wants to become a physician can put to use anywhere along the course of his or her premedical education. It will cover, from high school onward, the gamut of decision-making and the traumatic events that every premed must face, ranging from choosing a college and a major to accepting a medical school, and to what to do—short of suicide—if you are rejected by them all. Included are chapters on what it means to be a premed, the Medical College Admission Test, how to apply to medical schools, the way in which medical school admissions committees evaluate applicants, summer programs and preceptorships for premeds, amazing success stories including a lengthy Internet correspondence with a successful applicant, acceptance or rejection and your alternatives, a listing of noteworthy premedical Web sites, and a directory of all U.S. schools of medicine and osteopathy.

Since medical schools cannot absorb even 50 percent of qualified applicants, it may seem paradoxical to take an interest in the students who either drop out of premed or are unsuccessful applicants. My feeling, simply, is that surviving the rigors of the premedical curriculum is not the most important prerequisite for becoming a good physician. Although a medical school's first concern in admitting applicants has traditionally been, "Will they get through?" and not, "What kind of physicians will they make?" I prefer to reverse this order of importance. I do not believe, for instance, that organic chemistry should be the most highly regarded academic experience of the premed. The reason that it is so regarded is that an organic chemistry course may simulate the most rigorous tasks of first- and second-year medical school, and medical school admissions committees feel that anyone who can handle it satisfactorily can pass basic medical sciences. The person with a capacity to absorb a lot of data may be favored by admissions committees over an individual who thinks more abstractly.

Encouragingly, the times have brought change. More and more applicants to medical schools are showing a variety of backgrounds that may include not only a nonscience major but an interim period in their education as well. Some have worked; others have traveled. Many are older applicants. Once having taken the required courses, nearly anyone who is otherwise qualified can go to medical school today.

There is room in medicine for all types of interests. Contrary to popular myth, every doctor is not a scientist who sees patients one minute and makes great scientific discoveries the next. Although most physicians do direct patient care, not every doctor sees patients. Some work for the Public Health Service tracking down sources of contagious disease; others are employed by state and local health departments to run immunization and multiphasic screening programs. Many doctors prefer teaching and academic medicine to private practice, and a few find satisfaction in editing medical journals and in medical illustration. There are currently fifty-odd specialties and subspecialties in the area of medicine, and this number will certainly increase. In the future, more doctors will be involved in planning health care delivery systems on city, state, and federal levels. More young physicians will realize that preventing disease is easier than curing it and will come to consider health education, epidemiology, and community medicine as specialty fields. And with concern for our ecology increasing exponentially with time, environmental and occupational medicine and nutrition can be expected to attract more and more attention. Many doctors now combine their MDs with degrees in law and business.

Medicine today can find a place for artists, photographers, educators, and historians. It needs biomedical engineers and computer programmers, administrators and basic research scientists. Medicine is the meeting ground of the arts and sciences. Its potential is limitless. It welcomes all kinds of people because diversity works against stagnation and aids growth. I mean to encourage all students to consider medicine as a career, not just the biologist, chemist, and physicist, but also the psychologist, sociologist, and economist, the anthropologist, journalist, and philosopher—and, of course, the poet.

CHAPTER 1

Choosing a College, Choosing a Major

M any people know early that they want to be physicians. Some have never wanted to be anything else. Others make their career choices in high school and in college. And there are the few who, like myself, decide on medicine after completing their college education. A sufficiently large number of students settle on medicine in high school to justify treating the choice of a college as the first order of business.

It's Not Where You Go to School or What You Study

It may come as news to some that the undergraduate institution attended carries little weight with many medical schools. You can be accepted into medical school from virtually any accredited college or university, and your own academic credentials are vastly more important than the reputation of your school. It *is* true, however, that some undergraduate institutions are more successful than others at placing their graduates in medical schools. The student working the percentages in applying to college should ask to know the relative rather than the absolute number of graduates admitted to medical school from that institution during the preceding five years.

I suggest that it is foolish to see college merely as a steppingstone to medical school. College can be a unique experience and a great deal more fun than graduate education. So choose your college for reasons other than

1

its premedical program, which you can get anywhere. Attend a small school if you would prefer, or a large school if you want anonymity or an active campus life. Accept a school with an outstanding English or theater arts and drama department. Go to a region of the country where you have never been before. Take your junior year abroad. Experiment.

> **Remember that once you become a doctor, your patients won't care where you went to college.**

People won't even care where you attended medical school or ask about the grades you earned or if you graduated with honors. They will only be concerned that you understand them and their medical problems. So if you use your college years to broaden your base of experience, in the long run you'll be doing your patients a service.

The Myth of the Premedical Major

Wherever you go there are, of course, the exigencies of the premedical program, and I do mean to talk about them. First, however, let us explode once and for all the myth of the premedical major. You cannot go to college and major in premed. Following a premed curriculum means nothing more than taking the basic science courses required by most medical schools. Minimum requirements are usually one year of general biology, one year of physics, one year each of inorganic and organic chemistry—all with lab. Other required subjects vary with the medical school and may include English, mathematics, calculus, and other more specialized science courses.

Medical schools always look at an applicant's science and nonscience cumulative grade point average, with emphasis on the science GPA (into which math grades are averaged). This has numerous implications, for if you are a nonscience major, each science course you take will have a considerable effect on your science average, whereas those majoring in science can do poorly in one course without any devastating effect. On the other hand, it is true that science is a tougher major than either the humanities or social sciences, and science majors applying to medical schools have lower overall cumulative averages than their nonscience major counterparts. What follows from all of this?

Majoring in a nonscience will probably raise your overall GPA and put you in a more advantageous position when seeking admission to a medical college.

Medical school admission committees today welcome the applicant who did not major in science. However, they must be sufficiently impressed with your premedical course grades to admit you.

Getting A's in the Sciences

How, then, can you do well in the required sciences? In the first place, do not make the mistake that many premeds make. I hear students say that a grade of C from school X is the equivalent of a B from school Y or of an A from school Z. This is pure myth. An A goes down as an A and a B as a B. *There are no hard conversion factors in evaluating applicants' grades from different schools* although, informally, some schools are viewed more selectively than others. So if a required premed course is ridiculously hard, or the competition is especially rough, and science is not your strong suit, then do yourself a favor and take the course somewhere else. This is extremely important, because many medical schools will not even look at your application unless you have a B+ (3.3–3.5) average or better in science, as well as overall.

The extremes to which some universities may go to "keep students competitive" is astounding. My own undergraduate school is a case in point. It had early achieved a reputation as a science school, although it had excellent liberal arts departments. Naturally, it attracted many science students—far more, in fact, than it had the faculty or facilities to train. Most of the influx wanted to concentrate in biology, although physics and chemistry also received more people than they could comfortably handle. The situation was somewhat tolerable at the lower course levels, but would have become cataclysmic if all students had been permitted to advance to their junior and senior years with normal attrition rates. To ease matters, all students intending to major in biology and physics, as well as in engineering, were routed first through freshman inorganic chemistry along with all the budding chemists. "Into the valley of death rode the six hundred," including the premeds. I was so intimidated by my school's science department that I waited for the

Department of Earth and Space Sciences to open its doors before I dared fulfill my university's science requirements. When I finally did take premed inorganic chemistry, it was in night school at a local community college.

I do not mean to suggest that your professors are out to fail you, but some departments do believe in making things difficult on purpose, for reasons of either pride or practicality. My advice is simply not to bother with them. Take that inorganic or organic chemistry course in summer school or at a community college. Many of my premedical adviser colleagues feel strongly that premedical requirements should not be taken at a two-year school. I believe that it is appropriate for community college students to be premeds and that biology and inorganic chemistry may be taken there. Naturally, medical schools will want to make sure that students who get A's in community colleges also get A's at four-year schools when completing their premedical courses. I can also emphatically state that a grade of D from Harvard in inorganic chemistry will keep you out of medical school, whereas an A from a community college will not.

The Physician As a Scientist

The emphasis that has been placed on the basic sciences in recent years has given many people the erroneous impression that all doctors are scientists. This is simply untrue, but the evolution of the idea is an interesting bit of medical history. At this point, it might be helpful to examine it and see how the idea of the physician as scientist has evolved and influenced medical school admission policies during recent years.

The first medical schools in this country were those associated with established universities such as Harvard, the University of Pennsylvania, and the University of Maryland. These schools were, for their day, reasonably substantial medical schools with high academic standards.

During the years of the great immigration to this country, many of the newcomers already had a European medical degree, whereas others wished to study medicine in the European tradition after they arrived. In Europe, a physician who had attained any degree of eminence was called *professor.* A European who became sick did not go to a practitioner, specialist, or consultant, but to a professor at some medical center. When an immigrant became sick, he or she, too, wanted to go to a professor. It was part of the European heritage. However, in most states there were no medical schools and consequently no professors.

It wasn't long before groups of physicians began to band together and start medical schools of their own. Probably one of the motives behind this was that these doctors could then hold professorships in their own medical schools, thereby acquiring the title of professor. This type of school, known as the proprietary medical school, was organized for prestige and profit and flourished until 1906, when there were about 160 medical schools in the country. With the exception of those affiliated with the older universities, all the rest were proprietary schools.

In most cases, the proprietary schools had low academic standards and sometimes admitted students without a high school education. Virtually anyone was admitted who could pay the tuition, and when enrollment dropped, the professors went out to solicit students. There were no state agencies to regulate the practice of medicine. Persons attending proprietary schools, as well as those attending some major universities, spent two years after high school studying medicine and two summers of preceptorship with local practitioners. With this meager background, students then went out to practice. The licensure requirement was that the student merely have graduated from any of the medical schools then existent.

Abraham Flexner and His Flexner Report

By the turn of the century, the Carnegie Foundation for the Advancement of Teaching, which had been engaged in activities to improve the quality of teaching in general, employed Abraham Flexner, who was not a physician, to make a survey of medical education in the United States. In 1909, Flexner personally visited every medical school in the country and evaluated the schools on the basis of their requirements for admission, the caliber of their faculty, and the quality of their laboratories and physical facilities. When he finished, he formulated the now-famous *Flexner Report*, which was published by the Carnegie Foundation in 1910.

In this report, medical schools were classified as A, B, or C type schools. Many of the medical schools then operating received a C rating. All of those rated C were proprietary type schools. Following the *Flexner Report*, the states established boards of medical examiners and passed medical practice acts. These boards instituted examinations for medical licensure and said, in effect, that a person was not eligible to take the exam unless that person had graduated from a Class A school. This immediately put the

Class B and Class C schools out of business, so that by 1920 there were only 72 medical schools left in the United States.

It was recommended in the *Flexner Report* that medical schools, in order to qualify for Class A rating, become affiliated with universities that could provide the student with a reasonable academic background and good laboratory facilities. Requirements for admission to medical school quickly included a year of liberal arts education after high school. As time went on it was recognized that, as knowledge in all fields increased, more preparation was necessary.

> Gradually admissions requirements were changed from one to two years of college, from two to three years, and finally to four years.

Today almost all medical schools require that applicants have a bachelor's degree.

Emphasis on the Sciences

Another change occurred. As emphasis for admission to medical school was placed more and more heavily on the scientific disciplines, premedical programs in the liberal arts colleges came to center around comparative vertebrate anatomy, general biology, physics, and chemistry. By the 1930s, the broad liberal arts education fostered by the old premedical programs was subdued almost totally by scientific training. This attitude lasted until after World War II. Then, in the late 1940s and early 1950s, medical schools began to encourage applicants to take a fourth year and use it to study the humanities. For a short while, students began choosing non-science majors. Few who wanted to go to medical school intended to have careers in full-time scientific research or academic medicine.

In the late 1950s, the wheel again came full circle. There was an explosion in scientific and technical information beginning with Russia's *Sputnik* in 1957. Suddenly vast amounts of money became available for research. Medical schools, supported by government grants, hired more faculty for full-time research positions. Aided by government money, medical schools expanded their laboratories in the basic sciences. Less attention was paid to community medical care; medical schools began to favor students who had majored in biology or chemistry, with preference given to those who had taken higher-level courses. Premeds responded by studying the more advanced and more difficult sciences, resulting in an upgrading of the preparation of the matriculating medical student. The model for this generation of students became the academic physician who spent 70 percent of his or her time in research and 30 percent in patient care.

The situation remained unchanged until the mid-1960s, when a large number of students in the physical sciences began to apply to medical school with the intent of becoming biomedical engineers. It was the era of the pacemaker and other spectacular technical solutions to medical problems. Then, in 1968, the picture changed again. The majority of young people had turned against the Vietnam War, the poor were becoming increasingly visible, and the inequities in the American way of life stood out glaringly. Premedical students responded by becoming family physicians rather than specialists. Many of the graduates of the 1980s and 1990s were attracted to the subspecialties that have burgeoned from the technological advances of the last three decades—angiography and angioplasty, CT scanning, nuclear MRI, organ transplantation, and the medical laser, as well as computer applications to the medical sciences.

What Kind of Doctor Do You Want to Become?

With myriad alternatives in a medical career, the issue of what to major in is more a question of what type of physician you wish to eventually become and what you might want to do should you *not* get into medical school. If you want a life of medical research, by all means enter medical school with a strong background in the basic sciences. If your interests in medicine are more social, however, then ten years hence an undergraduate major in sociology or economics will probably be more advantageous to you than one in biology or chemistry. And if, like most entering college students, you are undecided, then major in whatever turns you on.

Choose a major according to your strengths, interests, and alternate career objectives. Do you think you'd like a major in music or drama? Does the study of anthropology intrigue you? Would you mind four years of reading great literature or sculpting, drawing, or painting? Do these things! As long as you take the required premedical courses, no college major will handicap you or make you less prepared to perform adequately in medical school. And where (except in college) will you ever again have the chance to study Chaucer, Egyptian hieroglyphics, or pre-Socratic philosophy? College is your opportunity to develop your full potential; use it for just that. Medical school will give you all the science you will ever need to be a competent physician, I assure you. You should enjoy and have ability in science, but that doesn't mean you have to major in it. It is true that nonscience majors usually find the first two years of med school, which is mostly basic science, to be more overwhelming than it is for science majors. However, once into the clinical experiences, which require more problem-solving and communication skills, everyone seems to be on equal footing.

Here's a letter I received several years ago from a premed student who took my advice:

> Dear Dr. Brown,
>
> Since I last wrote to you I've had a diverse and interesting undergraduate experience. Due to various requirements, being an English major and a premed at Harvard has been very challenging because, unlike biology majors whose premed courses count toward their major, I've had few electives. However, I do not at all regret pursuing a liberal arts education before going to medical school. I had the chance to go straight into a six-year medical program but felt my life would be poorer for passing up a four-year undergraduate education and I now know the decision to be an English major was a very good one.
>
> I thank you for not being pragmatic and advising premeds to major in the sciences but instead to try to have the best and most fulfilling undergraduate experience possible. Many of my friends have regretted majoring in the sciences. I don't see how undergraduates can be happy with constantly sacrificing the present for some vague future situation. Medical school should be a priority but not the only one. Undergraduates should keep the big picture in clear view and study what they find truly interesting. They'll probably end up with a more successful college career, gradewise, to boot!
>
> Ed Spillane

According to AAMC's *2006–07 Medical School Admissions Requirements*, for the 2004 entering class, students who majored in one of the physical sciences, mathematics, or statistics had the highest overall acceptance rate to medical school. However, nonscience majors—in fields such as economics and philosophy—had an acceptance rate higher than those who majored in the biological sciences (45.5 vs. 39.9 percent). Anthropology majors had a 53.5 percent acceptance rate; foreign language majors, a 52.7 percent rate; and English majors, a 50.5 percent rate! Interestingly, those who majored in other health professions, such as pharmacy or nursing, had the lowest acceptance rate—26.9 percent. Thus, it is obvious that a nonscience major is not a handicap but more likely an asset when applying to medical schools.

Here are the acceptance rates for the 2009 entering class (see chart below).

2009 Acceptance Rates by College Major

	Applied	*Accepted*	*Acceptance Rate*
Biological Science	21,630	9,141	42%
Humanities	2,041	1,020	50%
Math and Statistics	389	177	46%
Other	7,185	2,993	42%
Physical Sciences	4,676	2,329	50%
Social Sciences	5,110	2,282	45%
Specialized Health Sciences	1,238	448	36%
All Majors	42,269	18,390	46%

In summary, major in whatever you enjoy, and do well in the premedical science courses. Use your college years for personal growth and don't burden yourself with a major that's not intellectually satisfying. Not only will college become a more pleasurable experience, but you're bound to do well in courses that you enjoy and boost your GPA besides!

Avoid the Extra Science Courses

I often hear undergraduates talk about taking science courses that will "help" them in medical school, by which I suppose they mean courses in biochemistry, physiology, comparative anatomy, and the like. It is true that those courses may make the first year of medical school somewhat easier. However, the degree of simplicity of the course must also be seen as directly proportional to the amount of boredom it generates. Coming to med school with an English major, I found my first year truly difficult but quite fascinating, because everything I learned was new to me.

> **Unless you have a genuine interest in scientific material, you are not necessarily doing yourself a favor by taking extra science courses.**

This is only logical. In the first place, you always do one thing at the expense of another. That course in statistics may mean passing up the one in creative writing offered by the novelist in residence at your university. Second, the way a course is taught at one school may be totally unrelated to the way it is handled at another. For example, the freshman biochemistry course at my medical school was so atypical that former biochemistry majors had difficulty passing it. Third, medical schools may not care how many science courses you have taken as long as you meet their requirements and they are convinced you can do medical school work. In addition, some medical schools may not accept credit earned in these courses.

Also keep in mind those skills that will be essential once you become a physician—communications, logic, business, computers, language, and knowing how to work in a multicultural society—when you are searching for electives to take during your junior and senior years.

A survey that appeared in the Winter 1996 issue of *The Advisor* polled fourth-year medical students at nine medical schools and found that 42 percent cited philosophy and 18 percent bioethics as good to exceptional courses for premedical preparation. Science courses came in third with 14 percent. Students were unanimous in advising premeds to get a broad background beyond science courses, take courses for pleasure, and learn how to learn and to solve problems.

What undergraduates fail to understand about medical school is that, with diligence and perseverance, anyone with average intelligence can pass through it successfully.

> **The hardest obstacle to overcome in becoming a physician is getting admitted to a medical school.**

About 60 percent of those applicants considered fully qualified are rejected, whereas fewer than 5 percent of any entering class fails to graduate, and most of these failures are for nonacademic reasons. A friend of mine is fond of asking, "What do they call the person who graduates last in his medical school class?" The answer, of course, is "doctor."

I believe that performance in premedical courses, on the Medical College Admissions Test, or even during the first two years of medical school is no indication of the kind of physician you will become. Your success as a practitioner is more a function of your personality, character, and native intelligence than of your grades. Medicine has always been more of an art than a science. Science is but one of the tools the doctor uses to deliver total care to the patient. It is not the only tool.

CHAPTER 2

The Premed Syndrome

O nce you have decided to opt for medicine, you become a premed. It's that simple. It has nothing to do with joining a premedical club or acquiring a premedical adviser. Nor is it required that you be attending a college or university. It all has to do with consciousness.

The Premedical Mind

Being premed is a state of mind. Some people know when they're five years old, with their first chemistry set or doctor's bag. A friend of mine became a definite premed at age twelve, when his father gave him a copy of *Gray's Anatomy*—unabridged. When I was in college, the last thing I thought I would become was a doctor, so I wasn't a premed until after I graduated.

Most medical schools require completion of at least three years of college—and prefer four—before they will admit you. Many require or prefer that a bachelor's degree be completed prior to entrance. There are special six-year programs for high school seniors leading to the combined BA or BS and MD degrees. For those who wish to pursue them, the American Association of Medical Colleges' *AAMC Admissions Requirements* book offers an entire chapter of information on medical schools offering a combined college/MD program. These are highly competitive. If you're not in any hurry to become a doctor, I would advise spending four years in college and using your senior year for electives to take something other than premedical science courses. Many doctors who spent only three years in college often mourn the loss of that fourth year.

The Premedical Society and the Premedical Adviser

Once you are a matriculated college student, your school may offer facilities and services to assist you. Notably, there will be a premedical club and a premedical adviser. Regarding the former, I can offer the words of Marx (Groucho, not Karl), who said that he would not belong to any club that would accept him as a member. Apart from their annual pilgrimage to medical schools, the value of such clubs is debatable. Joining the club may even make you uneasy, because you will be seeing the same people you regularly compete with in your premedical courses.

It makes no sense for you to join because you think it will look impressive on your record. Also, it is important to remember that these societies are clubs sponsored by the students and are not considered a service of the university. Events they sponsor are open to all premeds and may include speakers on health-care reform, MCAT prep, different areas of medical practice, and even an admissions dean or two from a nearby medical school. On the other hand, the premedical adviser is a service of the university, and ignoring the adviser would be foolhardy, as he or she can be critical to your case.

My own premedical adviser, after hearing my story, asked me what I was going to do when I didn't get into medical school. Fortunately I was obsessed with the idea of becoming a doctor, and since he didn't give me the encouraging counsel I wished to hear, I simply did not hear him. The question of whether or not his advice was good advice never entered my mind. However, when I first realized that his position had no job description, I began to wonder about the premedical adviser's credentials and experience and about what exactly he could do for me that I couldn't do for myself. What follows is a profile of the premedical adviser that answers these questions and may also answer some others that you perhaps have.

First off, premedical advisers are rarely, if ever, physicians themselves. They are almost always faculty members at the university who have taken an interest in the plight of the premedical student. Although premedical advisers can be members of any department, they are most frequently from the science faculty. At some schools, the job is part-time and the adviser puts in a few mornings or afternoons a week without extra pay, although at some of the larger universities, health professions advising has become a full-time job.

The majority of schools have one premedical adviser; some have more than one, and others have none at all. In the latter case, the faculty itself assumes the role of adviser to the premed students. In many places, serving as the premedical adviser may take the place of having to serve on other faculty committees or on the faculty senate. As with most academic committee work, the term of a premedical adviser may be surprisingly short. Or, one adviser may serve for quite a long time and then (possibly in the middle of your own college career) relinquish the post to a fresh recruit. It is important for the student to know how long the adviser has held that post so that it will be possible to evaluate accordingly the advice rendered. Experience at this job is of key importance.

There is no required formal educational process for advisers to go through before they assume their position. The premedical adviser holds no degree or certification for the job, is not licensed, and is not subject to peer review. The adviser is only as good as personal interest and involvement allow. However, a National Association of Advisors for the Health Professions has existed for over twenty-five years and holds yearly meetings for the Northeast, Southeast, Western, and Central regions, as well as a biannual national meeting. The meetings offer a sort of refresher course on the state of education in the health professions and gives the advisers a chance to have their questions answered by the medical school admissions people who attend, as well as to make personal contacts. Matters taken up at the meetings may include how to write an evaluation for a student applying to medical school, current trends in admissions, and up-to-date information on the MCAT, as well as commentary on the way medicine is currently being practiced.

Does Your Adviser Attend the Meetings?

This organization offers its members a quarterly journal, called *The Advisor*, and a between-the-issues supplement. It also has a premedical advisers' reference manual available exclusively to active pre-health professional advisers that supplements the AAMC's *Official Guide to Medical School Admissions Requirements* with information not generally available to premeds. These publications, together with the yearly regional meetings and one national meeting of the association and a health professions advisor list server, constitute the prime opportunities for premed advisers to keep up in the field.

My advice to you is to find out if your premed adviser belongs to this association. If he or she does not, then look for someone who does. This, in addition to experience, is the best way to judge your adviser's reliability. Most premedical advisers will talk to you even if you're not a student at their college, so don't be shy about calling up and asking for an appointment.

It is noteworthy that the NAAHP has several publications for sale to premeds. They are *Medical Professions Admissions Guide: Strategy for Success; Write for Success: Preparing a Successful Professional School Application;* and *The Medical School Interview.* Cassette tapes from the national meetings are also available. NAAHP offers a travel program with discounted airfares for students going to health professions school interviews and the organization has information for students on its Web site **www.naahp.org**. You can also contact the NAAHP at P.O. Box 1518, Champaign, IL 61824-1518, or by phone at (217) 355-0063, or by fax at (217) 355-1287.

The question arises, "What can my premedical adviser tell me that I can't find out for myself?" The core of the premedical adviser's knowledge comes from publications that are readily available to the public. The core book is *Medical School Admissions Requirements,* put out by the AAMC. Included are chapters on selection factors for each school, specific admissions requirements, tuition figures, financial aid information and sources, minority admissions information, combined degree programs, MCAT and AMCAS data, and much more. This book is updated yearly and is truly the official guide. In addition, the adviser receives a newsletter, published by the AAMC, which may have occasional nuggets of information. A very helpful publication is the *Journal of the American Medical Association,* which can be found in most libraries. Each year this journal gives a complete profile of the entering freshman class to medical school. Included are the number of applications and applicants, their GPAs, average MCAT scores, the number accepted and rejected, and pertinent analyses of factors affecting medical school admissions. As far as printed matter is concerned, you can probably lay your hands on as much stuff as your adviser. If you don't feel like digging up your own information, you should feel free to ask your adviser if you can peruse the office files. As far as I know, there are no secret documents there, so I see no reason for objection.

Certainly your adviser can provide valuable help, and if yours is conscientious you may not even have need of this book. Most of the things I talk about—e.g., choosing a major, taking the MCAT, applying to medical school, and facing alternatives—should be covered adequately by your adviser during your four years as an undergraduate. One of the functions of this book is to serve as a primary adviser for students who have none at their school and to offer a second opinion for those dissatisfied with what they have already been told.

Get Acquainted . . . See What They Write About You

Now, it is most important to get acquainted with your premed adviser because most medical schools require a letter of recommendation from the premedical committee, which may be made up wholly or in part by the premedical adviser, and the majority of colleges and universities nationwide offer committee or composite adviser letters of some kind.

Later we will talk about the kinds of recommendations faculty members may write. It is important for students to remember, however, that in most cases these recommendations are not sent directly to the medical schools to which you apply. The premedical committee drafts and sends a composite letter. Though your professors may describe you in the most glowing terms, the *tone* of the committee's letter will clearly depend on how well you are known to the person drafting it—usually the premedical adviser.

The following are two actual letters from premedical committees. They appeared in an issue of *The Advisor* that reported on a symposium of letters of evaluation sponsored by the Western Association of Advisors for the Health Professions. The presentation from which these two letters are excerpted was made by Dr. John P. Steward of the Stanford University School of Medicine. The comments following the letters are Dr. Steward's.

FIRST LETTER:

Premedical Adviser:

    Not much need to add to underscore the fact that _____ is a gem. I enjoyed my first encounter with this very bright lad three years ago when, as a freshman who had already traveled abroad as far as _____ and _____, he was then plowing through all kinds of advanced courses, displaying the energy and enormous enthusiasm which were to mark every step of his journey through _____. He had come to college imbued with the drive to become a doctor from the earliest age and with the simplest of explanations: "I just want to be able to help people." His next greatest ambition was to get back to Europe, to get to know people; and he has done every kind of menial labor, even jerking sodas, to earn the money. Sure enough, the next summer found him working for _____ in _____, and now he has only just returned from the greatly enriching experience of a junior year abroad where he was registered in school exactly the same as _____ students, not as a foreigner, in an experimental center in _____, a development of the University of _____, but the cosmopolitan life has in no way diminished his single-minded con-centration on becoming a physician. Furthermore, it is perfectly clear that here is a young man who has pursued the epitome of the lib-eral arts program not in the least with any idea of minimizing the sciences, as his very high standing in all the required courses testify—he is only saving them up for medical school! It is not possible that we will be presenting a stronger or more engaging candidate this year—a star.

COMMENTS ON LETTER:

The helpful parts of the letter were . . . the way the premedical adviser summarized his candidate. This excellent letter is typical of letters coming from this academically excellent institution.

SECOND LETTER:

Premedical Adviser:

_____ is enrolled in the premedical curriculum of this University and is applying for admission to your School of Medicine. He is expected to graduate with a Bachelor's Degree in June 1971.

At the present time, _____'s cumulative grade point average is 3.64.

The premedical faculty of the College of Science acts as a committee to pass on applicants for recommendation to medical school. After due consideration of his case, the five members of _____ committee were unanimous in recommending him as an excellent candidate.

One committee member commented that he had a pleasant personality—on the quiet side—and would expect him to be in the upper half of his class.

The possible ratings given to applicants who receive the recom-mendations of the Committee are not recommended, fair candidate, good candidate, excellent candidate.

COMMENTS ON LETTER:

This is an instance where we have no choice but to say here is a student that, as far as we are concerned, we don't care what his GPA is, and we don't want to know anything else about him if this is all the premedical adviser could say.

Again, we will interpret what you write in light of the fact that we assume you have done your best.

Once you have developed a personal relationship with your adviser, you can be sure that the letter of evaluation will show the admissions committees that you're more than just another premed.

The Premedical Student

Having discussed the premedical adviser, the next order of business is the premedical student. What do other people see in him or her? What is the student's self-image?

Peer group evaluations usually label premed students "grade-grubbers," "gunners," or "greasers," depending on the part of the country they come from. Other disparaging adjectives used for the premed are ruthless, antisocial, narrow-minded, insincere, cutthroat, dull, and brown-nosing. On the other hand, students who see the premeds more as a benign than as a malignant force have described them as idealistic, dedicated, and brilliant.

Among faculty members the premedical student is usually highly regarded. Unfavorable comments from this group are that premeds are more concerned with grades than subject matter and are not fully interested in participation in the whole college experience. On the favorable side, professors often remark that premeds are desirable students who make many contributions to the extracurricular program of their colleges.

What of the premed's own self-image? Certainly many students exhibit elitist tendencies—all the more so the longer they remain premeds. Others, for whom the curriculum is an ordeal, see what they are sacrificing in time and may actually feel relatively deprived when comparing themselves with their classmates. Still others may have no self-image at all connected with being premed. In the true democratic spirit, they do not see themselves as fundamentally different from their peers. At the core, though, if the premed is motivated by a desire to aid others, by a need for self-gratification, for financial security, or for power, prestige, knowledge, or a challenging and varied career, that student is likely to feel good about what he or she is doing and to have a positive self-image. If, however, the student has an unsatisfied, subliminal yearning to be a physical education teacher but a parent in the medical profession is calling all the shots, then that student is not going to be very happy as a premed or in medical school.

Consider this letter that I received several years ago from the anxious father of a premed:

> Dear Dr. Brown,
>
> Sorry to bother you, but I need the favor of your advice. My daughter is a premed in her junior year at Cornell University. She made the very mistakes in her first two undergraduate years that you have advised to avoid in your book.
>
> She was brilliant in her high school studies even though she began school in this country in the eighth grade (we immigrated from India about eight years ago). She got accepted at Cornell University as an Early Decision student.
>
> At Cornell she took a chemistry major. She thought this would help her get admitted to medical school. This involved taking higher chemistry, math, and physics courses. She got a C in chemistry, C+ in physics, and B in math. Her grades in nonscience subjects are B+. Her grades in biology average B.
>
> In her junior year she changed her major from chemistry to microbiology and she did better academically last semester. She wants to repeat some courses to raise her GPA but she is being advised that, after completing higher science courses, she should not retake lower courses (although the lower courses meet the requirements of medical college and her new major).
>
> We shall appreciate your advice and guidance in the matter as we are totally ignorant of the system in this country. We do not mind if she spends an extra year repeating her courses.
>
> Raj Mulati

Although I can appreciate this father's concern, I somehow wonder why this letter didn't come from his daughter. I am always suspicious of queries that come not from the premedical student themselves but from family members or friends. I ask myself, what is the source of this person's desire to study medicine? Is she self-directed or other-directed? Is she pursuing a premedical program because she wants to be a physician, or just to please her parents? Admissions committees ask the same questions. Studies show that attrition among medical students has more to do with motivation than any other single factor. If a person genuinely wants to become a physician, the medical school curriculum is a minor obstacle. The major obstacle is getting into medical school in the first place. Academically, medical students are sound. But if a physician parent is pressuring a son or daughter to follow in their footsteps, or a parent wants a physician in the family and that student would rather be sailing, then flunking out is a real possibility. My medical school classmates were not geniuses; they were hard workers. Medical school involves long hours, tedious work, and requires a high degree of personal sacrifice. With proper motivation, it can also be highly rewarding and a lot of fun.

The Premedical Syndrome

For those who don't genuinely want to become doctors, the premed curriculum, not to mention medical school, will be sheer hell. To those at peace with themselves, it can be a joy. Yet some students who genuinely want to study medicine are not at all at peace with themselves, and they let the rigors of the premed curriculum interfere with their self-development. They suffer from what I call the premedical syndrome.

The affliction is readily diagnosed. On any college campus, those suffering from the premed syndrome are the students who look as if they've been in a pressure cooker. Worn and haggard, but very determined, they are the last to leave the library at night and the first to arrive in the morning. They don't go out much, unless there's a lecture on diabetes or heart disease. Their extracurricular activities consist of membership in the premedical society and flipping a Frisbee for physical fitness. Artistically, all of their drawing is done with a number two lead pencil on IBM sheets. Musically, they are satisfied with AM radio. Ask them to demonstrate or sign a petition, and they say, "What, and blow med school?!" Psychologically, they are anal-retentive types who make up daily schedules so they won't forget anything.

> **Their lab notebooks are impeccably neat. Major headings are underlined in red, minor ones in blue.**

They never miss a class without getting the notes. All homework assignments are handed in on time. Before examinations they study incessantly, develop a tachycardia, and become diaphoretic. This anxiety is theoretically linked with an impending sense of doom, but the symptoms promptly abate after they "ace," "gun," or are "all over" the exam. If they do poorly, they are miserable and hard to live with.

The syndrome is marked by exacerbations (failures) and remissions (successes) culminating in a crisis (acceptance or rejection). The individual may recover completely (is accepted), be left with permanent residual damage (is rejected), or may pass into a carrier state (reapplies again the next year).

This was written in gross caricature, of course. All the same, it is not hard to see why the premed is maniacal in the pursuit of medicine. In our society the premedical student runs a particular risk and has far more to lose than any other pre-professional. Of all the professions, none turns away qualified applicants as frequently as does medicine. In addition, one quarter of your college career will be spent taking courses that, should you complete them successfully, will serve only to qualify you for admission into a medical school. Contrast this situation to law, for which no specific academic preparation is required of aspiring students.

The premedical student may have majored in science with no intention of becoming a scientist, or studied literature without any desire to teach. The primary goal is medicine, and unless prepared for the possibility of not gaining admission to professional school, the student may have nothing at all on which to fall back.

Failure Is Always a Possibility

The sad fact is that the students who are not admitted have most probably lost out not because they are at fault, but because the system cannot absorb them, even though they may be competent, sincere, and dedicated. There are alternatives for the rejected applicants, and I will be talking about them later; however, *the ambitious pursuit of medical school acceptance is not a guarantee of success.* If you are prepared to make the commitment and to cope with possible failure and uncertainty about the future practice of medicine, then read on. Otherwise, if you haven't already marked up the pages, see if you can't get some money back at the bookstore.

CHAPTER 3
The Medical College Admission Test (MCAT)

The Most Important Criterion

Besides your GPA there is probably no single more important criterion for admission to medical school today than your performance on the Medical College Admission Test (MCAT). Because it is hard for admissions committees to rate one college against another, the MCAT provides a level standard by which all candidates may be compared. The MCAT is one path in the admissions process that everyone must follow. Virtually all schools require you to report MCAT scores.

Now, if you have been anything other than a superior undergraduate student, the MCAT is especially for your benefit. It is your chance to show off and show up all those compulsive premeds who study incessantly and give you a guilty conscience for going out and having a good time. Even if you have a borderline GPA, high scores on this exam will indicate to medical schools that you have the potential to do work that will be up to their standards. On the other hand, low MCAT scores from a student with a high GPA might indicate someone who has reached his or her limits in college and may not be able to handle the more difficult workload of medical school.

After all, don't you spend countless hours studying to boost your grade point average? How much time have you spent to assure yourself high scores on this all-important test? It is a fact that your performance on this exam will help or hurt you as much as that GPA you sweated for during your entire college career.

MCAT—a Means for Comparison

By now, I hope you are wondering why the MCAT is of such great consequence and what you can do to be ready for it. To begin with, you must realize that in selecting applicants, medical schools are eternally looking for the single most consistent predictor of medical school success. In the past, success has correlated most reliably with GPA, but using grade point averages has caused two major problems. One is that grades are not always comparable from college to college. Any attempt to evaluate institutional rigor and grade inflation is informal at best. Admissions committees may err at the extremes—either by assuming more differences between schools than actually exist, or by not accepting the fact that colleges actually do differ in their academic standards.

The second difficulty with grade points has emerged more recently: a modification of the grading system at many universities, with evaluations replacing letter grades as a more meaningful way to assess a student's ability. Indeed, this pass-fail trend has been adopted by some medical schools, with the result that many have done away with class rankings and today operate exclusively on a satisfactory-unsatisfactory grading system. At this point, however, medical schools feel justified in using nonletter grades because, by the process of selection, they have prejudged the student to be capable of becoming a physician and see little advantage in continuing to foster a competitive atmosphere. However, many medical schools are trying to incorporate a high pass and a low pass in their grading system. The reason is that greater distinction is needed in monitoring medical student performance in response to competition for residency programs. On the undergraduate level, these changes may be beneficial to the students seeking self-improvement, but they have made the task of selecting among applicants to medical school increasingly difficult.

To briefly recap, medical school admissions committees must consider whether the grade itself is a valid measure of the applicant's performance. If the applicant presents a "pass" instead of a letter grade, the task of evaluation is that much harder, since what constitutes satisfactory completion of the course is usually not described on the transcript.

When admissions committees finally do lose faith in the GPA as a means of selecting students who are bright enough to graduate from a school of medicine, there will be only one objective criterion left—the MCAT. It will be the last bastion of objectivity left to the medical school, the only means by which applicants may be differentiated in an impartial manner.

Although it is unfair, the initial selection of medical students by factors other than grade point averages and MCAT scores poses other logistic difficulties. Picture the dilemma in the modern medical school's registrar's office. Every year four to six thousand applications arrive for one to two hundred freshman class places. How to sort them out? Clearly, there are two alternatives. Either you can have an admissions committee of seventy-five to one hundred people so that each applicant will get personal attention, or you can feed GPAs, MCAT scores, and lesser factors into the computer and review only those applicants who make a certain cutoff. The former approach happens at a minority of medical schools. The latter method is more universal, for obvious reasons. Large admissions committees are unwieldy; smaller ones function more easily. Consensus is easier to reach, and decisions among applicants can be made more quickly. But small committees do not have the time to read through thousands of applicants—hence, the initial, nonpersonalized screening.

Now, if students are going to be judged initially by a computer, there must be a way to turn their academic achievements into a score. A formula is devised which varies from school to school. Essentially, grades are weighed along with MCAT scores. Some college years may be weighed slightly more than others (junior over freshman) and perhaps some majors over others or some colleges over others, but this is minor compared with GPAs and MCATs. Standardized test scores give medical schools an impartial way to rate students from different schools, with different majors, of different races and sexes. For all their differences, these premeds arrived at a testing center at the same time to sit through an all-day marathon exam that is designed ultimately to lend an air of fairness to the decision of who does and who does not get into medical school.

I am no fan of the MCAT. I think it is basically unfair because it favors students who are good at taking tests (although it also gives the applicant from Podunk U. a better chance). It does not differentiate between good and excellent medical students and sheds no light on an applicant's suitability to be a physician. The only purpose it serves is to make the admission committee's job easier. And it is also in the proprietary interest of the AAMC, which owns and writes the MCAT and keeps the fees.

Rather than rant about MCAT's imperfections, it would be simpler to accept the reality that taking the MCAT, like death and taxes, is inevitable for anyone wanting to attend a U.S. medical school. As can be observed in the following sections, the exam has changed and will continue to change as more people demand that it becomes more relevant to the kinds of physicians we would like to produce. But for now it is important to do well enough on it to be invited to a personal interview, where an admissions committee member can see more of who you really are.

The Test

Although the test is scheduled for five and a half hours, the actual test-taking time is four hours and twenty minutes. The rest of the time is for a tutorial, three breaks, the void option, and a satisfaction survey. As of 2007, the MCAT has been administered entirely as a computer-based test. The computer-based test is identical in content to the paper-and-pencil-based test; however, it requires the examinee to complete the entire test on the computer. The exam has four components: verbal reasoning, physical sciences, a writing sample, and biological sciences. Seventy minutes are allotted for each 52-question science section, one hour for 40 verbal reasoning questions, and 60 minutes for the two writing samples. The verbal reasoning section does not test for subject matter knowledge; all the information needed to answer the questions is provided in the passages. It is meant to test critical thinking and reading comprehension. The science sections, on the other hand, do assume knowledge of the premedical science requirements, even though data may be presented in graphs, tables, or charts. The essay section is meant to evaluate applicants' writing skills. Two written essays are required; neither is about why you want to be a physician or on the technical aspects of the sciences. Rather, they are on social, cultural, or emotionally charged issues and are not meant as much to elicit a right answer as to see how you think and organize your thoughts. On a past MCAT, for example, test takers were asked to consider these two statements—*Price is not necessarily a reflection of value* and *In politics, good intentions cannot justify bad actions*—and write two essays explaining what these statements meant. Another statement I wish the AAMC would consider using is *The best test takers do not necessarily make the best doctors!*

Registering for MCAT and Test Day

As a result of the transformation of the MCAT into a computer-based test, the AAMC is able to administer the exam at a higher frequency. Throughout the year, the AAMC offers the MCAT at least 25 times. Depending on the test date, exams are offered as morning administrations (8 a.m.), afternoon administrations (1 p.m.), or two administrations (8 a.m. or 2 p.m.). You can register for the MCAT on the AAMC Web site, **www.aamc.org/ students/mcat**. There are times when students still do not feel prepared for the MCAT, despite the fact that their test dates are quickly approaching. In such instances, there is no need to panic because the AAMC allows you to switch your test date within two weeks of your scheduled exam. The AAMC charges $55 each time you change your test date and/or location.

Many examinees wonder what they should and should not bring to their test sites. At the test center, you will be provided with scratch paper, pencils, and noise-canceling headphones. One item you should not forget to bring with you on test day is a government-issued form of identification (e.g., a drivers license, passport, etc.) with your photograph on it. Without this, you will not be able to sit for the exam. When you arrive at the test center, you will also be issued a locker to place snacks or other belongings for safe keeping.

When you register for your exam, you will be provided with procedures for your test date. The AAMC encourages you to arrive at the testing center approximately thirty minutes early. This is because the check-in process is quite time-consuming, since each test taker needs to be seated for the exam individually. Thus, since all the examinees do not start the exam together, if you have an emergency—such as being stuck in unexpected traffic or having your car break down—do not panic because you will still be able to sit for your exam. Unnecessary stress will only hinder your performance. That is not to say, however, that you should idly take your time making it to your exam. In fact, it is advised that you scope out the test center the day before your exam so you know precisely where you are supposed to go and do not have to worry about following directions to an unknown location on test day.

At the close of your exam, you will be provided with the option to either have your exam scored or to cancel your exam. Be careful when marking your choice. The AAMC will have your exam scored within 30 to 35 days of your test day. You will be able to check your scores on the AAMC Web site. For exams taken post-2003, your scores will be released automatically to AMCAS.

Future Changes to the MCAT

The AAMC is currently reviewing the science and research methodology and behavioral science content of the MCAT. It has administered surveys to faculty, students, and residents of U.S. and Canadian medical schools, asking them to rate the importance of topics in the areas of biology, general chemistry, organic chemistry, physics, biochemistry, and cell/molecular biology. The AAMC hopes to use this data to determine the material that should appear on future MCAT exams.

Following its current review, the AAMC will turn its focus on developing a test that will assess higher-order thinking skills. According to the AAMC, its goal is to "develop conceptual frameworks for testing critical analysis, scientific reasoning, and other skills and competencies on the future exam." Additionally, the AAMC is exploring ways to examine personal characteristics and skills in admissions through its Innovation Lab, through which the AAMC hopes to discover methods to measure integrity, altruism, dependability, and other personal characteristics.

The AAMC is currently considering the idea of adding a Communication Skills section to the MCAT. According to the AAMC Web site, if this section is added, "it would be a computer-based test, administered as a set of video scenarios followed by questions in a number of different question formats" **www.aamc.org/students/mcat**. Examinees would be asked to respond to the scenarios—played out in a medical environment—using opinion rankings, true/false, or multiple-choice answers. While the effectiveness of adding this section is still under research, the AAMC finds it necessary to put emphasis on the importance of interpersonal skills within the medical world. The AAMC Web site states that "with the growing emphasis on humanism and professionalism in medicine . . . 126 schools currently teach and assess communication skills in the first two years of medical school, either as separate required courses or as part of a required course." Adding this section would also allow admission committees to evaluate applicants' non-academic attributes beyond the personal interview. According to the AAMC Web site, this change would not take effect until 2014 at the earliest.

How Is It Scored?

According to the *MCAT Student Manual*, "your total score is a reflection of your right answers only. This means that a wrong answer will be scored exactly the same as a no answer." In other words, do not leave any space blank; answer every single question, even if you have to guess. You will not be penalized, so the best policy is to fill in every answer space. This is crucial to remember.

The scores are reported on a scale ranging from 1 (lowest) to 15 (highest). Raw scores are converted to a score on the 15-point scale. Let's say you get 44 out of 52 questions correct on one section; this would probably convert to an 11 or 12 on the scale. In this manner, even though there might be a slight difference in the raw scores among several students, their interval score (1 to 15) will be the same.

The essay sample is scored on an alphabetic continuum of J through T, with T representing the clearest, most coherent, and best organized writing. Although scores among accepted applicants vary with race/ethnicity and sex, most students will have to score 9s or better and P or better to remain competitive for medical school. However, the range of acceptable MCAT scores varies from school to school.

Preparing for the MCAT

To the question "Can I prepare for the MCAT?" the answer is an emphatic YES. Some of the ways to prepare are obvious, and you probably already know them. If you are at all conscientious, you may already have purchased one of the books that have questions simulating the MCAT. Those I have seen pattern their questions after the actual MCAT and should give you a good idea of what to expect. A few tips—start using these books early (don't wait until a week before the exam) and look up the things you do not know. Get into a routine of doing a number of pages or questions each day and stick to it. Once you are comfortable with the types of questions asked in each section, it is advisable to take practice tests using the allotted amount of time available in an actual testing situation. This way, you can see where your weaknesses are and what areas you need to focus on. Computer-based practice tests can be downloaded from the AAMC Web site at **www.aamc.org/students/mcat**. This kind of discipline, incidentally, will also get you through medical school.

Many students feel the need to take additional, advanced science courses to further prepare for the MCAT. However, while this may increase a student's general science knowledge, it will not necessarily lead to an increase in MCAT scores. The online *MCAT Student Manual* states that the MCAT tends to test one's problem-solving skills using basic scientific concepts rather than testing for rote memorization of more advanced scientific topics. As a result, an effectively organized program of courses in the basic premedical requirements, coupled with the ability to comprehend and interpret fundamental scientific data, are the most valuable tools for success on the science-based portions of the MCAT. However, courses in the humanities and composition may help you prepare for the verbal reasoning and writing sections, respectively. Any exercise that fosters expository or argumentative essay-writing will be of benefit in the writing sample section. Similarly, the more practice you get at reading and analyzing works of literature, the better you will fare on the verbal reasoning section of the MCAT.

It is a very good idea to take this exam as seriously as you took organic chemistry. If need be, pretend that the MCAT is simply another premed course in which you must do well in order to get into medical school. It would be wise to start your systematic review procedure about six months before you plan to take the real thing. Get psyched up early and build up your confidence so that you can perform really well on the test.

Preparatory Courses

There is currently much controversy surrounding the merits of taking a special prep or cram course for the MCAT exam. Inasmuch as these types of commercial courses are expensive and time consuming, you really have to be seriously committed to doing well on the exam.

However, the MCAT preparation centers can help you prepare for the exam in one very important way—building confidence. If you've paid good money for a course, then you will force yourself to study and review your notes. In this manner you will increase your confidence because of a sense of preparation and knowing that you are not facing the test cold. If you are confident in your own performance, this will decrease the anxiety level that accompanies the MCAT, and your scores are bound to be higher. Remember, it is a two-way street. The prep courses won't help you if you don't give the necessary hours to review and to do practice problems.

Data from the AAMC, makers of the MCAT, shows that review classes have no statistically significant impact on students' scores, suggesting that the student can successfully prepare for the test without extracurricular MCAT courses. In other words, all of the material covered on the MCAT should have been taught in "pre-med" undergraduate courses. Nevertheless, MCAT preparation classes may help some students who require help in particular areas.

Practice exams allow the student to attack the MCAT more efficiently. Taking multiple tests and analyzing the results will help pinpoint which area of undergraduate coursework that most needs review. Though the AAMC sells practice tests, it can prove difficult for the student to replicate the exact environment of test day. Since understanding the routine of test day can greatly improve the chances of success, most preparation courses hold diagnostic exams under the same conditions as the actual test. Also, students who do not maintain the best composure during high-pressure tests can use the all-day mock exam to discover an ideal routine for the days leading up to the MCAT (sleep schedule, diet, etc.).

Many companies sell MCAT training products on the Internet. For this reason software review packages (with formats like those provided on the AAMC's MCAT Web site) may seem increasingly attractive. Review courses like Princeton Review and Kaplan cater to different poles of the student's preparation. Anecdotally, Princeton Review's classes do not focus on test-taking strategy as much as Kaplan's do. Instead, Princeton Review courses examine subject matter in more detail. Both programs give lectures on the format of the test and lecture on how the test is scored. The quality of instruction can vary; PhDs teach some classes and undergraduates teach others. Regardless, all instructors have performed extremely well on the MCAT. Review classes usually cost a hefty fee and demand a great deal of time both in and out of the classroom.

Many summer programs, in addition to research projects, provide lectures for students on MCAT test-taking strategy. Some say taking the August MCAT can ruin the fun of summer; however, MCAT programs included along with summer research programs may at least attenuate the arduous task of reviewing for the most important test on the path to medical school. Considering the difficulty of managing a prep course and a full course load during the spring, summer prep courses look even more attractive.

Lastly, save all your notes and tests from all the important science courses—biology, general chemistry, organic chemistry, and physics. In this way you will be able to review your own material and look over your review sheets from previous study binges. Why waste all that work that you had to do anyway? Good students keep their notes in binders or folders so that they are still legible a year or two later. It wouldn't hurt to retake some of your class tests as practice to help point out to yourself areas in which you may need some extra work. If possible, you may even want to sit in on lectures for concepts that you need to review more thoroughly.

The major preparatory courses are offered in most cities. The local offices of these commercial centers can be found online and in the yellow pages—or just ask around at your college and you will be surprised at how many people have taken the course themselves. In other words, you also should keep your eyes and ears open about what is going on at your school and what the going rates are for such courses. Many times, premed organizations provide their members with discounts for review courses, so inquire with officers in your organizations.

I posed the question of preparatory courses to Dr. Thomas L. Pearce, premedical adviser at the University of Virginia. This was his response:

"Students must not expect that 'review' MCAT courses are really *science review* courses. Usually they are simple courses in examology; they try to teach students how to take a specific test on a specific date, namely the MCAT. This entails teaching test-taking techniques as much as, or more than, reviewing the required premedical sciences. Obviously topics covered in these 'review' courses include premedical subjects, but the emphasis is on taking the test, not reviewing comprehensively the material to be tested.

"I believe that students are just as well off by reviewing *extensively* and *independently* the subject matter on which they will be tested. All undergraduates I have taught these past thirteen years have been experienced test takers, for they have been taking standardized tests for many years. I advise my students to take any 'review' courses they wish; I *never* advise them to rely completely on such courses. I urge them strongly to review all their class notes, every page of their introductory texts in biology, inorganic and organic chemistry and physics, and to buy the science review book written by James Flowers. In addition I urge all of them to reference the *MCAT Student Manual* (available online at **www.aamc.org**), which contains useful information about parameters of subjects on which they are to be tested, as well as *Barron's Medical College Admissions Test,* which contains reviews of subject matter as well as full-length practice exams. There are several books available which contain *only* practice MCATs; generally these are good to use as well, but only after the review studying has been done."

Before leaving the subject of the MCAT, I must take up two frequently asked questions: "When should I take the MCAT?" and "When is it necessary to take it more than once?" There is no doubt in my mind that the

MCAT should first be taken in the spring of your junior year. Unless you plan to pick up a summer course, the additional time afforded by taking the exam in the fall will not be a distinct advantage. In fact, you will lose a great deal of momentum. By taking the MCAT in the spring, you will have your scores by summer, and you can begin to apply to medical schools June 1 for AMCAS schools and often earlier for non-AMCAS schools. However, if you wait until the fall of your senior year to take it, your scores won't be posted until October (it takes 30 to 35 days for you and the medical schools to receive your scores). By the time the schools receive the scores, add them to your file, and move your application on for processing, it could be November or December. By that time, many of your friends will have already had interviews, and some may even have been accepted by a medical school. This will do little to lessen your anxiety. So unless there are unusual circumstances (e.g., you don't decide until your senior year to become a premed), take the MCAT in the spring. Of course, candidates for early admission to medical school (after three years of college) should take the exam in the fall of their junior year.

There is only one situation in which the MCAT should be repeated. This is if you have scored poorly in science and are positive your score was a fluke or know that you can do better. If you were sick on the day of the exam, misunderstood directions, or simply had other things on your mind and were distracted, then by all means repeat the MCAT. But if you have no good excuse for your performance and do not intend to do intensive remedial work, remember that two mediocre scores look worse than one.

The MCAT is a tough exam by anybody's standards. You must do well on the test or your chances of acceptance are very slim. It is better to take the exam very seriously and to prepare for it than to be angry with yourself after having done poorly. Everyone must take the MCAT. The more confident you are, the better you will do. That confidence comes from good study habits and a well-planned review procedure prior to the test.

What follows is a list of academic resources to prepare you for the MCAT. All are available from the AAMC.

1. *The MCAT Student Manual.* An absolute must-have reference.

2. *AAMC MCAT Practice Tests.* Actual MCATs from the 1990s–present.

3. *Scoring the MCAT Writing Sample.*

CHAPTER 4

Applying to a Medical School— When, Where, and How

W e have finally arrived at the really big step. So far all your energies have gone into fulfilling the requirements for medical school acceptance. You have completed most, if not all, of your premedical courses, taken the MCAT, and amassed a portfolio of recommendations from professors. Now it is time to put those grades, test scores, and plaudits to use and to couple them with some hard-core facts. Getting into a medical school is often a matter of having information that other people never bothered to find out or were never told. In this game, a little knowledge is an essential asset.

Like being a good doctor, getting into medical school requires multiple talents. Premedical students often focus on the purely academic aspects of the process, getting good grades and performing well on the MCAT exam. But being admitted to medical school requires more than academic achievements. Each year there are students with outstanding academic achievements who fail to get into medical schools because they never took the time to be informed about the process involved in applying to medical school.

Where to Apply?

In the United States, people who are licensed to practice medicine have either obtained an M.D. degree from an allopathic medical school or have a D.O. degree from an osteopathic medical school. Around 95% of the

33

licensed physicians are M.D.'s, and most medical schools are allopathic medical schools. By and large, allopathic medical schools are more difficult to get into, M.D. degrees are considered more prestigious, and M.D.'s are more likely to be higher in medical field "pecking order." Osteopathic medicine is often described as being more "holistic" and D.O.'s are most commonly found as primary care physicians. Students with high GPA's (over 3.5) and high MCAT scores (over 30) may be justified in considering only allopathic medical schools (assuming that they don't find the osteopathic approach to medicine appealing). Other students should spend some time finding out about osteopathic medicine and consider applying to osteopathic schools.

How Many Schools to Apply To?

MANY! Probably 15–20! Why should you apply to more than one school? Because it dramatically increases your chances of admittance!!! Consider a situation where you have a 50% chance of admittance. Like the winning of a game based on a single coinflip, you have only a one in two chance of "winning" (getting into medical school) if you only apply to one school. But if winning the game requires that you only get "heads" once, then flipping the coin multiple times is a great advantage; if you flip the coin twice you have a 3 out of 4 chance of winning, and if you flip the coin four times then you only have a one in 16 chance of *not* winning. Obviously getting into medical school is not a mere matter of chance, but some aspects of the process are. In any group of applicants there are a few applicants who would always get in everywhere they applied, and a few more that would never get in anywhere they applied. But there is a substantial group in the middle who will get into some schools, but not all. Why? Not because the admittance committees flip coins, but because the schools and committees weigh and evaluate pieces of an applicant's record differently; even within the same school, different committees will be different; even the same evaluator will rank students differently depending on change factors (how much sleep they got the previous night, what the previous application was like, etc., etc.). Your best weapon to guard against the vagaries of the admittance process is to apply to multiple schools.

There are a few rules of thumb to observe when choosing the schools to which to apply. First, it is always advisable to apply to schools in your part of the country, especially to schools in your home state—or, if there is no medical school in your state, to those that have contract agreements for residents of your state. State-supported medical schools are required to give priority to qualified in-state residents, and usually consider only exemplary out-of-state students. At many state schools, those few nonresidents who are admitted may be only or primarily MD/PhD candidates, underrepresented minority students, or students with ties to that state (former residents or nonresidents who are currently attending school in the state). A number of private institutions are also heavily state-supported and lean toward taking in-state residents. Very few schools, in fact, are truly representative of the entire country. Few accept more applicants from any state other than their own, and fewer still accept more out-of-region than in-region enrollees. In 2005, 62% of acceptances went to in-state students.

Consider the schools in your geographic area as primary targets. Always include a number of private schools, particularly those that profess to be geographically egalitarian. However, if you are an underrepresented minority student or a qualified MD/PhD candidate, you may have more of a chance in the nonresident pool. Also be aware that there are a few medical schools whose main mission is to educate underrepresented minorities and educationally or economically disadvantaged students.

Furthermore, with the growing need for physicians over the past few decades in rural and disadvantaged areas, programs targeting applicants who intend on practicing medicine in these underserved communities are on the rise (some programs will even offer scholarships if a student commits to practicing primary care in an underserved community). One of the largest of these underserved educational programs is the University of California's Program in Medical Education (PRIME). The PRIME program began in 2004, when the UC Irvine School of Medicine launched its PRIME program targeting the underserved Latino communities in California. Since then, the remaining four UC medical schools have launched their own PRIME programs: UC Davis's Rural-PRIME program, UC San Diego's Health Equity program, UC San Francisco's Urban Underserved program, and UCLA's Diverse Disadvantaged Communities program. All five of the PRIME programs require five years to complete and offer a combined M.D. and master's degree. Applicants to these programs should be aware that they are extremely competitive (each program only has around 10 to 20 students per class). However, with increasing demand and funding in recent years, the class size of the PRIME program at each UC is likely to increase in upcoming years. Also be aware that some of the PRIME programs may have special requirements (e.g., being fluent in a second language).

For those applicants who aren't California residents or who aren't interested in applying to schools in California, Columbia University in New York offers a program similar to the PRIME program called the Columbia-Bassett Program. Students in this four-year program alternate between attending Columbia's main campus in New York City and Columbia's Cooperstown campus in rural upstate New York. Like the PRIME programs, the Columbia-Bassett program is extremely competitive, so it would be advisable to apply to both the Columbia-Bassett program and the regular program if you are interested in attending Columbia University.

Another area of interest that has become increasingly popular over the past decade is global medicine and health policy. In fact, many of today's medical schools have affiliations with medical colleges throughout the world and provide opportunities for students to study abroad during their rotations in third and fourth year. In particular, the University of Minnesota School of Medicine has agreements with over 25 universities around the world and is a good fit for applicants who have a strong interest in global medicine. Also, the George Washington University School of Medicine offers specialized tracks in both global health and health policy, and its location in Washington, D.C. makes it an ideal choice for students looking to become leaders in the global medical community.

These are only a small sample of programs available for students with special interests in medicine. To find the medical schools that are the best match for you, please check individual school Web sites, and carefully read the information in the annual publication by the AAMC, *Medical School Admissions Requirements for the U.S. and Canada*, which profiles every med school and indicates the numbers of nonresidents admitted and other admissions criteria. Also contact the schools if you have questions regarding the admission of nonresidents.

Above all, apply early!

When to Apply

Medical schools operate on a yearly cycle, with most schools offering rolling admissions. They start accepting applications in June of the year prior to when you would start school (i.e., 14 months before you would start classes). Because admissions are rolling, applicants are at a disadvantage if they apply late; for borderline candidates (and this is a substantial portion of candidates!), a late application keeps them out of medical school, at least for a year. Applying the fall of your senior year is TOO LATE; students should plan to apply in June and doing this requires preparation.

How to Apply

Nearly all allopathic and osteopathic medical schools use online application services known by acronyms: AMCAS (American Medical College Application Service) and the AACOMAS (American Association of Colleges of Osteopathic Medicine). These services make the application process easier than it would be otherwise (although it is still time-consuming). They allow applicants to fill out one set of online forms, and an application is then sent to all the schools to which the applicant wishes to apply. The service has a set fee ($160 for AMCAS in 2010) with additional fees depending upon how many schools you apply to ($30 for each school after the first for AMCAS in 2010). Applicants need to arrange to have their transcripts from all institutions where they took college courses sent to AMCAS/AACOMAS.

The application is straightforward, although it does take some time to complete. You do not need to complete the application all at once; you are able to store in online and log on repeatedly to review, add information, and modify what you have already put down. You are asked for a variety of information relating to coursework and grades, biographical information, awards and honors, extracurricular activities, employment, volunteer work, and medically related experiences. Do not feel that you have to completely fill up the spaces; activities and awards from high school generally are not relevant unless they are sustained through college. A long list may simply reveal that you have done lots of little things, which usually is not as valuable as having done a few things that are more substantial. Having had some medically-related experience is nearly essential, so make sure that you get some! Activities that demonstrate compassion for others and ability to work with and for others are also very significant. The form also asks if you have been subject to any disciplinary action. Be honest here, as the same question should be addressed in the letter from your premedical advisory committee (they are expected to check your standing with the Dean's office). Being subject to disciplinary action does NOT result in an automatic rejection, but being dishonest does! If you have questions, talk with your premedical advisor.

The part of the application that takes the most time is "personnel statement," an essay about you and why you want to be (and would be) a good physician. For most applicants—including applicants who write well—this is a difficult task, because you need to strike the right balance between being too boastful and being too unassuming. Most of all, the essay should be personal and revealing. This is the part of the application that requires the most preparation, and in order to apply in the summer you need to start working on your personal statement in the spring. It is a document that needs to be both inspired and well-edited; while inspiration may come in a flash for some, it is much slower for others and good editing always takes time. PLAN AHEAD!

The AMCAS/AACOMAS application is the "primary" application. After finishing your primary application, you will begin receiving supplementary secondary applications from some or all of the schools to which you applied. These secondary applications will begin arriving at or around June 20, which is the date that AMCAS begins releasing your primary application to medical schools. Similar to the AMCAS application, these secondary applications can be filled out and submitted online (although some schools may require you to print and mail in a hard copy). In the secondary applications, schools will ask for information regarding the courses you took to satisfy their medical school prerequisite requirements as well as additional biographical information. Some schools may also ask for a recent $2'' \times 2''$ passport-size photo, which you should probably get done professionally at a photo shop. Depending on the number of schools you applied to, you should request around 15 to 20 printed copies as well as a computerized jpeg file (you will need to submit these photos throughout your interviews as well).

Like the AMCAS application, the most difficult and time-consuming portion of the secondary applications is the supplementary essays. While these essays are usually much shorter in length than your personal statement (with a word limit of 200 to 250 words), each secondary application on average has two to three required essays and thus will still require a decent amount of time to plan and produce. These essay prompts can range from a variety of topics and subject matters, but by far the most common essay prompt (and arguably, one of the most difficult to answer) is some variation of, "Why do you want to attend our medical school?" While you should hopefully have a general idea of why you want to attend a particular medical school, to answer this essay prompt well you will need to cite specific details about the school's medical program. Thus, you should spend some time researching each school's Web site, reading the school's informational brochures, and if the opportunity presents itself, talking to a current medical school student at that school.

One important fact to note is that in the modern-day application cycle, most medical schools do not screen applicants between the primary and secondary applications (meaning that practically everyone that applies receives a secondary application), and even the schools that do screen primary applications tend to rely on a computerized screening that will automatically send you a secondary as long as you meet a certain GPA and MCAT cutoff. What this means for you as an applicant is that shortly after your AMCAS application is verified and sent out to medical schools, secondary applications will start piling up in your inbox. Thus, you cannot sit on one secondary for too long, and turnaround time becomes an important factor in the secondary application cycle.

Why is a fast turnaround time important? Firstly, the medical school application is a rolling process and consequently, the faster you submit your secondary, the faster you'll get an interview and the faster you'll potentially get an acceptance (interviews begin around September for the majority of schools and you can receive your first acceptance as early as October 15). Having an acceptance early in the cycle will not only make you feel good, but it will also potentially save you a lot of money because you can begin to narrow down your list of schools and be more selective about what interviews to attend. Also, some admissions committees may consider the turnaround time of your secondary when reviewing your application, and a turnaround time of a month or even a few weeks can raise a red flag that you're actually not that interested in their school.

However, do not sacrifice quality for the sake of a quick turnaround! While you shouldn't be spending weeks and weeks on one secondary, you also don't have to click "submit" within a day of a receiving your secondary. A good turnaround target to shoot for is three days, but if you need more time to write a solid essay it is all right to spend a bit more time. In the end, a powerful, well-written secondary essay will have a much bigger impact on an admissions committee than a quick turnaround time.

Early Assurance Programs

A number of schools offer programs that admit exceptional students during or after their sophomore year and some schools even offer eight year programs for students straight out of high school. These programs have the allure of assuring a student that they are into medical school early, and some have the benefit that they allow the student to skip the MCAT exam. Some of the programs encourage accepted EA students to be more adventuresome in selecting courses, since their GPA is no longer critical to admittance; however, some EA programs actually discourage this by setting rigorous GPA standards that must be maintained or the students will lose their "assurance." Competition for EA acceptance is intense because there are very few early assurance spots. As a consequence, the accepted students are students who would have no trouble getting accepted, probably at some more distinguished schools, had they waited and applied in the normal manner. For most students these programs are probably not worth the effort; however, for a few students it may be a desirable program.

Early Decision

With reference to early application, some students may wish to participate in the Early Decision Plan (EDP). With this program, highly-qualified students with a strong preference for one particular school may apply to that single medical school by the August 1 EDP deadline and await, hopefully, an acceptance by early fall. This is a binding agreement—if you are accepted, you must attend that school and cannot apply anywhere else. Because of the early deadline, it is also necessary to have taken the MCAT prior to August.

The EDP has several advantages. For the successful student, it means the heat will be off by the beginning of the senior year. It is also a tremendous savings of dollars that would have been spent applying to other med schools, and you are in a small (although very competitive) applicant pool. At some schools, candidates who are not accepted EDP are automatically deferred to the regular decision pool and even given a second set of interviews; thus, you are looked at twice. To the medical schools, it represents savings of both time and paperwork, because EDP students would otherwise have applied to an average of 13 schools each, and, as most EDP candidates are highly qualified, their applications would have been processed in detail. It also gives the med schools a chance to select some top candidates who might otherwise get away from them if those candidates applied to other schools.

On the other hand, there are several limitations to the EDP program. The first is that, if accepted by the school applied to, the student is obliged to go there and may not apply elsewhere. The big disadvantage, however, is that the applicant is not certain of admission until October 1 of their senior year and may not apply to any other schools before that date. Thus, the rejected EDP applicant will be applying late to other schools. There are 94 medical schools that offer EDP.

It is important to weigh your choice of applying EDP carefully. If you feel you are competitive for EDP at the school you have chosen and that school is truly your first choice, then go for it. But have your backup list of schools ready to go in case you are not accepted EDP. If you do not get accepted EDP, you will need to quickly get out your applications to the other schools, and even then you will be initiating your application quite late for some. With the current large number of applicants, this can truly be a disadvantage. Some private schools (where your chances might be the best after your state/regional institutions) are currently receiving 10,000 or more applications. Applying late in those pools can be a problem. You may wish to check with some of the other schools you are considering to see how much of a disadvantage this would be. Note: Some state schools require nonresidents to apply through the EDP.

Combined MD/PhD Programs

Combined MD/PhD programs are intended for students who are seriously committed to a career in research. A competitive applicant should have excellent MCATs and GPA, usually have majored in science, have participated extensively in research prior to application, and have strong letters of recommendation from faculty singing praises as to his or her research abilities. These programs are very small and most are highly competitive.

The combined MD/PhD allows you to complete both degrees in a shorter period of time than if you did them separately. The programs usually take seven years to complete, not including residency training. Because the student is pursuing a long training in research and planning on a less lucrative career in academic medicine, programs usually offer annual stipends, cover the cost of PhD tuition, and sometimes pay for part or all of medical school tuition. In addition to the standard medical school application, the student is usually required to file separate materials to the PhD program. It also requires that you research the medical schools that offer the PhD in the area of your interest.

Most medical schools offer an MD/PhD in one form or another. These programs are listed in the AAMC's *Medical School Admissions Requirements* book. The most highly regarded programs are Medical Scientist Training Programs (MSTPs) funded by the National Institutes of Health (NIH). For more information on MSTPs, contact: Medical Scientist Training Program, National Institute of General Medical Sciences, National Institutes of Health, 45 Center Drive, MSC 6200, Bethesda, MD 20892-6200, or phone (301) 594-0828.

Cost of Applying

Beg or borrow the money you will need to apply to medical schools. There will be two fees to pay for those schools that are members of the standardized application service AMCAS (American Medical College Application Service): the AMCAS processing fee and the individual school fees. If you apply to 15 schools the AMCAS fee will be $650 and secondary applications will cost around $1,500 more for a total of $2,150. It is possible to spend upward of $3,000 filing applications, but if you have picked your schools carefully enough, it is worth the coin. Let's face it—should you be admitted, compared to what you will spend on your medical education, $50,000–$200,000—exclusive of costs of living—application fees are just a drop in the bucket. Consider this an investment in your career goal and its potential return on your investment.

For those students with extreme financial limitations whose inability to pay the fee would discourage their application to medical school, AMCAS does offer a fee waiver for up to 10 member schools. The waiver form is included in the AMCAS packet.

I do not mean to suggest that you should apply to 100 medical schools or even 50 of them. Medical schools like to know that you want them as much as they want you. It is expected that you will apply to a healthy number of schools, but if you have made arbitrary application to too many schools, your contention that you really want to go to one of them will seem hollow. However, if you have applied to a reasonable number of carefully selected schools, you can safely expound at your personal interview your reasons for wishing to attend each of them without your word being doubted. It will not appear that you want to go to any medical school that will accept you.

At your personal interviews, you may be asked to how many other schools you have applied. Being less than truthful will get you into a great deal of trouble, because all your applications are known to the AAMC. This is another reason to choose carefully.

Meeting the Costs

The rising cost of medical education and the amount of debt you are likely to incur is a concern for almost every applicant. It should not deter you from your career goal, however. Financial aid is available to cover the cost of education and living expenses, but it is mostly in the form of loans. The average indebtedness for students who graduate today is over $150,000. Students who come from upper-class families may not give the cost of medical education a second thought, but it must be kept in mind that most students do have to borrow to attend medical school. Financial aid remains a major problem for most minority students. Many come from families whose parental annual income is below $20,000.

Many organizations do offer financial assistance, some specifically for minority students, such as the Indian Health Services or the National Hispanic Scholarship Funds. Do research on the Web, in the financial aid office, or in the library at your school, and inquire at the minority affairs offices at the medical schools to which you are applying.

The following is just a partial list of loans and fellowships available to students entering medical school. Once you are in medical school, there are also some scholarships for second-, third-, and fourth-year students. (All federal programs require that you be a U.S. citizen, U.S. national, or U.S. permanent resident.) Don't forget to check the American Medical Association Web site, which has a section on paying for medical school.

1. American Medical Women's Association, Inc., 100 North 20th Street, 4th Floor, Philadelphia, PA 19103, (215) 320-3716 (**www.amwa-doc.org**). Scholarships and minimal loan programs for active AMWA members. Minimum renewable loan programs are available. Applicants must be women students enrolled in their second, third, or fourth year at an accredited U.S. medical or osteopathic school. Repayment of loans begins six months after graduation.

2. Armed Forces Health Professions Scholarship Program. U.S. Air Force, Army, and Navy. Scholarship recipients, who must agree to serve on active duty, are awarded tuition, associated educational costs, a stipend, and annual pay allowances. Air Force: Medical Recruiting, Division HQ, USAFRS/RSOHM, 550 D Street West, Suite 1, Randolph AFB, TX 78150-4527 (**www.airforce.gov**); Army: U.S. Army Recruiting Command, Attn. RCRO-HS-MC, 1307 Third Avenue, Fort Knox, KY 40121-2716, 1-800-USA-ARMY (**www.goarmy.gov**); and Navy: Commander, Navy Recruiting Command (Code 32), 801 North Randolph Street, Arlington, VA 22203-1991, 1-800-USA-NAVY (**www.navyjobs.gov**).

3. National Medical Fellowships, Inc., 347 Fifth Avenue, Suite 510, New York, NY 10016, (212) 483-8897 (**www.nmfonline.org**). Fellowships, based primarily on financial need, are given on a competitive basis to minority students already accepted into medical school. They are renewable and cover tuition and living expenses. Their helpful publication, *Informed Decision Making Part 1: Sources of Financial Assistance for Medical Students,* available for $15, lists many different scholarships and loans for minority and nonminority students.

4. Indian Health Service (IHS) Scholarship Program. IHS, a bureau of the U.S. Public Health Service, provides scholarships that include tuition and fees. Loan repayment program also available. Contact IHS at 801 Thompson Avenue, Suite 120, Rockville, MD 20852 or (301) 443-6197.

5. National Health Service Corps Scholarship Program, 2070 Chain Bridge Road, Suite 450, Vienna, VA 22182-2536, 1-800-221-9393 (**www.bphc.hrsa.gov/nhsc**). Scholarship recipients, who must agree to serve in federally-designated health manpower shortage areas, are awarded tuition, associated educational costs, and a monthly stipend. To be eligible you must be going into an approved primary care specialty. Loan repayment program also offered.

6. State-sponsored scholarships or loan repayment programs for individuals committed to choosing a primary care specialty and are willing to practice in an underserved area of the state. Check with the individual state's department of health or a school of medicine in that state. Listings for state programs can also be found at **www.aamc.org/stuapps**.

In addition to the sources just listed, financial assistance is usually made available to medical students in the form of a mix of direct scholarships and loans. The amount of a scholarship award is determined by most schools primarily on the basis of economic need and not on academic performance. Thus, the student with a greater need and an adequate to above-average academic record usually receives more scholarship assistance than loan money. Funds for either of these two types of assistance come from a variety of sources. Some are:

1. Directly from the medical school itself, usually from endowments made to the school for use in the support of students.

2. The federally-supported Primary Care Loan provides funding to students who demonstrate need and are committed to a career as a generalist physician (i.e., family practice, general internal medicine, general pediatrics, or preventive medicine/public health). Regardless of tax status, the expected contribution of parents or spouse is considered. Currently, a student may borrow up to the cost of attendance, payable over a period of 10 to 25 years at an interest rate of five percent, subject to change.

3. The Federal Perkins Loan is a federally-supported loan program that awards loans based on need and available funds at each school. The maximum yearly amount is $5,000, with up to a ceiling of $30,000 and an interest rate of five percent during repayment.

4. The Federal Subsidized Stafford Student Loan works this way: the student borrows money from a private lender, and the federal government subsidizes the interest on the loan while the student is enrolled. The student may borrow up to $8,500 per academic year, with a maximum cap of $65,500; repayment begins six months after graduation with an 8.25 percent interest cap.

5. Under the Federal Unsubsidized Stafford Loan, students may borrow from a private lender regardless of need at the same interest rate as the subsidized, but the borrower is responsible for accrued interest. Maximum annual amount is $38,500 less Subsidized Stafford, and total borrowed is capped at $138,500 less Subsidized Stafford.

6. Other loans and scholarships targeted at students in primary care: Scholarships for Disadvantaged Students (SDS), Loans for Disadvantaged Students (LDS), and Financial Aid for Disadvantaged Health Professions Students (FADHPS).

7. Private comprehensive loan programs such as Medloans, MedCap, and the Access Group are private lenders through which medical students may obtain some federally-sponsored loans as well as private loan funds. Through these loans, qualified students may borrow private funds beyond what is covered with federal funds up to the cost of education. Interest rates vary.

8. Check Web sites **www.fastweb.com** and **www.finaid.org** for a large general listing of scholarships nationwide.

Minority Students

Increasing the numbers of underrepresented minority physicians has been a priority of medical schools for many years. The underrepresented are defined by the AAMC as African-Americans, Native Americans (American Indians, Alaskan Natives and Native Hawaiians), Mexican-Americans, and mainland Puerto Ricans. These four groups are underrepresented in medical schools and in the profession and have also had a history of discrimination and exclusion in the United States. As our population becomes increasingly more diverse, the medical community is striving to provide our country with a more equitable representation. African-Americans account for 12 percent of our population, but only 6.5 percent of all medical students. Hispanics constitute 9 percent of the population and only 7 percent of the nation's medical students, whereas Native-Americans are 0.8 percent of the population and 0.2 percent of all medical students.

According to AAMC's *2000–01 Medical School Admissions Requirements,* in 1998 the nation's medical schools enrolled 1,872 new underrepresented minority students, only 11.6 percent of all new entrants. Although minority student enrollments have made great strides since the 1960s, a disparity still exists. The number of minorities entering medical school peaked in 1994 at 2,014, but as the total number of applicants has declined nationally, so has the number of minority applicants. Only 7.4 percent of first-year students in 1998 were African-American. Of these 1,201 students, 146 (12 percent) were attending Howard University, Meharry Medical College, and Morehouse College, predominantly African-American institutions. This is a dramatic change since 1969, when 75 percent of African-American medical students were enrolled at Howard and Meharry. However, historically African-American schools still provide African-American students with attractive features, including more faculty role models, lower cost, fewer socialization problems, and extensive mentoring and support programs.

Looking at test scores, it is obvious that underrepresented students have been held to a different standard. In 1996, the average verbal reasoning score on the MCAT for accepted white males was 9.9, and the average cumulative GPA was 3.58. For accepted black males, it was 8.1 and 3.23. For rejected white males, it was 8.0. This is not to say that grades should be the be-all and end-all of admission criteria, but critics contend that assuming that noncognitive skills such as kindness, dedication, and altruism are possessed at greater rates by underrepresented student categories is improbable and being used as a pretext to admit them over whites in lieu of favoritism based on race and ethnicity. Countering this, affirmative action proponents state that diversity is desirable, and we need to level the playing field.

What follows from all of this? The bottom line is that, I believe, there are incredible opportunities today for underrepresented applicants, from financial aid to enrichment programs, many of which occur during the summer. Most of the U.S. medical schools offer some version targeting high school students, college students interested in entering the health professions who need to enhance their basic study skills or gain exposure to a particular field of interest, and graduate students. They run, on the average, six to ten weeks. Many are stipended and most include room and board and a travel allowance. The AAMC's *Minority Opportunities in U.S. Medical Schools* includes a comprehensive list of summer enrichment programs; AAMC also runs its own excellent summer program, the Minority Medical Education Program (MMEP) at various med school sites around the country. You can access information about MMEP at **www.aamc.org/meded/minority/ mmep/start.htm**.

As for financial aid, underrepresented students have all the resources available to any applicant with financial need, including loans made directly from the medical school, federal funds, and low-interest bank loans. Additionally, National Medical Fellowships provide grants-in-aid to minority group students to reduce the amount of their loan indebtedness. Every medical school has a contact person or office for minority affairs to assist applicants with financial hardship. The AAMC guidebook provides a comprehensive listing of these.

An engaging chart I came across lists undergraduate programs with the most underrepresented minority students accepted to medical schools. Although the relative percentages of premeds admitted were not given, it did make for interesting reading:

Xavier	70	Michigan	33
UCLA	42	Morehouse	30
Duke	42	Texas (Austin)	30
Howard	39	Berkeley	29
Spelman	35	Illinois (Urbana)	28
Harvard	33	San Diego	28
Stanford	33		

Staying In Can Be Harder
Than Getting In

As long as their representation in medical schools is disproportionate to their percentage of the total population, qualified underrepresented students should consider themselves prime applicants. As their premedical preparation improves, so does their medical school performance, and fewer are failing to complete the curriculum and become MDs. Financial aid remains available for all, in the form of loans and scholarships, and as more African-Americans, Native Americans, Mexican-Americans, and Puerto Ricans matriculate, their feelings of isolation and alienation are reduced. Medical schools are bending over backward, not only to accept them, but also to see to it that they graduate. The attitude no longer seems to be, "We accepted you, now show us how good you are," but, "We accepted you because we want you to become physicians. We will help you because we have an investment in your future."

Women

Women are applying to and entering medical school in greater numbers than ever before. At some medical schools, half or more of the entering classes are women. However, in the practice of medicine, women are still underrepresented—in some specialties more than others. (About 25 percent of U.S. physicians are women, up from only 8 percent in 1970.) Thus, admissions committees continue to seek a gender balance in their entering classes. As more and more women have entered medicine, medical schools and the profession have learned to work with them on issues specific to gender, such as family planning. In the past, women medical students had a higher attrition rate than men, and there was some concern about how a woman would use her medical education. Would she soon leave the profession to have and raise children? Today, most women physicians take a short leave of absence from their practice for childbirth and new infant care, as any working woman would do. There is also some indication that current health care reform trends, e.g., more physicians in salaried positions in group or HMO settings—allow women even more flexibility. However, a few admissions committee members seem to be still living in the past, and women may still encounter some interview questions about their plans and how they fit with medical education and practice.

"Woman has so apparent a function in certain medical specialties and seemingly so assured a place in general medicine under some obvious limitations that the struggle for wider educational opportunities for the sex was predestined to an early success in medicine." That was written by Abraham Flexner in the famous *Flexner Report* of 1910. However, although women were freely admitted to medical college in those days, only a small percentage of those who matriculated eventually graduated.

Flexner's conclusion was that "as the opportunities of women have increased, not decreased . . . their enrollment should have augmented if there is any strong demand for women physicians or any strong ungratified desire on the part of women to enter the profession, one or the other of these conditions is lacking—perhaps both."

Had Mr. Flexner interviewed some of those women, he might have discovered other reasons why only 15 percent to 20 percent of the matriculants graduated from medical school in 1909–10. Family commitments, social pressures, and economics were doubtless on the list of reasons a woman had for leaving medical school before graduation. These pressures are still present, but today most women who enter medical school not only graduate but their attrition rate is less than that of men.

AAMC statistics show that the percentage of women enrolled in medical school is increasing every year. The female portion of the total number of applicants increased from 41.9 percent in 1994 to 50.8 percent in 2003, but has since declined slightly to 49.8 percent in 2005. The female portion of the total number of matriculants increased from 41.9 percent in 1994 to 49.6 percent in 2003, but also declined slightly to 48.5 percent over the last two years.

The number and the percentage of women in residency programs have also been increasing steadily. As recently as 1977, one-third of all specialties had no female residents. Today, women are represented in all specialty and subspecialty areas. Most women physicians are concentrated in three specialties: internal medicine, pediatrics, and family practice. Many are also in OB/GYN and psychiatry. Very few women go into the surgical fields, and discrimination still seems to exist in some of those areas.

Special Interest Groups

Many people still believe that there are special interest groups influential in getting students into a medical school. Thus, alumni associations take on an undue importance, as does the private individual who makes a substantial contribution to the medical school library. Rarely does it happen any more that anyone gets into a medical school simply because a close relative went there and, contrary to the mythology, nobody buys his or her way into a medical school today. It just isn't done. There is that occasional student who, by directive of the dean, must be admitted, but this is by no means a common occurrence. Indeed, sons and daughters of faculty members gain admission no more easily than anyone else. Given personal idiosyncracies and individual preferences, it may safely be said that medical school admissions committees are about as democratic a group as you will find anywhere.

What Makes You Different?

Medical schools are also impressed by work that, although not dealing directly with other people, involved the completion of a task. Thus, editing your school newspaper or literary magazine, researching, writing, and publishing a paper, or being a fine artist are all relevant to your application. Indeed, anything about you that makes you different from most everyone else is precisely what *is* relevant. If you are a top basketball star, a golfer, a tournament chess player, airplane pilot, or writer, you must say so. Medical schools look for diversity in their freshman class. Diversity can mean many different things: an unusual major, where you are from, where you grew up (foreign country, rural background, moved around a lot), ethnic background, economic background, or special accomplishments such as those mentioned earlier. It is not hard to find students with high GPAs and MCATs—they are plentiful. It is hard to find students who bring unusual backgrounds to the study of medicine.

One way to stand out from the crowd is to publish in a medical magazine. This does not have to be original research; that would be a tall order for most undergraduates. Essays in humanities and social sciences are much more achievable. For some, this can represent an expansion of their personal statement, or it can be a reflection of a medical experience that touched them deeply. Several magazines have been known to publish the work of premeds. *The New Physician*, an AMA publication, comes to mind, as do e-zines *Pulse—Voices From the Heart of Medicine* (**www.pulsemagazine.org**) and *The Sun Magazine* (**www.thesunmagazine.org**). Here's an example of an essay that grew out of a premed's personal statement and was picked up in an issue of *The New Physician*.

Shoving the last of a Rice Krispies treat into my mouth on my way to speak to a patient group, I thought about the day's presentation, my summer plans, and that evening's dinner. I was not thinking about the fully functioning beta cells in my pancreas, or about the insulin soon to be released into my bloodstream. I am oblivious to the harmonic convergence of my perfect digestion: the release of enzymes, the contraction of smooth muscle, the efficient utilization of insulin receptors—all parts working together in concert to keep my blood sugar within normal range.

I opened the meeting room door to a group of people who hadn't been so lucky. They all had diabetes, and the last time they thought about their blood sugar was probably two minutes ago. As the health educator for this weekly diabetes group, I was expected to deliver pertinent information in an accessible manner.

This particular day, we were talking about diabetic complications. "The point of today's discussion," I announced in an enthusiastic voice, "is not to scare you about the complications of diabetes, but to highlight the importance of self-management. Lowering your risk of these complications is within your control." The group of diabetics I worked with every week looked up at me; some stared blankly, some nodded their heads in agreement, and others avoided eye contact.

The youngest group member, a Type I diabetic named Julie, spoke up. "It is easy for providers to say, 'Manage your disease,' but what does that really mean? It means I need to take my blood sugar every day, measure and administer my insulin, watch what I eat, and live with the fear that I could go into a coma again."

Her comment ended my enthusiastic delivery. Beyond being correct, she reminded me of my health status in this room of diabetics. I was thinking about dinner, eating a sugary snack, and daydreaming about a summer of possibilities while everyone else in the group was checking their blood sugar. How can I possibly understand what it is like to live with a chronic disease?

Although this is changing, medical providers today are disproportionately wealthy, white, and capable of making the same assumption that I did: that their patients share their reality. This can be detrimental to care. Telling a patient to eat more vegetables can mean very little if they lack the income to buy fresh food. Giving out health education materials is disempowering to a patient who can't read, and advising a patient to walk around her neighborhood for exercise overlooks the fact that some people live in dangerous areas.

During my junior year of college, I—a financially secure, educated white woman—acted as the health educator for a school in

West Oakland, California, predominately made up of students of color in a low-income neighborhood. At that time, the school had no health education program, so it was my responsibility to develop and implement one. I chose to focus on sex education. I figured that sex ed was my biggest need in high school, so why wouldn't it be the same in West Oakland? After three months, my curriculum was up and running, and the students seemed to be enjoying and learning from the presentations.

Then the first wake-up call came. During a sex ed session with 11th graders, I was explaining that about 30 percent of men get prostate cancer in their lifetime but, because of slow growth, most die of something else first. A male student then asked, "What would they die of first—getting shot?" I was taken aback by his comment. Addressing homicide as a primary cause of death is something that would have never crossed my mind.

About a month later, a shooting on school grounds punctuated the distinction between my uninformed perception and their reality. There was no school assembly, no outreach or grief counseling, and a general attitude among the school administration that the students could cope because it "happens all the time." Though I was outraged by the lack of response, the truth was that violence was ever-present: The homicides in Oakland numbered 148 in 2006, with 47 percent of the victims under age 25. Students at the clinic shared heart-wrenching tales with their doctors, counselors and, over time, with me, about being raped, abused, or losing a sibling.

In Oakland, I began to understand the invaluable role that self-reflection and awareness play in the delivery of health care. I had come into this school, this clinic, and this neighborhood with an agenda to help the youth make better choices.

The logic seemed easy enough: Tell the students how to take care of themselves and they would do it. I was basing these assumptions on my personal experience growing up. When I learned how to better take care of myself, I did it because I could. I had access to necessary medical services, a supportive and financially secure family, and, most importantly, I felt safe.

These youth did not have access to the same tools I did when I was their age. This compromised my effectiveness as a health educator; I had very little to offer the students until I understood where they were coming from. I had to start over.

Violence was the pertinent issue for West Oakland youth, so I began to work outside my comfort zone and focus on violence prevention. I also needed to examine my social location and role as an educator. Talking about violence and working to prevent it meant having open conversations about race, racism, oppression, *and power imbalances in society. Who was I to present on these topics? They were the experts and I was the amateur. It was not appropriate for me to take on a leadership position, so I stepped out of the spotlight and asked the students to assume that role.*

Immediately, I noticed a difference in the reception of the presentations. Youth leaders were talking candidly with their peers about their real-life experiences. Youth were able to talk about difficult issues from their perspective, and not that of an outsider. What's more, by acting as a support person, and not a leader, I gave the students a chance to build community in the classroom, empower one another, and strategize collaboratively to combat violence in their neighborhood.

This is when I first realized the concept of alliance: the ability to join forces with others in pursuit of a common goal. In this case, the goal was violence prevention. For someone with a significant amount of privilege, the best thing I could do was back off and let those who may not have had a voice take a leadership role. But what happens in cases where there is little choice in the relationship? Doctors, for example, cannot allow patients to diagnose and treat themselves. In clinical situations, as with the diabetes group I worked with, the concept of alliance can mean something else entirely.

Delivering good medical care is a constant interplay between self and others, a chance to scrutinize assumptions and act from a place of understanding and respect.

In educating diabetics, high school students, or any other patient group about their health, we must constantly ask ourselves, "How can I teach this population?" I can by incorporating open conversation and peer teaching into the curriculum whenever possible, truly valuing the abilities and experiences of group members, and giving them the chance to educate each other. This is the best health education we can offer.

I believe premeds should tout their nonacademic achievements—their work experience and published writing. I am particularly partial to medical narrative, as I believe in the importance of telling a story to make medicine more humanistic. I'm still not sure how much weight it carries with admissions committees. I'm afraid that the overriding criteria are still GPAs and MCAT scores, with life experience merely becoming a prerequisite for consideration. But in some admissions offices, it could make the difference between being asked to come for an interview and not. So not only get medical exposures, but also write about them! It will make your experiences even more meaningful, and you will feel the elation of being a published writer as well.

Besides the AMCAS personal statement, many medical schools also require additional essays as part of the secondary application. Some ask that you write about why you want to become a doctor or other specific topics, whereas others let you do with the space as you wish. In all cases, the page should be used and under no circumstances should it be returned blank. If you are coming to medicine late in your college career or after you have been out of school for a while, then you should offer some explanation. If you are from an economically-disadvantaged background, are the first person in your family to attend college, or have overcome some difficult personal obstacles, you might want to talk about how this has influenced your life experience and the achievement of your educational goals. Admissions committees always want to know when and how you have decided to study medicine. You can use this space to tell them.

Dr. Woodrow W. Morris, associate dean of the University of Iowa College of Medicine, made these comments about the personal statement page on application forms quite some time ago in an issue of *The Advisor*. His comments are still applicable today.

"The way in which applicants use this blank space has already proved useful to admissions committees in the realm of affording them a little insight into the personality make-up of the writer. And some of the ways the space has been used have been wonderful to behold. Among these are: straightforward appeals for admission, autobiographical sketches, philosophical dissertations on everything from the state of mankind...to the essential qualities of the complete physician. Other uses have included doggerel verse such as the student who apparently wanted to impress the reader with his knowledge of anatomy by writing:

> The cow is of the bovine ilk,
> One end is moo,
> The other milk.

Still others have filled the space with more ambitious creative poetry, again on the various kinds of topics already listed. Perhaps the most unusual of all have been those creations produced by applicants with an artistic flair—everything from chiaroscuro productions to caricatures. Finally, it should be noted that there are occasionally those brave souls who dare look at the blank space, and leave its pristine surface alone. (This, it should be observed, often leaves admissions committees in doubt as to whether the student did not wish to reveal his [*sic*] or herself, or whether the applicant simply had nothing to say.)

"It would be a service to both applicants and admissions committees if preprofessional advisers would encourage their students to make optimum use of the opportunity provided to them for expressing their individual thoughts and talents. Similarly, it would be helpful if future AMCAS materials provided both more space for 'personal comments' and more detailed instructions concerning the use of this important space."

The essay should be typewritten and grammatically correct at the very least. A great deal of care should be taken in organizing it. A good idea is to write a rough draft, put it away and pull it out a few days later, and see how it looks to you. In the meantime you might think of things you wish to add or delete, or you might consider a different focus to give the essay. You might also want to show your essay to a few trusted individuals for some feedback—a professor, an adviser, a med student, or a physician. Under no conditions should you turn in essays that have not been read by someone who knows you, writes well, and is willing and able to critique your writing. This little essay is far more important than any paper you will write in college, so judge the time you spend on it accordingly. Given the fact that many incoming medical students cannot even write a coherent paragraph, a well-written essay is downright impressive.

Recommendations

After MCAT scores and GPA, recommendations are another important criterion for admission to a medical school. Although they are usually not given quite as much weight as the interview in the final analysis, recommendations are read carefully for positive, lukewarm, and negative comments that provide further insight into you as a candidate. It is true that most recommendations are positive in their appraisal of a student, but some are more positive than others, and some are just negative enough to keep you out of medical school.

The usual way of obtaining recommendations is to use the services provided by the premedical adviser at your undergraduate institution. Although the precise manner that premedical advisors/committees draft letters varies, it often involves using extensive excerpts from individual letters of recommendation to produce a "composite" recommendation, often with additional insights that the advisor/committee has based on their knowledge of you, your school, and your curriculum and activities.

The professors and others you choose to write on your behalf need to know you well. If all they can say is that you received a high grade, the letter will not be particularly useful. You can help get better letters of recommendation by taking the time to interact with faculty or other possible recommenders. When you visit with them, make them aware of your goals, ambitions, and accomplishments. Try to maintain contact with people whom you interact well with and don't just show up two years later asking for a letter.

While it is expected that most letters of recommendation come from faculty, good letters of recommendation may also come from employers, leaders of groups that you volunteer for, and from workers in health care (especially physicians) testifying to your experiences and suitability for the field. Obviously, it helps to obtain letters from distinguished sources, but only if the person knows you well and this is revealed in the letter.

The premedical student might also want to make the faculty member whose recommendation is being solicited aware of the kind of letters medical schools like to receive—namely letters that reflect real knowledge of the student and his or her past performance. Comments that help put the student's performance in perspective and make clear the letter writer's opportunity to evaluate the student are very helpful. A comment such as "He is one of the best premedical students I have had in his laboratory class for some time" or "She ranked in the upper third of this seminar for laboratory students" help the medical schools interpret the comments made on the student. If the class is one for majors or has special qualifications for enrollment, that should be noted. The basis for evaluation—e.g., two midterm examinations and a final test, or two three-hour laboratory sessions a week throughout the quarter—helps the medical school interpret the evaluation.

Medical school admissions committees tend to think in terms of rank categories. For example, if you received an honor, they would be delighted to know just how selective an honor it was. If you were "highly recommended" by the premedical committee, what percentage of all the premeds were similarly recommended? Being elected to Phi Beta Kappa as a physics major may be more significant than gaining the same honor as a humanities student if, at your institution, it is rare for physics students to be elected. Or if, for example, you have received a highly competitive summer research fellowship, you may ask your professor to comment on the conditions of the competition. If, on the other hand, you were the only applicant for the position, the less said the better.

The student should attempt to solicit a recommendation from the faculty member with the highest professorial rank, provided that person is well enough acquainted with you. An outstanding recommendation from a full professor is much more impressive than one from a laboratory instructor, and it carries far more weight.

Some students simply have had no personal contact with their teachers and have difficulty obtaining recommendations. Medical school admissions committees feel that it is the student's responsibility to get to know professors, especially the faculty adviser. The reason is that student-teacher contact is an integral part of college education, and the good student will make an effort to establish it—even if only for the sake of getting a recommendation. Medical schools do not frown on aggressive students!

Reference letters written by relatives, clergy, or friends are not only absurdly flattering, but there is rarely any pertinent character content. These recommendations often have nothing whatever to do with your ability to perform in medical school or to be a physician, plus they are considered to be very biased. Also avoid politicians and prominent business executives who are friends of the family, unless you have actually been employed or supervised by them in some way pertinent to your career goal. Admissions committees are most interested in hearing from people who evaluate you in an objective manner.

> Recommendations from people outside the academic sphere—the family minister, priest, or rabbi, relatives, or friends—are usually uniformly laudatory and should be avoided.

Certain types of recommendations, however, may be helpful. If, for instance, you have worked in a research lab during your summer vacations, you might ask the director to write a recommendation for you, especially if he or she was favorably impressed with your work. A letter from any physician, health care administrator, or community service supervisor under whom you have worked in a nonacademic setting can be of use. In fact, anyone who has known you in a professional context should be considered as a source of letters of recommendation. Letters may be mailed to your school's premedical advisory committee or sent directly to the medical schools to which you have applied.

The importance of the recommendation is not merely to reaffirm your academic competence; your grades and MCAT already attest to that. Rather, recommendations serve basically to assess your character and to explain any discrepancies that may exist on your academic record. If you are a more capable student than your transcript indicates, perhaps your recommendations will state this. If your grades dropped sharply one semester because you held a part-time job to earn enough money to continue in school, your recommendations should make this clear. On the other hand, if you argued incessantly for grade changes or are an antisocial dolt with no personality, your recommendations are likely to say so, and they will be a severe handicap to your getting into a medical school.

One issue connected with recommendations concerns the confidentiality of the evaluations. When you ask each recommender to write a letter or evaluation, you are given a choice on the form to waive your right to see what is written and keep it confidential, or to reserve the right to review the letter and designate it nonconfidential. Your rights are protected under the Family Educational Rights and Privacy Act of 1974. Most premed committees will *only* write letters that are confidential, and it makes sense to waive your rights for the individual letters of recommendation that you ask for as well.

Choose your recommenders carefully. Go for quality, not simply quantity, and complete your recommendation file or committee evaluation early. Courtesy demands that you allow a person at least a month to complete a recommendation. Help your recommenders. Make a personal contact (don't just leave the request in their mailbox), volunteer information about yourself and your decision to enter medicine, and perhaps provide a brief resume and/or copy of your transcript. When you ask recommenders for a letter, give them a deadline by which *you* need to have it in—not the schools' final deadlines.

AMCAS Letter Service

Beginning in the summer of 2009, the AAMC introduced the AMCAS Letters of Evaluation/Recommendation service, which allows letters of recommendation to be sent directly to AMCAS instead of each individual school. Once received by AMCAS, letters can be sent electronically to designated schools via the AMCAS application. Since its introduction, all but five accredited allopathic medical schools in the United States accept letters exclusively through the AMCAS letter service.

There are three different classifications of letters that AMCAS will accept: a committee letter written by the pre-health advisor or committee at your school, a letter packet composed by your recommenders, or an individual letter. Note that if your school offers a committee letter, most medical schools require that you choose this option. Each of the above classifications (the committee letter, the letter packet, and the individual letter) will count as one entry in the AMCAS letter service, and you can store up to ten entries. Storing multiple entries in the AMCAS letter service gives you the flexibility to send different groups of letters to different schools.

There are four different ways that you and your letter writers can send letters of recommendation to AMCAS: AMCAS Letter Writer Application, Interfolio, U.S. mail, and VirtualEvals. Interfolio and VirtualEvals are specialized letter services that are usually only used if an applicant's institution or letter writer already has an account with these services (if you are interested in using these services, please refer to **www.amcas.org** for more detailed instructions). However, the majority of applicants and their letter writers will choose to use the AMCAS Letter Writer Application or send letters to AMCAS via U.S. mail. The AMCAS Letter Writer Application allows your letter writer to upload your letters as PDF files and send them electronically to AMCAS.

In addition to having your letters sent directly to AMCAS by your letter writers, some institutions offer a career center or letter service organization that will store your letters until they are ready to be sent out. Since the AMCAS application only begins accepting letters in May of your application cycle, using the career center letter service at your undergraduate institution allows you to gather and store letters of recommendation. This can be especially useful if you plan on taking some time off between graduating from your undergraduate institution and applying to medical school, as it will allow you to secure letters from your undergraduate professors. However, please be aware that your letters should be written by professors that have instructed or worked with you recently, and letters that are outdated may hurt you (you should probably avoid using letters from professors that taught you freshman or sophomore year).

Also, even though the Letters of Recommendation section is part of your primary AMCAS application, you can still add new letter entries and assign letters to schools even after your AMCAS application has been submitted and verified. However, be aware that if you mail in your letters to AMCAS via U.S. mail, it can take up to 15 business days for your letters to be processed by AMCAS, Thus, even though you technically don't need to submit your letters until you are ready to submit your secondaries, you should have your letters in order and sent to AMCAS well ahead of when you plan on submitting your secondary applications (probably in early or mid-June around the time you submit your AMCAS application). Remember that secondary applications will be complete and ready for review until a school has received your letters of recommendation. Do not let letters of recommendation delay your application!

The Interview

According to a survey of U.S. medical schools published in *Academic Medicine,* the interview was ranked the highest of five preadmission criteria listed, the others being MCAT, science GPA, nonscience GPA, and letters of recommendation. When medical schools were asked to list the purpose of the interview, most responded that it was used to assess the applicant's noncognitive skills, to predict success as a medical student, to clarify written application information, to assess the applicant's fit with the individual school's mission, and to determine potential psychological problems or immaturity. Another important purpose listed was as a recruitment tool to "sell" students on attending.

For the most highly qualified candidate, it is true that the interview may be somewhat of a formality; however, particularly while applicant numbers remain high, it is an important selection criterion for *all* candidates. Besides allowing the medical schools to evaluate an applicant's characteristics, as mentioned earlier, the interview also affords the candidate an opportunity to take a look at the medical school and ask whatever questions are considered pertinent. In almost all cases, interviews are required for admission.

The survey published in *Academic Medicine* also indicated that an average of 42 percent of candidates who had *completed* applications were interviewed. The percentage of students interviewed varies at each medical school, and this percentage can indeed fluctuate depending on the number of applications received at a school in any given year. At state schools, residents always have a better chance of receiving an interview than nonresidents. You also might want to note that usually the figure quoted for number of applications received is on *all* (including incomplete) applications. Many students never complete their applications and are thus not even considered for an interview. Today, some schools who are receiving 10,000 or more total applications may interview well over 1,000 students for an entering class of 150. So even though you've made it past a major hurdle at the interview stage, you must still convince the committee of your qualifications and desire to attend their particular school of medicine. In other words, being granted an interview is great, but your job isn't over yet.

It was pointed out at one recent medical conference dealing with admissions interviewing that too many applicants fail to realize one very important factor—physicians, by nature of their training, are professional interviewers. Doctors are experts at fishing out information from people even if these people resist initial attempts at probing. Doctors are trained to interview patients and to look for signs that a patient is holding back information or harboring false ideas about his or her individual condition. If you are unsure of yourself or unconvincing as a future doctor, then the interviewing physician will easily spot this and take note.

Actually, the interview is the most humanizing aspect of the medical school admissions process. This is your chance to sell the product you know best—yourself. The interview gives you the opportunity to see the particular school and to meet some faculty members and students. Take advantage of the situation and explore the school, ask questions, and try to form an impression of the school in your own mind. The interview is a mutual exchange; make it work for you.

The interviews are established to explore several different areas of the applicants' backgrounds. They test the motivation, preparation, commitment, and sincerity of the applicant. Believe it or not, these seemingly intangible factors can be easily assessed. Motivation we have discussed before in terms of summer work and understanding the role of the physician in our society. Preparation is another important aspect of any application. The interviewers will want to know if you took the proper science courses at your college or if you substituted "physics for poets" for the required course. How well did you perform on the MCAT, and did you take it seriously enough to prepare for it in advance? What is your level of commitment to medicine, as demonstrated by your knowledge of the different types of specialties and practices? Do you follow newspaper articles about medical issues, or is your only desire in life an MD license plate? Lastly, is your sincere desire to become a physician rooted in your own desires and intellect, or are you a last-minute convert to the medical mode? How seriously have you considered the alternative health careers, and why did you choose medicine as opposed to social work?

Being able to answer these questions for yourself is the primary goal here. You have to be honest with yourself before you can be honest with your probing interviewer. Review the evolution of your career decision and your qualifications. You cannot anticipate every question you will be asked nor should you have stock or memorized answers ready for your interview, but it is helpful to put in some preparation. Be aware of some of the commonly asked questions and give those some thought. Practice answering open-ended questions, such as "Tell me about yourself," "Describe your strengths and weaknesses," and "Why are you interested in attending _____ School of Medicine?" Some students participate in mock interviews, some practice with a friend or adviser, some just talk to the mirror. This exercise can help you collect your thoughts, build your self-confidence, and help you be a little more at ease at the real interview.

If you are lucky enough to be invited for a personal interview, you should certainly try to learn as much as possible about the school you are visiting. Don't go to the interview ignorant. By all means read the school brochure or catalogue beforehand. It is also a good idea to skim over your application to the school to refresh your strong points. Of course, this also means that you should copy everything before you mail your applications away. Think of the mail as a conspiracy against you, and you'll see how easy it is to learn to copy everything first.

Never, never be late for an interview. If your train or plane is late, then it is your responsibility to phone the school and explain the circumstances involved. This is a signal to the school of your maturity level and coolheadedness. Try to arrive early for your interview if possible. This way you will have some time to look around and start to relax a little. If your interviewer is late, do not make any reference to the amount of time you had to wait. Believe me, he or she was probably doing something more important at the moment than you. Don't worry, you were not forgotten.

Dress appropriately. Although this should be obvious to any college senior, you wouldn't believe what some people look like for an interview. Men don't have to look like an advertisement for Brooks Brothers, but certainly wear a suit if you can. If money is a problem, then a quiet sport coat and unobtrusive tie are in order. Avoid jeans and sweaters—they may go over well in certain parts of the country, but certainly aren't going to help your case. If you generally wear glasses, then wear them to the interview; don't sit there squinting at the interviewer for the sake of vanity. Interviewers are not interested in filling a class with Robert Redford types.

For women, the rules are similar: Slack suits, no matter how appealing, should NOT be worn to a formal medical school interview. A skirt suit, tailored skirt and blouse, or conservatively cut dress is far more appropriate. Avoid frilly things, miniskirts, excessive makeup, and fancy jewelry. You won't impress anyone with that kind of approach. Dress for the seriousness of the situation, and you should come out looking just fine.

Probably the most important recommendation anyone can make is the necessity for being completely honest at an interview. If you don't know something, don't be afraid to say so. This will demonstrate your own level of self-confidence and bearing. If you have certain questions about the school's program, then voice them at the appropriate time. Be honest about your financial needs and be prepared to discuss them intelligently if the situation arises. Be prepared to discuss any deficiencies in your record and try to avoid buttering up the interviewer at all costs. Do not second-guess the person questioning you; just try to be yourself. What you say and how you say it are what count.

Definitely try to assert your positive aspects during the medical school interview. If you are particularly proud of a certain research project you completed, then say so in a matter-of-fact way without pontificating. Try to convey your own enthusiasm for a particular field to your interviewer. If you did poorly in one course because of a teacher conflict, then tactfully explain the situation without attacking the professor involved. Never berate your own school, as this is a sign of immaturity. Of course, it is also important to be a good listener as well as talker. Keep your eyes on the person talking to you and pay attention.

Use the English language to your advantage and avoid the pitfalls of everyday usage. The interview is no place for *like* and *you know*. You don't have to sound like a walking thesaurus, but do avoid hackneyed expressions. Put your best foot forward and think before you speak. It is better to pause with silence than to say *um* twenty times in one conversation. Absolutely avoid impressing the interviewer with the small amount of medical talk you may know. This could be disastrous if he or she follows up this line of conversation and your knowledge runs out after two sentences.

Try to relax and be yourself. I realize that for some individuals this will be the most difficult part of the interviewing process. If you really are excessively nervous, then say so. It may help to caution the interviewer to be a little more understanding about your anxiety. If you approach the interview with PMA (Positive Mental Attitude), then you will be much cooler and self-assured without being cocky. If you are the knee-trembling type, then try this simple, proven technique used by public speakers and politicians. When sitting facing the interviewer, simply curl your toes up as tight as you can (of course without grimacing or removing your shoes!). The tension created by this simple maneuver will relax the rest of your body, and the shakes will miraculously disappear. Practice this trick if you want when you go out on a first date, and you'll see your nervousness vanish. Good public speakers may be a bundle of nerves inside, but outwardly they are the essence of cool. This little trick helps you relax and makes you more confident.

Lastly, remember to write down the names of the people who interviewed you. This serves two functions. It is always a good idea to send a brief thank-you card to an interviewer, stating the following:

> *Dear Dr. _____ ,*
> *Thank you for taking the time to discuss my application for the (Name of School) on (Date). I am looking forward to hearing from you soon.*
>
> *Sincerely,*
>
> _____

This will help to reinforce your name in the interviewer's mind and also demonstrate your level of breeding. Good manners are *always* good policy. Secondly, if you have occasion to write to the school for more information or for another reason, don't hesitate to include your (properly spelled) interviewer's name in the note or, even better, write directly to the admissions committee, care of that particular individual.

Questions most frequently asked at the medical school interview include those about your family background, extracurricular activities, employment or volunteer experiences (particularly those that are health-care- and community-service-related), your ability to work well with people from diverse backgrounds, your hobbies, what you do to relax, and how you handle stress. Other types of questions deal mainly with standard yet very important issues about your possible fields of interest:

why medicine, and your thoughts on current issues such as AIDS, abortion, euthanasia, and health care reform. Remember, the interviewer wants to see how you reason and how you react under fire. He or she is not concerned with your own opinion *per se*. Total truthfulness is the best approach for the interview confrontation.

Some students, particularly women, may be faced with questions that they feel are inappropriate or possibly discriminatory. According to a recent American Medical Student Association (AMSA) survey, 33 percent of responding students reported having experienced questions relating to such issues as gender, age, and religion. Women are sometimes asked questions regarding marriage and family plans, and in most cases these questions are considered legal if they are asked of the same number of men. Although some of these questions may be illegal, many interviewers still ask them anyway, and you have to decide how you will answer them. Outright refusal to answer may be legitimate but may not be the approach to take in this situation. Another approach might be to politely and pleasantly question the perhaps inexperienced interviewer as to the relevance of this question to your medical school application, giving them a chance to back off. Most applicants, as uncomfortable as it may be, simply answer the question as succinctly as possible in order not to jeopardize their chances for admission. Some schools offer you the opportunity to provide feedback or fill out a post-interview questionnaire, and if you feel strongly that you have been asked an inappropriate question, you may report it in that manner.

Under certain circumstances, an interview can assume even greater importance. Sometimes committee members are reluctant to accept a candidate because of special questions raised by his or her application. The only advice I can give in this case is to answer all questions at the interview and to be yourself. Remember that the ultimate question is always: "Who is this human being who will someday take care of other human beings?" Make the committee feel as good about you as you feel about yourself.

Sample Personal Statements

As mentioned before, writing a strong personal statement is a challenging and often confusing part of the medical school application process. To make it easier for you as an applicant to tackle these components, we have provided a sample of two exemplary personal statements that you can use as guidance for writing your own.

I will never forget the night that the man in the yellow jacket walked into the Berkeley Free Clinic. It was almost nine o'clock and I could still hear the rain pouring outside. For the third night in a row, the clinic had been overfilled, and as I was closing up, I noticed people still waiting patiently in the lobby. That's when I heard the front door open and saw a man wearing a drenched yellow jacket enter the clinic.

"I have no money and every other place turned me away; please help me," he begged. His plea was familiar to me: the declining economy had left many low-cost clinics in the area without sufficient funds to accommodate the growing number of people without health insurance. Sadly, the Berkeley Free Clinic was no exception to this worsening reality.

"I'm sorry, sir. We're completely full tonight."

"But there are still people in the lobby. Why can't you help me?" I could see the emotional pain in his pale, almost lifeless eyes. I knew he had nowhere else to turn, but how could I help? A deep sense of helplessness suddenly came over me. "Why can't you help?" he pleaded one last time, but sensing the hopelessness of the situation, he proceeded toward the exit and disappeared into the night.

As a child, I had been fascinated by the world of physicians. I remember attending my cousin's white coat ceremony and attempting to wear her coat, which was several sizes too big for me. I dreamed of one day being able to fit into that coat, and my determination to become a physician took root. But the feelings of despair associated with that night almost ten years later had me questioning, for the first time, whether I'd ever be able to fit into that white coat.

I soon began to accept that I could not single-handedly fix the health care system or the economy. Nonetheless, I undertook small tasks to improve the clinic, such as translating our flyers to Spanish to assist our large Hispanic clientele. Several weeks later, I translated for a Spanish-speaking client named Rosa during her tuberculosis test. Interacting with a client in Spanish for the first time was difficult, and although I struggled at times to find the correct medical terms in Spanish, we ultimately were able to communicate successfully throughout the procedure. Afterwards, Rosa took my hands and said, "Gracías por todo," a gesture of appreciation that transcended all language barriers That night, I realized that while it may be impossible to help every single patient, the emotional reward associated with those we can help makes the journey of a physician worthwhile. My desire to wear the white coat suddenly found new life.

My experience with low-income clients at the Berkeley Free Clinic had opened my eyes to the financial difficulties facing many Americans. As I began to understand the importance of the economy in medical decision-making, I decided in my third year to pursue a second degree in economics in addition to my degree in biology. As a physician, a background in economics will allow me to relate to the financial situations of both my patients and the medical institutions that I join.

While my passion for medicine was evolving at the clinic, my interest in biology grew in the classroom. As a Biology Student Instructor in my second year, something was apparent to me on my very first day: teaching students about the Law of Independent Assortment would be much more difficult than learning it. However with time and a bit of creativity, I developed strategies to help my students, creating diagrams and forming analogies that would simplify complex biological concepts. I soon discovered the inherent beauty of my teaching experience: for each topic that I taught, I learned something new as well. Every semester reinforced my understanding of biology and helped me grow as a mentor and communicator.

In my third year, I took my first steps into the laboratory setting, where I explored how zinc finger nucleuses can be used to induce targeted double-strand breaks in the genome and how mutations in DNA double-strand break repair can lead to carcinogenesis. In addition to gaining exposure to various laboratory techniques, I witnessed the scientific method in action and realized that medicine can only advance as quickly as research is translated to practice. As a physician, I strongly wish to be a part of this intricate bridge that links basic science discoveries to clinical practice.

While my initial interest in medicine arose from idolizing the physicians in my life, it has evolved into a deeper understanding of the challenges and responsibilities that come with the privilege of wearing a white coat. I understand that after becoming a physician, I still may not be able to help every man in a yellow jacket that comes my way, but a medical education is the first step in developing the tools to maximize my contribution to the welfare of my community. In my eyes, medicine is more than just a career path. Medicine represents a language, a form of communication among doctors across the world, a bridge that links a researcher's lab bench to a patient's bedside and to a student's classroom. Medicine is the only path that can possibly fulfill my goals and dreams by providing me with the satisfaction of being a mentor, a researcher, and a physician.

* * * * * * *

Three years ago, had I been asked why I wanted to become a physician, I would have said my desire came from working closely with my father, who is a family physician, running his medical office and watching his interactions with patients. Or perhaps I would have said that it came from the excitement I felt when assisting with an ultrasound on a pregnant woman in Mexico. I might even have cited my passion for science and my fascination with the intricacies of the human body. Indeed, all of these experiences have influenced me to choose medicine as a profession. None, however, has given me the same conviction to be a doctor as a simple conversation about race that I witnessed during my junior year at college.

At the time I was an intern at a high school-based health center in a low-income African-American community. In addition to creating and implementing a health education program for the school, I had the opportunity to accompany doctors during their medical visits with students. One day, I observed a visiting white physician conducting a sports physical with a fifteen-year-old student who was black. The young man sat stiffly as the doctor went through a list of standard questions. In the middle of the list she asked, "What is your favorite subject in school, History?" He shot back at her, "Why did you say History, 'cause I'm black?" The doctor stumbled over her words for several moments and then quickly changed the subject.

Although not part of the verbal exchange, I was, like the doctor, uncomfortable talking about race. I felt ashamed by this reaction, but it was not unfounded. Up until that point, my awareness of race was limited. I grew up in a predominantly white, relatively wealthy community, where I was rarely challenged to explore any reality beyond my own. I had access to medical care, healthy foods, transportation and an excellent education. I never talked about my race with my friends, and I most certainly would not have brought it up at a medical visit.

When I attended college, I was once again surrounded by people of similar socioeconomic status. However, my awareness changed because of classes I took in my social justice major. I read Meredith Minkler, bell hooks and Paul Farmer and, through the words of these activists for change, I began to understand the ways in which social and economic factors influence health. For the first time, I saw how my personal background made it easy for me to grow up as a healthy individual. Conversely, I was able to grasp the struggles that historically oppressed groups face when they try to achieve good health. I learned to appreciate, from an academic perspective, the significance of health disparities and the roots of these disparities.

Yet, my reaction in the exam room showed me that my academic background alone had not fully prepared me to be an effective health care ally in a community where homicide was an almost daily occurrence and drive-by shootings occurred on school property. As a result, I reexamined the health education curriculum I had created for the high school. When I first arrived, I had focused narrowly on sex education, with little discussion of the social determinants that affect health. After hearing students talk about losing loved ones to violence, I realized that I could not address any one area of health without talking about race, economic status, and other social factors that influenced their lives.

With this in mind, I decided to work with youth leaders to create a violence prevention program at the school. I had to look outside of my initial role as a health educator imparting information in one direction. Instead, the students became the teachers and were able to talk candidly with each other about their real-life experiences. They started to discuss difficult issues from their own perspective, including how to work together to combat violence in their neighborhood. I realize now that giving up my leadership role allowed me to enter into an alliance with the community and was the best form of health education I could offer.

My experiences during this internship compelled me to continue work with the underserved. I am currently an Americorps volunteer at a community health center, where I provide one-on-one counseling to patients with chronic illnesses who need support and education to make healthy lifestyle changes. This often means we spend a significant amount of time navigating the housing, food access, and mental health barriers that so often impede these changes. I try to meet people where they are, socially and mentally.

As a physician, I will be able to take my services a step further and provide high quality primary care that meets both the medical and social needs of the underserved. For me, being a doctor is about applying my interest in science to my profession, finding and prescribing the best treatment plans for my patients, and using the latest research and medical technology to give the best care possible. Equally important, it is being aware of patients' socioeconomic barriers to achieving health and collaborating with them to overcome these obstacles. I will strive to deliver medical care that honors the reality and needs of the people I serve. I am eager and ready to begin my journey.

CHAPTER 5

How Medical School Admissions Committees Evaluate Applicants

S ince I have never been a member of a medical school admissions committee, my information in this chapter is admittedly secondhand. It is true that some schools do have students serving on this committee, but, in most cases, admissions committee members are recruited from the medical school faculty to serve varying periods of time, usually from one to three or four years. The assistant or associate dean of student affairs is commonly a permanent member, whereas other members rotate, because the job is time-consuming and most faculty members have other obligations.

An admissions committee may have as few as five or as many as 25 members, selected from all areas of the clinical and basic sciences. They will try to be fair, but, like most human beings, they see the ideal applicant as someone who is quite like themselves. Therefore the more members a committee has, the greater your chances of finding an advocate.

Can the Applicant Make It?

Medical school admissions committees look for three things when they evaluate applicants. First they ask, can he or she get through the program? This is crucial. There are many who have the desire to become physicians, are congenial enough, and perhaps have the capacity for genuine concern and empathy for others. However, unless the committee feels that an applicant has made the commitment and can do the work, they will not recommend

71

acceptance. Medical schools are acutely aware of the need for physicians and do not want to waste a precious place on an applicant who is not likely to complete the program. Second, admissions committee members are concerned about the character of the people who will one day practice on the public. They feel it is their job to select students who will not only become competent physicians, but who are also stable and responsible. Finally, they ask whether it is fair to admit a specific applicant in preference to someone else, and while all members of admissions committees will admit to personal biases about what constitutes a desirable applicant, there is a universal attempt to be fair and impartial. To avoid pressure, members of the committee often remain anonymous.

With the enormous number of applicants to medical school each year, it is not possible for every member of an admissions committee to review each application. The number of applications may vary from 1,000 to as many as 10,000 for anywhere from 50 to 200 places. Your application may be reviewed by one or several members of the committee, but certainly not by all of them.

The usual procedure is as follows: The admissions committee won't even consider your folder until all the information is at hand. In other words, it is best to complete your application as early as possible. Once all the information is assembled, your folder is completed and ready for review.

Many schools differ in their review process. Unfortunately, due to budget and personal constraints, many public medical colleges have resorted to a computerized check-off system for folders. All the numbers are fed into a computer formula, and if a certain cutoff-point is reached, the applicant may be invited for a personal interview. If the cutoff point of a specific GPA and MCAT combination is not attained, the applicant may be summarily rejected.

At other schools the folder is assembled, and the applicant may be invited for an interview based on the essay or personal comments section of the application. This is a very time-consuming process but, in an important way, is a reflection of the caliber of the school and its faculty's commitment to the students. Several schools utilize a two-stage process where grades and MCATs are first reviewed and then, if satisfactory, the committee reviews the essay portion of the application.

To review, cumulative grade point averages, as well as grades obtained in science courses, scores on the MCAT, descriptions of extracurricular activities, letters of recommendation from faculty members, and letters from past employers are evaluated. If the application is given a high rating by each of the people who did the screening, the applicant will most likely be invited for the prized personal interview. At least he or she will have cleared the first hurdle.

Determining the Motivation

After a candidate clears initial screening, his or her whole application is carefully evaluated. Special attention is given to five areas. First, the admissions committee ascertains what courses went into producing the student's GPA. Required and science-related courses are noted, as well as those that show breadth of education. If there is a discrepancy between GPA and MCAT scores, a candidate's coursework is looked at for a possible explanation. Basically, however, the admissions committee is interested in what turned the applicant on in college. The same can be said for extracurricular activities. However, good grades and no extracurricular activities may be indicative of a person who used up all available energy supplies just to do well academically. Students who list many extracurricular activities and have also done well in class are thought likely to be capable medical students.

Just as extracurricular activities provide the admissions committee with insight into the applicant as a human being, the personal statement also lets the student seem more of an individual. The personal statement details the applicant's motivation for seeking a medical career. The expressed attitude toward service takes a particularly high priority in the committee's evaluation. If you state a strong desire to work with people but have no clinical medicine exposure and your transcript shows you took only science courses and your summer job was as a lab assistant, the committee will sense a discrepancy and will begin to doubt your suitability as a medical student. The committee must feel that society is going to profit when you become a physician, that your motives are service-oriented rather than self-aggrandizing.

Committee members are adept at judging such an amorphous concept as motivation. Ideally, they look for a certain group of characteristics in a potential physician. In an Ethics of Health Care study performed by the National Academy of Sciences, the top seven personal attributes used in the selection process were as follows: 1) humanitarian beliefs and sincerity, 2) evidence of psychological maturity, 3) initiative, perseverance, and enthusiasm, 4) ability to communicate effectively, 5) interest and knowledge of medicine, 6) general intellectual interest and cultural development, and 7) imagination or creativity. Furthermore, in the same study, faculty members on the admissions committee of a particular school endorsed *alert, conscientious, enthusiastic,* and *honest* as the adjectives used to describe the best candidates they had seen or folders they had reviewed at one time.

According to Dr. Marvin Fogel of the Mount Sinai School of Medicine, "the verbal and action offerings apparent in your credentials will be the following: the undeniable fact of your desire for knowledge and its implementation against disease; your quite evident compassion for the ill and the solving of their problems; your positive ability to work with people even under vexing circumstances; your unequivocal understanding of the continuing, unceasing education process that the practicing physician must undergo; the inescapable sacrifice of outside interest time in order to devote yourself to the 'jealous lover,' which is the profession of medicine."

Lastly, another favorite guidepost or indicator of a candidate's motivation level is the summer activities. Were the applicant's months away from school used to get a great tan, or did he or she attempt to learn more about the complex medical field? More on this appears in Summer Programs for the Premed; be sure to see this information before planning your next beach bum summer!

Family background is important in only two instances. The first is if the applicant's family is poor. This is usually taken as an indication of a highly motivated student who has had to fight all the way along the line. However, the committee may want to know why this candidate decided on medicine and what the choice means financially to the family. The second case is that of a physician's son or daughter who applies to medical school. The committee may become suspicious and want to be sure that the student's decision was not influenced by family pressure. The committee knows that attrition rates for the sons and daughters of MDs are higher than for the offspring of any other professional or nonprofessional group.

Letters of recommendation from undergraduate faculty members assume great importance in the committee's evaluation of an applicant. Not all recommendations are uniformly glowing. Some are merely perfunctory, while others may be ambiguous and need clarification, and still others may be unfavorable. In these letters, admissions committees look for statements regarding the candidate's motivation or commitment to medicine, his or her integrity, originality, and dependability. Any inconsistencies between GPA, personal statement, and faculty recommendations must be explained.

On the basis of the appraisal of the application, a student may be put into one of four categories:

1. Invited for interview—if satisfactory, accepted.

2. Invited for interview—use interview to clarify problems or inconsistencies in the record. Explain red flags. Give the student an opportunity to explain parts of the record that cause committee members some concern before acceptance is offered.

3. Hold category—hold until another group of applicants has been evaluated or until additional information is received, such as grades of courses in progress.

4. Rejected on the basis of the record.

If the candidate falls into either category one or two, he or she will be interviewed.

The interview itself serves two functions. It gives the interviewer a chance to see the candidate as an individual rather than as a collection of papers in a file somewhere. Second, it enables the interviewer to clarify items in the application if that is necessary.

Being invited for a personal interview is an accomplishment in itself. Once invited, you can be assured that your folder will get a very thorough going-over. Beware, however, that an interview appointment does not mean automatic acceptance. Several hurdles lie ahead.

CHAPTER 6

Rejection and Your Alternatives

Rejection and Reapplication

A favorite question posed at the end of medical school interviews is, "What will you do if you don't get into a medical school?" This is not usually asked out of any genuine concern for your future but to assess the strength of your conviction to pursue medicine. Don't say, "There's always teaching biology or selling encyclopedias."

The person who really wants to become a doctor will outline specific plans to wait, perhaps do some more coursework, and reapply the next year. If again unsuccessful, a foreign medical school would be the next step. Or even more confidence can be shown and the student can say that all other alternatives are second rate, no serious consideration had ever been given to being anything other than a physician, and he or she feels perfectly capable of completing the medical school curriculum.

This is an appropriate answer to the examiner's question, but is certainly not the most realistic way to think about the problem. In other countries, where medical school enrollment is open to all who have college degrees, the question of alternatives would be superfluous. Here, where demand for places in medical school far outstrips supply, the issue is crucial. To preserve your sanity, not to mention your livelihood, the issue of alternatives must be faced early in your premed career. To be sure, there are three possibilities for the rejected applicant: choose an alternative profession, reapply, or attend a foreign medical school. Although any combination of alternatives may be pursued simultaneously, it is necessary to plan for the first one well in advance of your graduation date.

To be able to select a suitable alternative career while still a premed, you must be very sure of your motives for wanting to enter medicine. This will also be an asset when, should you become a physician, it comes time to choose a field of specialization. Basically, you must have an accurate picture of *what* it is doctors actually do, and then ask yourself, "*Why* do I want to become a doctor?" The *what* problem can be taken care of by visiting medical centers and physicians' offices and observing what goes on. Work in a hospital for a summer. Read medical periodicals. Talk to physicians. Talk to patients. The *why* requires more insight, and you might avail yourself of help from a therapist in order to get it all straightened out.

Once you've gotten your head together, the question of alternative professions can be faced intelligently, should the need arise. If your motives for entering medicine are strictly materialistic, then for the amount of time invested, the business professions and dentistry yield much higher dividends. If the motivating force is status and prestige, law or politics is a suitable alternative. Anyone interested in basic medical research can pursue it almost as easily with a PhD as an MD. Altruistic motives will probably find gratification in the service professions—notably social work or psychology. The clinical aspects of medicine can be duplicated in nursing and physician assistant programs, as well as by training in the alternative health fields such as acupuncture, chiropractic, massage, and nutrition counseling.

Consider Reapplying

The issue of reapplication to medical school deserves some discussion. Clearly, it is more difficult to get into a medical school the second time around, although many students have entered by this route. In fact, of the 42,269 applicants in 2009–10, 11,206 were repeat applicants. These students most often have strong academic records and either applied to the wrong schools or sought admission in an especially competitive year. They are not marginal students. As a rule, they are the students who are most surprised at being rejected. They fully expected to be admitted to a medical school, and their premedical advisers expected them to be as well. They are the students who can point to others with lesser credentials who were successful where they failed. For such students reapplication is feasible. The questions are when to reapply and what to do in the meantime.

Reapply to any school that has encouraged you to do so and to any school where you were interviewed or put on a waiting list. If you initially applied to the "wrong" schools, as previously defined, find out what the "right" schools are for you and apply to all of them. Reapply early. The question of what to do in the interim has various answers. A school may urge that you take additional courses or enter a special program with the incentive that if you do well enough they will accept you, reconsider you, or something in between these extremes. The choice is yours. I would only suggest that the more positive the incentive, the more you should consider following the recommendation.

Many students with bachelor's degrees enter graduate school for a year as a steppingstone to medical school. There is a growing feeling in medical schools, however, not to accept candidates in the process of obtaining a higher degree until after that degree has been earned. Thus, entering a graduate school might result in a two- to three-year delay before acceptance by a medical college. In addition, you will once again be under the same pressure to perform academically as you were when an undergraduate. I would not recommend this route to the nonscience major, and would advise it only for science majors who feel the extra science will be useful to them in their medical field.

Actually, medical schools do not necessarily look favorably at students with either advanced or multiple degrees. Primarily, they wonder why the student could not find satisfaction in their first field of study. If the student has spent little or no time practicing in the area in which he or she was credentialed, then committee members may regard this as wasted education. For example, a person licensed to practice nursing and radiology technology who does neither and then applies to medical school has deprived the health professions of two health care workers. This person is usually viewed as a student with uncertain motivation instead of one who can achieve what he or she sets out to do.

Rejection by medical school requires a careful consideration of the applicant's weaknesses. Academic shortcomings can be remedied by repeating courses or taking extra ones as a special student. Low MCATs necessitate retaking that exam after extensive preparation. A student with a one-sided education stressing academics exclusively may find two years in the Peace Corps or performing other service-oriented jobs will prove an asset.

Reapplication to medical school is itself a testimonial to the applicant's persistence and desire to become a physician. Indeed, such students often graduate at the top of their medical school class. Before investing time in the reapplication process, an applicant must proceed from a realistic appraisal of their position. With competition for medical school places becoming stiffer each year, it would be self-defeating for someone with a weak record to stay in the race. Solicit an objective evaluation of your chances for success from the premedical adviser or other counselor. It is important for your own mental health to know when to quit and do something else.

A past issue of the *Journal of Medical Education* offers an excellent study of unsuccessful applicants to medical schools. Using questionnaires, the authors compiled data on a group of 98 rejected students. Information was solicited on the respondent's college major, accomplishments in the physical and biological sciences, MCAT scores, application patterns, the influence of various forces on the decision to enter medicine, perceived reasons for rejection, and factors related to subsequent academic and career decisions. Of particular interest is the large percentage of rejected applicants who chose careers related to the health professions; e.g., dentist, podiatrist, optometrist, pharmacist, health educator, sanitary engineer, medical laboratory technician, medical and scientific writer, or pharmacologist.

In a similar study conducted at Johns Hopkins, some interesting results were obtained. Almost 2,000 rejected applicants were questioned about their future plans. As explained in the *National Premedical Newsletter:*

The majority of the 1,933 who responded to the questionnaire had reapplied to medical school. Of these, 27 percent had succeeded in entering either U.S. or foreign schools. Because women comprised only 12.8 percent of the total applicant group, the entire available number of unaccepted female applicants was contacted. Of all who responded—men and women—most tended to have higher MCAT scores and were more likely to gain admission when they reapplied. Of the unaccepted applicants then engaged in study in foreign schools (96), 90 percent intended to practice in the United States.

Among those who were rejected after a second try, many were still intending to reapply, a fact that would indicate that the original intention of becoming a doctor dies hard. It was found that the earlier in life the applicants had decided on a medical career, the less willing they were to give up, *especially if they had no contingency plans.*

Most of those reapplying who sought counsel from nonprofessional sources (family, friends) were urged to reapply and were more apt to do so.

Such nonprofessional advisers were not apt to suggest alternatives to a medical career.

What of those who did not reapply? The study found that 53 percent of the men and 42 percent of the women were still pursuing studies in graduate or professional schools, both in health-related and nonhealth-related fields. Of those pursuing studies other than medicine but in health-related fields, 18 percent of the men were in dental school. The largest group of women were studying microbiology, bacteriology, or other medical sciences.

Most of the remaining group were employed, 55 percent of them in the health field—17 percent of the men and 31 percent of the women in clinical laboratory technology.

The doctors who conducted the survey were concerned that about half the unaccepted applicants were not attracted to alternative health careers when there is such a vital need for additional health manpower in specific geographic areas and in particular aspects of health care. If this situation is to be turned around, the doctors felt that knowledgeable counselors should be available at the undergraduate and high school levels (rather than for the applicant to rely on family and friends *after* being turned down).

They also raised questions as to whether or not medical schools are selecting the appropriate numbers and types of applicants in view of current and future health care needs. Do the paramedical health careers need to be upgraded in terms of status and income to attract the appropriate personnel? They concluded that the answers to such questions will help determine the best use of this country's qualified health-oriented labor force.

Several years ago I received a most interesting letter from a student who, by all established criteria, should have been admitted to medical school, but wasn't. His letter was the most articulate I have ever received, his questions the most serious, and his situation the most instructive. In his rejection there is a lesson for even the most outstanding applicant:

> Dear Dr. Brown:
>
> I'm one of your readers and have a special interest in the sixth chapter of your book Getting into Medical School. I've just gone through an agonizing six months of interviewing and waiting for replies from various medical schools across the country. Things have not gone well and I'm now seeking sound advice about rejection and reapplication. Unfortunately, I can't seem to find anyone I can really talk to about the matter and I thought perhaps it might be helpful to contact you.

My circumstances are a little unusual, I suppose, and that may be part of the problem, so I should fill you in on some background. I'm a graduate student in biochemistry at the University of Illinois at Champaign-Urbana and plan to finish my PhD in the next few months. I wish dearly to attend a good medical school and become a research physician; I feel I have the credentials to be admitted to some of the better medical schools in the country. Therefore, this past year I submitted applications to nine schools, most of them probably ranked in the top twenty in the United States, hoping to be admitted for the fall of _____ (by which time my thesis will be complete). I got the applications in on time, not as early as I had hoped, but within the deadlines. I then received some promising news in December of last year: a letter from Washington University in St. Louis, asking for an interview and inviting me to apply for a Distinguished Student Scholarship, and a letter from Harvard asking for an interview. The Harvard interview came first and was held in Chicago. I felt it went well and the one interviewer, who was a member of the admissions committee, talked very encouragingly to me, though he did say he could not guarantee anything. The Washington University interviews went all right, but I was told that my application was submitted kind of late.

Next, I had interviews with representatives of the University of Miami. I felt I handled myself fairly well at the interviews but the last interviewer told me that, although I was a well-qualified applicant, I did not stand a chance of getting into a school like Harvard. He said it was obvious that I did not know how to "play the game," that the only way to get into a top school was through "contacts." His comments upset me very much, but I put them aside and hoped he was just trying to convince me that Miami was a choice I should consider (it is not among my first several choices) or that he just didn't know what he was talking about.

Disappointing news began to arrive after this point. Washington University did not accept me but placed me on a waiting list and said I might hear from them later. Yale and Cornell sent me rejections. Then two more crushing letters arrived: rejections from Harvard and Johns Hopkins. I was very discouraged by this point. Then I received news that Stanford wanted to interview me in Chicago. I went, not expecting much to come of it because it was so late in the year. Several weeks later I found out I was on their waiting list and would hear from them later if anything developed. Nothing has developed.

I was accepted at Miami, but I had to turn the offer down. I knew I really did not want to go to Miami and, since the program is accelerated, it begins in mid-June and I felt I would not have completed my thesis by that time. Also, they required a nonrefundable $1,000 deposit, which was a little steep for me.

I've read portions of your book, particularly the chapter on rejection and reapplication, and I've settled it in my own mind that I must reapply and try to get into these schools one more time. However, I think, as you pointed out, it is imperative that I understand where in the application process I fell short. Obviously, of the schools I applied to, only one accepted me and the majority outright rejected me. I've tried to discuss the matter with several people (my adviser, health professions counselors, etc.) and have even written letters to the admission directors, trying to nail down specific areas where I was not competitive in relation to the accepted candidates. Unfortunately, no one seems able or willing to give me helpful answers. The typical response I get is something like, "Such a large number of very fine applicants apply to these programs each year that it is simply not possible to accept everyone," which, of course, tells me absolutely nothing.

What I need to know, and am hoping you can help me identify, are the factors in my application or background that hurt me the most. Obviously, since I was interviewed by some of these schools, they must have at least entertained the notion of accepting me. What factors did they look at then which caused them to say no or maybe instead of yes? I do not believe the interviews themselves were the problem; the feedback I got from the interviewers was largely positive. Also, my letters of recommendation were good and there is no indication that they presented any kind of problem. Do you think it could be my age? I realize I'm a bit older than the average applicant, but I was told that older candidates are not discriminated against so much any more and are even looked on more favorably by some schools. Was it because I did not have any "contacts" within the schools, someone who could put in a good word for me directly to admission committee members? Was the fact that I didn't have journal articles published yet considered significant (they're in preparation)? Or do medical school admissions committees simply frown on PhDs seeking a medical degree (I've heard some do)?

It may seem a little odd that I'm trying to get advice from a stranger so far away, but I just can't seem to get substantive answers from anyone I've contacted. Perhaps it is unrealistic to hope you can provide some insights into my problems, but I felt I must try, and the invitation in the preface of your book to write caught my eye. I apologize for the length of the letter and hope I have not infringed too much on your time. I realize you cannot be absolutely conclusive about the matter. Yet, I would appreciate any ideas you might have about specific shortcomings in my

application in relation to the schools to which I applied. I've
included a copy of my AMCAS application to give you more infor-
mation to go on. If it is more convenient for you to call than write
or if you have specific questions, please feel free to call collect.
Once again, thanks for your time.

Robert A. Mock

Mr. Mock included a copy of his AMCAS application along with his letter. It is impressive. His academic record is a compendium of A's and
honors; his undergraduate GPA was 3.98 overall and his graduate GPA was
4. He had many extracurricular activities as well as interesting school-year
and summer employments. His page for personal comments was extremely
well-written.

What went wrong? How could such an applicant be denied admission to
medical school? Is there no justice in the universe? I was so intrigued that I
took Mr. Mock up on his offer to call him rather than write. It proved to be
well worth doing.

Over the phone, Mr. Mock came across as a sincere but unenthusiastic
speaker. He spoke in flat unmodulated tones. It made me wonder if his
interviewers might not have found him a bit too unemotional. But, to be
fair, they might have interpreted this as being even-keeled or steadfast. On
the whole, however, I feel that the interview is a place to strut your stuff.
It's the time to make a lasting impression and state your case for why you
should be admitted. Conveying your excitement is OK.

Actually, Mr. Mock is not so unusual an applicant. In point of fact, he is
your run-of-the-mill extremely well-qualified candidate. There are hundreds like him with similar profiles—perpetual students with near perfect
grade points, high test scores, obviously bright, well-motivated, and capable of becoming physicians. Many of them get admitted to medical school.
Some do not.

Mr. Mock's mistake was in not realizing that the prestigious schools to
which he had applied get many applications from students of his caliber. At
less renowned schools, he would have been more of a standout and probably would have gained admission. Mr. Mock should have applied to more of
these; although there is wide variance in this, nine is almost an insufficient
number of applications when they are all to "top twenty" schools.

Mr. Mock's refusal to accept Miami's offer perplexed me and I asked him
about it. Apparently, he would have had to start medical school before completing his PhD, and this he was unwilling to do. This was a mistake, I

believe, since medical school places are so prized and Mr. Mock was not unusually competitive in his position (a near PhD without publications). Sometimes you can't have your cake and eat it, too: sacrifices must be made.

I encouraged Mr. Mock to pursue his ambition. I advised him to reapply to all schools that put him on their waiting list and to more of the less prestigious institutions. He was a strong candidate who simply applied to the wrong schools and may not have been aggressive enough at his interviews. His application timing may have been off, too. I fully expected to see him admitted the next year, after earning his PhD. His interviewer would then address him as Dr. Mock!

The Post-baccalaureate

For applicants whose GPA is bordering on the weaker side for applying to medical school (such as having a sub-3.3 GPA), attending a post-baccalaureate program may be an option. In recent years, post-baccalaureate programs have become increasingly popular for applicants who would like to improve their academic coursework. These programs serve mainly as potential GPA boosters or help nontraditional applicants fulfill course requirements for medical school.

Post-baccalaureate programs fall into two general categories. The first kind is a basic sciences program that is mostly aimed toward people who have not completed their premedical course requirements. These are usually people who have majored in non-science fields or have decided to go into medicine later in their careers. The science courses can be completed on your own at your local university without a formal program. The obvious benefit of this program is that you will not have to spend the money and time to formally apply to a program. You can also take courses at your own pace, and you will have more flexibility in terms of your schedule. However, attending a formal post-baccalaureate program comes with significant benefits such as advising, faculty support, and opportunities for clinical and research exposure. The downside is that such programs are expensive and are often very intensive, and they can become a one- to two-year-long, nearly full-time commitment.

The second type of post-baccalaureate program is the enhancement program. Unlike the "basic sciences" programs, enhancement programs are targeted toward people who have already completed their basic science requirements but feel they need to raise their GPA to be competitive. Like the basic science courses, enhancement courses can be taken on your own or with a formal, structured program.

In addition to improving GPA, structured post-baccalaureate programs can also offer the premedical student advising, preparation for the MCAT, and clinical and research exposure. In essence, once one is enrolled, such a program is intended to help the student enhance any lacking aspects of his or her credentials and ultimately help him or her successfully matriculate into medical school. However, it should be noted that the primary benefit from a post-baccalaureate program is to enhance the applicant's GPA. Other possible areas of weakness, such as low MCAT scores or lack of clinical experience, can be remedied through the student's own initiative. In other words, GPA withstanding, the student is better served to study for the MCAT or gain clinical experience independent of a structured post-baccalaureate program. This will allow the student to skip the expense (several thousand dollars per semester) and time (usually one to two years) required to complete a post-baccalaureate program.

There are several factors to consider when choosing the right post-baccalaureate program. Obviously, there is the issue of cost and convenience of scheduling and location. As previously mentioned, post-baccalaureate programs tend to be expensive—costing up to several thousands dollars per semester. A typical program lasts one to two years, depending on the pace and needs of the student. In terms of scheduling, there are programs that offer evening classes. However, for students interested in finishing the post-baccalaureate in as little time as a year, there are quite a few classes to cram in. Completing the academic coursework can become a full-time occupation—not to mention that the coursework is rigorous, and students must maintain very good academic performance to benefit from the program. Any grades—for better or worse—will need to be included in the student's medical school application and will be factored into the student's GPA. Ultimately, such issues of cost and time will depend on the student's individual situation, but beware that a post-baccalaureate program is a heavy commitment and should not be taken lightly.

When choosing a program, it is well advised to also carefully consider the program's name recognition, advising resources, and faculty support. Since post-baccalaureate programs are costly and non-degree granting, some people may feel a sense of profiteering associated with such programs. It is wise to select and attend a program that is closely linked with an established university. This not only helps to give a sense of authority and legitimacy, but it also assures admissions committees of the academic rigor of your coursework. Although there are not clear rankings of the prestige of a given program, several well-established programs come to mind, including Columbia; Johns Hopkins; University of California, San Francisco; University of Southern California; Mills, Scripps, Harvard Extension, University of Pennsylvania, University of Chicago, and Bryn Mawr. By all means, this is not a comprehensive list. Students can find many more post-baccalaureate programs through the official AAMC Web site (**www.services.aamc.org/postbac**).

Many post-baccalaureate programs also offer advising services and faculty support letters for their students. These are valuable resources and should not be overlooked. The faculty support letter is a committee letter that can serve as a recommendation letter for medical school applications. However, the general rule is that students must maintain good academic standing—usually above a 3.0 GPA—to receive the committee letter. Some schools also require a good MCAT score in order to receive faculty support. In addition, some post-baccalaureate programs offer linkage programs. Linkage refers to a formal agreement between the post-baccalaureate program and a medical school that allows for top students from the post-baccalaureate program to undergo an accelerated application to the medical school, significantly increasing the applicant's chances of admission. However, it must be noted that linkage is only awarded to a small top percentage of students, usually after their second year in the post-baccalaureate program.

So just how much exactly does attending a post-baccalaureate program increase one's chances of getting into medical school? Unfortunately, this is difficult to say, and there are no definitive statistics. Some of the most successful programs claim that nearly all of their students matriculate to medical school. However, such claims must be viewed with caution, as these programs may be reporting only applicants that have successfully completed the program and have received their full faculty support. These are the same students that have maintained good GPAs and high MCAT scores and are often already competitive applicants for medical school.

Here is some data that will give you a sense of some of the most successful programs. The Johns Hopkins post-baccalaureate program claims that nearly 100 percent of their applicants matriculate to medical school. However, their class size is very small, at fewer than 30 students, and the program's admissions policy is to admit students who already have competitive GPA and MCAT numbers. Other programs such as Columbia, Mills

College, and Bryn Mawr also report that more than 90 percent of their students successfully matriculate to medical school. However, keep in mind that such high percentages are not indicative of all programs, and students should thoroughly research a program before attending.

To enroll in a post-baccalaureate program, one must also go through an admissions process. While specific requirements differ from program to program, applications typically require college and high school transcripts. Some programs also require standardized testing scores such as MCAT, GRE, or SAT. A personal statement, recommendation letters, and an interview are also often required. The most successful programs have a GPA requirement of at least 3.0. However, the majority of successful applicants to such programs have at least a GPA of 3.2. Admissions for the fall semester typically begin in January and occur on a rolling basis for most programs. Fortunately, the application turnaround time is quick, at around one month for most programs.

Osteopathy

An alternative approach to allopathic medicine is osteopathy, a field that began as a systemic approach to traditional medicine with a philosophy rooted in traditional medicine. Osteopathy, or osteopathic medicine, views the systems of the body as interrelated, directly working together to maintain health, and incorporates distinct elements to promote holistic well-being.

Osteopathy was developed in 1874 by a pioneering surgeon named Andrew Taylor Still, who sought to encourage well-being by focusing on the entire body instead of just the symptoms of a disease. He proposed that stimulating the musculoskeletal system would facilitate the body's ability to heal itself. His theory introduced a greater understanding of the body's systems over traditional techniques in medicine that Still viewed as harmful.

In 1892, Still founded the first college of osteopathic medicine, the American School of Osteopathy, in Kirksville, Missouri. The field grew as the American Association for the Advancement of Osteopathy (today known as the American Osteopathic Association) was founded in Missouri in 1897, and more than 5,000 doctors of osteopathic medicine were in practice by the time of Still's death in 1917. By 1947, osteopathic hospitals were approved for residency training and, in 1950, the Aurdrain County, Missouri court defined the practice of osteopathy as the practice of a complete physician, with the rights to perform surgery and prescribe and administer medications.

Today, there are twenty-two osteopathic medical schools in the United States. Doctors of osteopathic medicine (DOs) are licensed physicians that can practice medicine in all 50 states of the United States. The American Osteopathic Association reported that there are currently more than 56,000 practicing DOs today. Osteopathic medical schools are located primarily throughout the east coast, west coast, and in the Midwestern areas of the United States; practicing DOs are concentrated in states such as California, Florida, Illinois, Michigan, Missouri, New Jersey, New York, Ohio, Pennsylvania, and Texas. Many doctors of osteopathic medicine practice in rural areas, and more than half of these physicians practice in primary care. As the current focus in health care is shifting toward preventive medicine, opportunities for osteopathic doctors have and will continue to increase.

Students studying osteopathic medicine will embark on a path similar to allopathic medical students, but with some notable differences. Prerequisite courses are similar to allopathic requirements prior to matriculation, and students must take the MCAT for admission. Admission is keenly competitive for osteopathic schools, but osteopathic admissions are reputed to place greater emphasis on personal quality and character versus numbers. The American Association of Colleges of Osteopathic Medicine (AACOM) reported that the average GPA and MCAT scores for osteopathic matriculants in 2009 were 3.49 and 26.2, respectively, as compared to 3.60 and 30.8 at allopathic schools. Though both types of physicians are trained to work in various medical fields, the doctor of osteopathic medicine is the minority profession in medical practice as these doctors comprise only 6% of America's physicians. Osteopathic students complete four years of medical school, an internship, and residency as allopathic medical students; the Comprehensive Osteopathic Medical Licensing Exam is taken for achieving licensure. A primary difference is the approach to medicine reflected through osteopathic coursework: osteopathic curriculum includes training in osteopathic manipulative medicine, manipulation of the musculoskeletal system, which ensures physicians' understanding of its effects on the body. Osteopathic medical schools focus on primary care and preventive medicine; this emphasis on primary care is demonstrated as osteopathic schools require that students spend more time during rotations in primary care areas than allopathic students do. Clinical work is divided throughout medical facilities and doctors's offices, as osteopathic medical schools do not partner with a teaching hospital.

Recipients of the osteopathic medical degree do not generally encounter limitations in practice in the United States, since they can specialize in medical areas like allopathic medical doctors. However, the career path for most doctors of osteopathic medicine is a clinical career versus a research-oriented career. While some states do not have a large percentage of practicing DOs, these physicians provide patients with some alternative methods that may not be available from allopathic doctors. Osteopathic physicians are trained to treat virtually any illness or trauma. Osteopathic medicine can be an ideal choice for the student seeking patient care through noninvasive healing methods while taking a partnership approach with the patient in treatment.

Attending an International Medical School

For many rejected applicants, international medical schools offer an alternative to either giving up medicine or reapplying to U.S. medical schools. Currently, there are about 10,000 native U.S. citizens and an equal number of naturalized citizens at schools abroad. These students attend medical schools in some fifteen countries but are chiefly in Mexico and the Caribbean nations of Grenada, Montserrat, and the Dominican Republic. Smaller groups are located in Belgium, France, Israel, Italy, Poland, the U.K., and the Philippines. Medical schools in Canada rarely admit Americans. In general, foreign, nonproprietary schools do not admit students from countries that have medical schools.

Americans who apply to foreign medical schools should know that most countries have to have at least one medical school that serves to educate native physicians. These schools are largely off limits to foreigners. Realistically, most foreign medical schools that accept Americans were not created to serve the local population; they were begun by entrepreneurs to offer medical degrees to all who could pay the price. In this respect they are similar to the proprietary type of medical school that flourished in this country in the nineteenth century. Organized for profit, these schools had low academic standards, poorly equipped laboratories, and undistinguished physicians holding the title of professor. The famous *Flexner Report* of 1910 effectively put these schools out of business, but they have resurfaced again, at least in spirit, during the last three decades. I am speaking particularly of the Caribbean Basin and Mexico, where the majority of all Americans studying abroad are enrolled.

I had the opportunity to visit the St. George's University School of Medicine in Grenada, where almost 1,500 Americans are enrolled. The school has two enrollments a year of 200 students, thus far exceeding the number of matriculants to U.S. medical schools, which average 100 to 125 students per year. Surprisingly, I was told that they had eight applicants for every place and, although they had students from all over the world, over 85 percent were from the United States. This school, as well as other foreign medical schools popular among U.S. students, is geared to getting their students to pass the United States Medical Licensing Examination (USMLE) parts 1 and 2, which is the primary requirement of the Educational Council for Foreign Medical Graduates (ECFMG) for admission into graduate medical education (residency programs) in the United States and the gateway to obtain a full and unrestricted license to practice medicine here. However, average pass rates for these students is under 50 percent, perhaps as much because they are not good test takers (which is why they may have been rejected by U.S. medical schools) as because of the quality of the training. But this can be uneven from school to school, and the good news is that the exam may be taken as many times as necessary to pass.

The laboratories at St. George's were well equipped and the library had a plethora of current journals. The lecture halls were spacious and comfortable and the professors seemed primarily dedicated to teaching. There were services for students who were having academic or psychological difficulty. Housing was available. And, most important, classes and textbooks were in English. It's hard enough studying medicine in a foreign country without having to also deal with a language barrier, although most foreign medical schools do conduct their classes in the language native to their country. Unless proficient in a foreign language, Americans would be best advised to first consider those schools that cater to them. These would include most of the Caribbean and Mexican schools.

Even with classes in English, the American medical student studying abroad faces other obstacles. Financially, they are on student visas and rarely permitted to work for money. Therefore, they must be adequately financed before they go, either from savings or loans. Medical education abroad is not cheap. In fact, tuition and living expenses rival that of onshore schools. Additionally, travel and incidental expenses would probably make the cost of foreign medical study in excess of that here. Psychologically, the U.S. student is at a clear disadvantage in a foreign country. Having been rejected from U.S. schools and not having gone abroad as a first choice, he or she may be embittered. Also, culture shock may be pronounced; living in a strange country is often an alienating experience even when there are other North Americans around, for as soon as you get off campus, you are in another world. The American student abroad may initially experience overwhelming loneliness and frustration.

Although the basic medical sciences may be taught up to a minimal standard, students need to be concerned about the adequacy of the clinical years. The third and fourth years of medical school give students exposure to patients and their illnesses. Unless clerkships give students sufficient clinical experience, they may be at a disadvantage when taking part 2 of the USMLE. The smaller foreign schools have attempted to deal with this by sending their students to other countries. Grenada, for example, has clerkships in the United States and the United Kingdom, and none on that small island.

Perhaps the biggest problem studying medicine abroad is the uncertainty about what will happen afterward. Candidates who do successfully complete their medical education at foreign medical schools must take extra steps to be eligible for accredited residency programs in the U.S., board specialty certification, and state licensure. International medical school graduates (IMGs), both U.S. citizens and not, are vital to the operation of many of our hospitals, particularly in the Northeast and Midwest. This is because there are many more residency positions than U.S. graduates to fill them. This shortage works to the advantage of the IMG. In 1988, 3,500 IMGs entered the first postgraduate residency year—20 percent of the total of U.S. grads. By 1994 their participation had increased to 7,500. The total number of IMGs in residency programs during the same time period increased from 15.3 percent to 23.3 percent of all residents in allopathic programs. In 2005, the National Resident Matching Program enrolled 3,813 programs in the match, which altogether offered 24,012 positions. A total of 31,862 applicants participated. Of those, 15,308 were 2005 graduates of accredited U.S. medical schools and 16,554 were Independent Applicants, including osteopathic graduates, Canadian graduates, and, mostly, foreign medical school graduates. In 2010, the National Resident Matching Program enrolled 4,176 programs in the match, which altogether offered 25,520 positions. A total of 37,559 applicants participated. Of those, 16,427 were 2010 graduates of accredited U.S. medical schools and 21,132 were Independent Applicants, including osteopathic graduates, Canadian graduates, and mostly, foreign medical school graduates.

The times they are a-changing. Experts disagree as to dates, but trends predict too many physicians per capita in the near future. There are already too many physicians in some medical specialties in some locations. This will ultimately lead to too many physicians in all specialties in all locations unless the trend is checked. How do we turn down the tap and limit the flow of medical school graduates?

Already some U.S. medical schools are reducing their class sizes. No new medical schools are being built in this country. But short of closing schools now existent, little can be done nationally to reduce physician output. And, indeed, what's the point in chiseling down a few U.S. grads when schools like St. George's are turning out 400 graduates a year and the University at Guadalajara probably a similar number? These schools are unabashedly operating for profit, have capable students, and are geared toward getting their students to pass the USMLE. Most of them do and, upon graduation, are eligible to apply for those residencies that U.S. graduates find undesirable. They go to places that depend on resident physician labor, generally in the inner cities and rural areas—places that, as a tourist, you wouldn't want to visit and, as a physician, you wouldn't want to train. And there's the dilemma.

If these hospitals—in cities like Newark, Detroit, Kalamazoo, Macon, Brooklyn, Hartford, and dozens of other places that even Humbert Humbert never thought to visit—don't get doctors, then they will be forced to close, thereby denying medical care to the indigent populations that they serve. Residency physicians are a cheap source of medical labor and traditionally form the house staff of teaching hospitals. Mass General and the Mayo Clinic need not worry; their positions will always fill. But Coney Island Hospital and St. Mary's in Waterbury may not be able to run without the international medical graduate. These are the kind of places that foreign graduates go to train, and the training is actually quite good because the hospitals are usually understaffed and the residents usually run them. Of course, studies show that the IMGs don't stay where they trained but seek out the same desirable locations as the U.S. graduates, leaving the inner cities still relatively deprived of physicians, and the suburbs overloaded.

I believe that we will see the closing of more and more of these hospitals as managed care makes inroads into their neighborhoods. Inpatient medicine will be handled in fewer facilities as ambulatory care centers abound. More efficient management will allow higher salaries for house staff, and they will be recruited from among the already-trained specialists and generalists who are the junior members of health maintenance organizations.

Furthermore, the outcry from organized medicine to shut the gates to the IMG will be hard to oppose once there is little demand for their services and more American-trained doctors find themselves under- and unemployed. I predict that in five to ten years, the well will run dry for the foreign medical school graduate.

But in the meantime, foreign study remains a viable option. These three Web sites are a fine starting place for information about international medical schools and the hoops the IMG needs to jump through to get into a residency training program in the United States:

www.ecfmg.org/annuals/ECFMG2009.pdf
Education Commission for Foreign Medical Graduates

www.imed.faimer.org/
International Medical Education Directory

www.nrmp.org/about_nrmp/index.html
The National Resident Matching Program

Another alternative, seldom mentioned, is for students to remain abroad and to practice medicine in the foreign countries in which they become licensed physicians. I have met retired people in their fifties and sixties who were studying medicine abroad with expressly that purpose in mind. They had comfortable retirement incomes and were fulfilling lifelong desires to become physicians. Furthermore, many of them brought to their study and practice of medicine technical expertise of great value in their countries of emigration. They knew that they were of an age when finding positions back home would be impossible, so they learned a new language and offered their skills where they were most needed. A while ago, I received a letter from a senior citizen studying medicine in Guadalajara!

> Dear Dr. Brown:
> I do definitely recall reading your book and writing to you several years ago. I tried all over Europe, especially Italy and Spain, and also happened to write to the Universidad Autónoma de Guadalajara. I got accepted here at UAG and am now in my second semester. It's been real exciting for me to begin a new profession—I think I told you I was 62 years old and a retired chemical engineer. I have to be very thankful to UAG for giving me this chance. There are about 500–600 other students here from the U.S. who are also thankful for their chance to pursue medicine.

As luck would have it, UAG turns out to be a very good medical school. They have started a program for Americans in which all the basic sciences are taught in English. The program is aimed at imitating American med schools. All our tests contain national-board-type questions and the depth of each science course is modeled after American medical colleges. Actually, UAG was forced into restructuring their curricula to compete with the Caribbean schools.

My wife, who was a biology major and a licensed laboratory technician in Illinois, decided to enter medical school with me. After graduation we hope to return to the U.S. to do family practice residencies wherever they might be available. We would love to return to California, since we are both natives, but that looks extremely impossible at the moment, as I'm sure you know. However, I am confident we will find an area of the U.S. where doctors are needed. Louisiana sent a representative down here to recruit good students for residencies in pediatrics and family practice because of physician shortages in their poorer areas. We have read of great health care needs among migrant workers in Utah. Also, we would not be unhappy remaining in Mexico since service is our ultimate goal.

Jim Watts

I know of no evidence that it is easier to get into an American medical school after a year in a foreign one compared to taking an advanced degree, more coursework, or simply reapplying. To recapitulate briefly: Going to an international medical school is better than going to none at all, if you are determined to become an MD. Graduate school should not be entered unless you sincerely want to earn a degree in one of the basic sciences. Extra coursework should be followed to correct obvious weaknesses. Work in medical areas is a definite plus. Simply reapplying the next year is a prerogative for the strongest applicants who, I would suggest, should take the year for personal growth.

CHAPTER 7

Amazing Success Stories

S everal years ago I had a novel idea for another book for premeds: a compilation of incredible stories from students with unusual backgrounds who had managed to get accepted into medical school despite overwhelming odds. I wasn't thinking merely of the non–science-majoring applicant, nor strictly of the minority or older student. Nor did I have in mind women (who were then a minority in most medical school classes), nor Doogie Howser types. I was thinking of *extreme* types: the grandmother who got into medical school, students without college degrees who got in, students who talked their way in; felons, deaf or mute students, amputees, impaired students, former alcoholics and drug abusers . . . All right, perhaps not *that* extreme. But I honestly did not know what to expect when I started running classified ads in the *Journal of the American Medical Association*, the *New England Journal of Medicine*, and *The New Physician*. The ads said simply: "Seeking unusual stories of how physicians got into medical school for forthcoming book." I also sent out similar requests to premedical advisers and medical school admissions directors.

The response was not overwhelming, but neither was it negligible; I received twenty or so letters of varying lengths from people who thought that they had unusual stories to tell. Many weren't, but some were *truly amazing*. I thought that my story was exceptional, but some of these people's stories were stranger than fiction. Unfortunately, I was not able to collect enough of them for a book, so I filed them away, awaiting a suitable opportunity to publish. This book's revision has provided me with that chance.

I have elected, at times, to change names, places, and dates to protect confidentiality, but have left the basic facts unaltered. If it's inspiration to continue pursuing your dream of medical school acceptance that you're looking for, then, pilgrim, your search has ended. These students beat the odds. Anyone who isn't heartened by their stories would probably do better to switch to a business or computer science major. If you can top them, write to me; you will make it into the next edition.

Dear Dr. Brown:

I received your letter the other day. I am anxious to tell you my story hoping that it will be published. Perhaps other premeds might learn from some of the difficulties and mistakes that I encountered.

In order to understand my unusual circumstances, it is necessary to realize that I was a competitive figure skater. My attachment to the sport turned out to be both my demise and greatest asset in regards to my application to medical school.

I entered college as a premed with a biomedical engineering major. I was a strong math/science student in high school and thought that I would have a stronger interest in the School of Engineering. My first quarter included the basic premed courses (calculus, chemistry, and biology) and I was still a competitive skater. This necessitated numerous hours at the rink for practice and also involved missing as much as two weeks of a nine-week quarter to attend competitions.

That quarter I won a bronze medal at the U.S. National Championships. Upon returning to school, I faced numerous midterms and unfortunately I either failed or did poorly on most of them. It was at that point that I had to decide whether to continue with school or to skate full time. I struggled with this decision and decided to dedicate myself to academics.

I continued in the School of Engineering for three years. Eventually I took six courses in calculus, numerous chemistry (general, organic, physical, and biochemistry) and upper-level biology/physiology courses. The quarter courseloads were rigorous because the majority of these were taken simultaneously and, as a result, my grade point average was mediocre. A crucial point came during the fall quarter of my junior year, in which I was taking biochemistry, mechanics, neurophysiology, and psychopathology. Additionally, I was working as an oral surgical assistant and teaching skating fifteen hours per week. The results of that quarter were disastrous. The courses proved too difficult to take simultaneously and I realized that I'd practically ruined all my chances of ever getting into medical school. My grade point average plummeted, and I was told point-blank by the premedical adviser, "Mr. Belmonte, you're never going to be a doctor." Those words will never be forgotten.

I subsequently switched to a major in biology. I rounded out my sciences with liberal arts courses and my grade point average improved steadily. I also got involved in student musical productions. I was in the school's premiere annual production, which involved many hours of rehearsals, yet I managed to keep up with my courses and two jobs. Unfortunately, I had an even bigger problem coming up—the MCAT. As luck would have it, the opening performance turned out to be the same day as the MCAT. I was excused from the afternoon performance, took the MCAT, and performed on stage that evening. It may have been exhilarating, but it was also unwise, since the results turned out average on the MCAT.

That summer I started applying to medical schools. I applied to nineteen of them. As I was filling out my AMCAS application, I sensed an impending doom. I was applying with a 2.73 grade point average with MCATs at or slightly below national means.

By senior year I was getting rejected by medical schools left and right. I knew that my academic credentials were not impressive, yet I was hoping that admissions committees would see past them. Even though my average was low, I had taken extremely difficult courses above and beyond the recognized standard. Many were graduate level in the sciences and math. Also in my favor were the experiences in the medical field. I had worked as an oral surgical assistant and even had one-to-one patient contact as a biofeedback therapist in a headache clinic with a prominent neurologist. I was hoping that these attributes would at least get me an interview, at which point I could prove to the committees that I had more potential than my numbers indicated. Eventually I did get an interview. However, after looking at my file, the interviewer bluntly stated that he didn't think I would get into their school. It really seemed hopeless.

I retook the MCAT, but my scores were basically unchanged. At this point, it was hard to keep everything in perspective. I continually agonized over skating. For the three years following my amateur retirement, my former competitors that I defeated were gaining national prominence and eventually went on to win a silver medal in the Olympics. When graduation came around, I found myself holding a bachelor's degree and sixteen rejection letters. Worst of all, I gave up a chance at the Olympics for a career in medicine. Unfortunately, neither of the two was going to come true.

I considered applying to foreign schools, even received applications from several of them, but decided it would be best to work for a year to help pull my shattered ego back together. I found a job in a cardiologist's office. I learned a tremendous amount there—the most important lesson being that I wanted to be the doctor, not work for one, as I had done so often in the past. I knew that I would eventually reapply to medical school, though I didn't know when, or how I was going to change my academic profile.

That year my life took a big change. A touring company of the Ice Capades was in town and holding auditions. I read about this in the local newspaper and auditioned on a whim. One month later I had a contract in my hand. I would join them in three months at the start of their new season. I joined as a member of the chorus and emerged three years later as one of their soloists. It was a chance to finish my unfulfilled skating career. Yet, in the back of my mind, I knew that I wanted to be a doctor, but was at a loss as to when I would try again. Three years later, when my contract came up for negotiation, I realized it was time once again to begin my quest for medical school.

It became apparent that the only way that anyone would remotely consider my application would be if something improved drastically. As I already had my degree, the most natural thing to improve would be my MCAT. Having been out of school for four years, the thought of studying for them was horrifying. Yet I spent three entire months, five days a week, taking a review course and becoming a very serious student. I studied seven hours a day after teaching skating in the morning. My scores improved tremendously, with my highest score in the 94th percentile.

I spent the year applying to several allopathic and three osteopathic schools. By December, I had two interviews—one at each type of school. Ironically, medical schools found my background as a skater very impressive and a definite asset. They realized very little as to how my skating hindered my previous application. Later that month, I was accepted at the osteopathic school and was placed on the alternate list at the allopathic medical school.

I was ecstatic, but yet still had sincere hopes of entering the allopathic school. Although I realized that the practice of osteopathy is much the same as "traditional" medicine, my heart was intent on becoming an MD and not a DO. I rationalized many months over this, realizing that at least I would be able to practice medicine in either case.

In July I was still on the alternate list and the time was rapidly approaching in which I'd have to matriculate at the osteopathic school. Eventually I matriculated and finally began my medical career. I was extremely insecure about being able to handle the academic load. I spent many hours studying the first week, being so paranoid after being out of school for such a long time. I made many close friends, yet only confided in a few of them that I was still on an alternate list elsewhere. On the day of our first biochemistry exam I was notified that I'd been accepted at my state medical school. I was torn by leaving my good friends and also faced the loss of $8,000 of my $13,000 tuition. I was back in Chicago the following day.

Unbelievably, the academics went relatively smoothly and I studied diligently. Even when the pressures and workload were intolerable, I would never take for granted the fact that I was finally in med school. I've done well enough to be in the top half of my class. This is ironic, as according to all other stats from AAMC I really should never have been admitted, much less survived the ordeal. As a matter of fact, I just finished with the basic sciences two days ago and will begin my clinical training tomorrow.

I feel that my story might be inspirational to many struggling premeds. I've faced adversity, but my perseverance was paramount in achieving my goal. Retrospectively, I was not honest with myself in college. I let many of my extracurricular activities detract from my priorities and failed to realistically assess my average performance by rationalizing that I had such tremendously difficult courseloads. Unfortunately, I learned how inconsequential my schedule really was. One must get past the numbers game before an admissions committee will consider motivation, potential, and past medical experiences. I would have been much better off taking standard courses, doing well, and maintaining a decent GPA. One needs to maintain this objectivity.

At times, I visit my undergraduate campus to study for my final exams, and I overhear many premeds speaking of the same concerns that I faced eight years previously. I will never forget my premed adviser telling me that I would never become a doctor. I proved him wrong.

Sincerely,
Ray Belmonte

Dear Dr. Brown:

If you are looking for strange stories, how about this one?

I graduated from high school and went to the University of Texas in Austin. I started out with advanced placement, having tested for placing out of seventeen hours of Spanish and three of chemistry.

As a long-haired, pinko, radical type, I never went to classes (or studied either, for that matter). I was also working as a paramedic starting my second year and as a research assistant in the department of zoology.

By the end of my second year or start of my third year, I was a full-pledged frat-rat (I must admit in all honesty that Animal House *was very reminiscent of my fraternity days).*

By now I was putting in even more hours working as a paramedic and less at anything connected with school.

During all this I was constantly taking off during weekends (almost every one during the summer and one or two per month during the rest of the year) to go to Native American Indian pow-wows (i.e., Indian dances).

I had started Indian dancing and craft work at age 13 and I must admit I am quite an expert in the field. In the middle of my fourth year in Austin, I was kicked out of school for having taken a Spanish achievement test for one of my fraternity brothers. At the time we did it, we thought it was rather funny. Unfortunately, the dean of students did not think so.

So I returned to Houston to work and think things over.

Well, I decided I really wanted to be a doctor above all things and registered for school at the University of Houston. Meanwhile, I was working in a pulmonary functions lab at the Methodist Hospital there. The University of Texas called me and told me they had decided to change my one-year suspension to a six-month one and I could come back, but I decided to stay.

When I arrived at U. of H. to speak to the premed adviser, he looked at my record—approximately 115 hours with a GPA of 2.05. He laughed and told me to beat it and I was totally wasting my time. I convinced him to approve my schedule and started school.

I took all upper-divisional science courses, taking six to ten hours a semester with a 3.65 GPA. During the same time I

> *—Became certified as a cardiopulmonary technician.*
> *—Took over a research project from a pulmonary fellow. It eventually was presented at the ACCP meeting and will likely have a follow-up publication.*

—Went to work at the University of Texas Medical School as a research assistant.

—Did extensive work helping people out with various technical problems in research projects and got my name on several abstracts and presentations.

—Started (with my brother) a DJ business playing music at parties. In three years it became so successful that, working part-time at this, I was making almost as much as my salary as a technician.

As the years passed my premed adviser laughed less and less. Finally, with his help and the very invaluable help of several friends on the faculty who were very supportive to me at work, I was accepted and started medical school at the University of Texas Medical School in Houston.

Now I'm doing a surgical residency that I started at age 30. I don't make Indian powwows like I used to (or party like I used to), but I'm still happy with myself and doubt I'd change anything I ever did.

Sincerely,
Eddie LaRouche

Dear Dr. Brown:

My mother taught me and encouraged me to pursue any field of study that interested me. In junior high and high school, I found myself very involved in music and science. Both of my brothers were into science, one receiving a degree in physics and the other in mathematics. I, on the other hand, decided that my career would be in music. Specifically, I had decided to become a bassoonist. Bassoonists are a rare commodity for most orchestras and bands, so I had ample opportunity to pursue my musical interests. My mother, who had been a widow since I was seven years old, encouraged me in music. The support of my private music instructor also strengthened my desire. When it came time to enter college, I had chosen to attend the University of Southern California as a music performance major in bassoon.

My four years at USC were a tremendous musical experience. I was able to play in the USC Trojan Marching Band (as a tenor saxophonist) each year as well as perform in the school's highly regarded performing ensembles. As a senior, I competed in the Coleman National Chamber Music Competition with the USC Woodwind Quintet. We won second place in the competition and subsequently performed in the winners' concert the following day. I graduated from USC and received the award of outstanding graduate in the wind and percussion area. A career in music appeared imminent.

However, instead of immediately beginning work or graduate school, I chose to serve a mission for the Church of Jesus Christ of Latter-day Saints (Mormon). I was called to serve a full-time prose-lytizing mission to France. My mission helped me reevaluate my career and life goals. I began having doubts about becoming a professional musician. In addition, my mother was killed in a bicycle accident while I was in France. The sadness I felt at that time caused me to reflect on a career in dealing with the health of others. Still, medicine had not yet really entered my mind.

When I returned to the United States, I worked for several months in Los Angeles before entering graduate studies at Brigham Young University. Still unsure as to my future plans, I was pursuing a master's degree in music. Perhaps a career in academic music would be of interest to me. After two semesters, I first approached the idea of medicine as a profession.

I am still uncertain as to how exactly I came to the decision to attempt getting into medical school. I do remember an incident that occurred at my fiancé's apartment. A couple of students were visiting her and her roommates while I was there. One of them mentioned that he had a married friend with children who had suddenly decided to go back to college and try to get into medical school. The fellow talking thought his friend was crazy. I, on the other hand, was motivated to find out what I needed to do to go to medical school.

This was a very radical idea for me. I was about as far away from a premedical student on the educational spectrum as one can be. Not only was I in music, but I had not even taken a science course as a college student. In high school, I had taken physics, chemistry, and calculus, but it stopped there. In addition, my GPA at USC was a none-too-impressive 2.95. My goal had been to come out of USC as a fine bassoonist, not an honors student. The fact that my graduate adviser and the professors in my specialty area would not be pleased with such a choice clouded the situation. I disregarded these complications for the moment and went to see the premedical counselor. I was not aware of how much my life would change starting with that important step.

I felt very inadequate as I sat at the desk of the premedical counselor and explained to him my desire to go to medical school. He listened intently as I explained to him that, even though I had woefully neglected my classes at USC, I felt I could do well in the required science studies. I believe he was intrigued by the opportunity to work with a musician. With restrained encouragement, he wrote out a schedule and timetable: In a year and three months, I would complete the courses required for the MCAT. The list included such standards as inorganic and organic chemistry, noncalculus-based physics, and biology. He also recommended anatomy, genetics, and physiology. The goals were an MCAT score of 30 or better and a 3.5 (or better) GPA. He emphasized that a good MCAT score was a must. I was, in general, encouraged and excited about my chances.

I took two courses (inorganic chemistry and anatomy) during the summer term. At the end of August, I returned to my counselor's office and emphatically (and naively) told him that I would take the calculus-based physics course starting in the fall. He was less than encouraging and clearly doubtful of my calculus skills (as was I, though I didn't admit it!). Nevertheless, he told me which class to take and added that if I were able to do reasonably well in that specific course, he would be favorably impressed.

The next two semesters for me were very challenging. I took twelve credit hours of science classes each semester in addition to continuing work on my degree in music. I had decided to finish my degree, as that had been my original goal. This meant that I spent about twelve hours in rehearsals each week in addition to scheduled concerts. I also found it necessary to work between ten and fifteen hours each week. In addition to my schedule, my new wife and I were adjusting to the first year of married life. Despite the busy schedule, five-hour physics exams, and memorizing organic chemistry reactions, I really enjoyed myself during those two semesters. I had the feeling that the choice to pursue a medical career was the correct one.

The next summer was considerably less taxing. I was taking no music classes and was completing organic chemistry, taking physiology, and preparing for the August MCAT. I also filled out my applications and sent them in near the beginning of July. I feel that the decision to get my applications in early was crucial. Despite not having my MCAT scores, most schools (I applied to nine) sent me supplementary applications. When my MCAT scores were available in early November, most schools then had a complete file for me. This kept me from being too far behind the applicants who had taken the April MCAT.

The application process was certainly not a simple task. Two of the schools I applied to did not accept the AMCAS (American Medical College Application Service) forms, so additional time was required to fill out their applications. In order to satisfy the requirements of my premedical committee and the medical schools, I solicited no less than six letters of recommendation. In addition, almost every school required a supplementary application. My decision to be very prompt and complete in completing and returning these items was, as I have mentioned, important to the success of my overall application.

In November, I received my MCAT scores. At that time, I evaluated my records to assess my competitiveness as an applicant. I had attained a 31 cumulative on the MCAT and my science GPA was 3.54. My overall GPA had crawled up to about 3.20 (including my undergraduate grades). Despite the latter statistic, I felt that I had a chance at several of the schools to which I had applied.

My first interview offer came from the University of Utah. As a Utah resident, Utah was the only public school to which I applied. Utah gave me two interviews during my visit, both of which I enjoyed very much. I was, as was to be expected, nervous. One interviewer went down my list of classes at USC and asked me about each of my low grades. I was also asked about such topics as euthanasia, my favorite composer, what books I had read recently, Einstein's theory of relativity, and trichinosis. Within two weeks, on Christmas Eve, I had a letter of acceptance from the University of Utah School of Medicine. That was a wonderful Christmas present!

Within the next several months, I withdrew from two schools and received interview invitations from five other schools and a rejection from one school. I accepted only one of the interviews, at the University of Rochester, after my acceptance to Utah. At Rochester I had three very positive and enjoyable interviews. In contrast to Utah, the interviewers at Rochester had not seen my application and therefore approached me without any prior knowledge. It was interesting for me to compare and contrast the two different interviewing philosophies. In each case, the interviewers were very positive about my background in music and all seemed to feel that it would not be a detriment to my success in medicine.

I had to make a difficult decision in the summer when Rochester accepted me. I finally decided to attend Utah. Upon receiving my master's degree in music at BYU in August I enrolled, at the age of 27, as a first-year medical student at the University of Utah School of Medicine. I am a little older and certainly a little out of the ordinary when compared with most of my classmates.

My first year of medical school will soon be completed and I have enjoyed it very much. I have found time to spend at home with my wife and daughter and to play in the Salt Lake Symphony Orchestra. I feel quite certain that the challenging premedical schedule I had helped me cope with the rigorous coursework I've had this year. Playing in the orchestra, spending time with my family, and remaining active in my church have proved to be very effective stress relievers.

The entire process of preparing, applying for, and beginning a medical education is a great challenge. I suppose the future will prove to be no less of a challenge. I would, however, not change the way I approached my premedical and present medical education. I am convinced that many medical schools are looking for a diverse student body and for a variety of experiences in a student's background. In my situation, I was acutely aware of the need to prove myself in basic science skills, but I believe all applicants must somehow do the same. Once this is accomplished, all other interesting and extraordinary life experiences tend to add dimension to the medical school applicant.

Sincerely,
Ray Patterson

Several replies to my ad came from premedical advisers, from among which I have selected these two vignettes.

Dear Dr. Brown:

You may be interested in interviewing one of our graduates, Portia Smith. She is now a second-year student at the Philadelphia College of Osteopathic Medicine.

Portia is black, in her mid-late thirties, and the mother of five children. She saw her husband through school, had her children, and then began her college career. Portia first completed an associate's degree at Philadelphia Community College and then transferred to our campus to pursue the baccalaureate in premedicine. She commuted approximately eighty miles round trip a day to and from Philadelphia to our suburban campus on public transportation. This required the use of three to four vehicles and a good hike. Money was always scarce. Her husband was usually unemployed. Once she apologized to me for missing class because she did not have sufficient money for transportation. In spite of this and other almost insurmountable obstacles, she told no one of her circumstances, never asked for special consideration, and proved to be a solid student. She was recognized as an outstanding continuing education student by the Commonwealth of Pennsylvania in her last year here.

Portia's story would make most students count their blessings and would encourage many others to pursue their goals despite obstacles.

Sincerely,
Barbara Hoffman, PhD
Premedical Adviser

Dear Dr. Brown:

    Hooray! Brian Smothers got in; he's gonna be a doctor!

    Brian was a high school dropout in the tenth grade; he became a bricklayer. The story of this amazing young man's eventual progress into medical school is heartwarming and inspiring. At age 30, Brian received his acceptance last weekend.

    I had wanted to write you in response to your card last October but decided I'd better wait until I knew for sure Brian would make it. I had a pretty strong inkling as his premed adviser, but you need genuine success stories for your new book.

    A few more details on Brian: he injured his back as a bricklayer and went to a chiropractor. While undergoing treatment, it occurred to him that the chiropractor made a lot more money with a lot less work than he did as a bricklayer. He got his GED, gained two years of spotty college work, and entered chiropractic school. There, he decided the profession was, shall we say, hokey, was not impressed with its quality and dropped out. Totally lost as to what to do with his life, he retired to a log cabin on an Indian reservation in Montana for two years, basically living off the land. There, he met the reservation doctor. That did it. Brian finally knew.

    Returning to the University of Arizona, Brian's goals were clear, and the change in his grades and success was dramatic. His record shows 3.85 and 4.0 consistently. He works in the lab of a major research biochemist who was, at first, reluctant to take on this unlikely assistant. But the letter that biochemist wrote the med school in recommendation is the most glowing I have ever read. Brian has become a top student and researcher.

    The medical school wisely overlooked his checkered background and focused on his steady recent achievements.

    Finally, there is one other story, Karen's, of a 39-year-old woman whose interest in how people learn led her into psychology, then neurology, thence, to med school. She proved herself by taking twenty-four units one semester of premed requirements, earning a 4.0. The med school overlooked her low MCATs, as she had not even completed the coursework before the exam. It's a story I use to encourage my older students and to illustrate the value of a truly focused purpose in attending medical school. It is my observation that an older applicant is more successful if he/she has a specific goal in mind, a specific topic of research, for example, rather than a vague desire for a career change "in order to help people."

                                                Sincerely,

                                              Christine Jones

                                              Prehealth Professions

                                              Program Adviser

Next, the most amazing success story of them all. My writer was rejected by all the medical schools to which he applied the first time around. He was shocked, but was told by a medical school dean that they felt he needed another year to prepare himself. He didn't quite know what he needed to prepare himself for; he already had a master's degree. But he took a job as a research assistant in a molecular genetics lab and continued to plug away. He made early application to the same state medical school that had rejected and then encouraged him, was the first person interviewed that year, but got another rejection letter "on Friday, October 13." He was crushed and thought his life was at an end. But he was also astounded and furious that they had again rejected him. This second rejection prompted him to write back to the admissions committee the following letter:

Gentlemen:

I believe that your recent decision to reject my application for a place in your class was hastily made. It is my opinion that I am deserving of a closer and more thorough evaluation. Therefore, I respectfully request that you reconsider my application. There are several factors that lead me to ask for this reexamination.

First, I felt that my interview did not allow me the opportunity to verbally express my sincere desire and motivation toward the study and practice of medicine. The brevity of it led me to believe that my character could not have been easily evaluated. Further, it may not have provided an unbiased evaluation of my more subjective qualities. I feel that a second interview would allow me the opportunity to express myself, answer pertinent questions, and provide you with another opinion of my personality.

Second, I prefer you not consider my grades as an entity unto themselves. They are inextricably linked to my need to provide for myself, thus, explaining the cause of the obvious disparity between my test scores and grades. I believe my MCAT scores should be the measure of my innate knowledge. Allow my academic and work experiences to provide you with a clear picture of my ability to work long hours, beyond the capacity of most individuals. Consider how well I could perform if my extracurricular employment were reduced to zero.

As a state resident, of course I desire to attend your school. My AMCAS form clearly indicates my desire to serve my state, biasing other schools against me. At present, I work about eighty hours per week because I desire to bear as much of the financial burden as possible. I wish to devote my life to the study and practice of medicine here in this state, in an area where those services are needed. I want your school to provide me with the education necessary to do this. It is my honest and sole intention to attend your school and excel.

Finally, I am acutely aware of the fact that my application is atypical. As you reconsider it, be aware of the difficult road I have traveled. Take into account my willingness to sacrifice and my intense desire to excel in your program. It is my belief that, allowed to direct the totality of my personal energy to the study of medicine, my ability to excel cannot be doubted.

Respectfully yours,
Ronald L. Perry

Basically, Mr. Perry said that he felt the admissions committee had made a mistake and they ought to take a better look at him. They did this and, lo and behold, he received his acceptance in the mail shortly thereafter:

Dear Mr. Perry:

It is with very great pleasure that the Committee on Admissions is able to offer you a place in our Class. This offer is contingent upon satisfactory completion of the requirements of entrance as stated in our current catalog and the satisfactory completion of all college courses as stated in your application. The Committee assumes that you will maintain your present high level of scholarly achievement.

A reply to this offer, at your earliest convenience, would be appreciated. This offer does expire two weeks from the above date. In order to matriculate, a remittance of fifty dollars ($50), by check or money order should be returned to the Committee.

This remittance, an advanced deposit of $50 on your tuition, will be credited to your first-semester charges when you register. In the event that you withdraw before registration, it will be returned upon request.

You will receive a receipt for the amount sent us. This receipt must be presented to the Comptroller's Office at the time of registration in order that it can be credited to your first semester's charges.

For the purpose of tuition, our records show you to be classified as a resident.

Prior to matriculation in September, the University requires that you have sent to this Office, official transcripts of all courses taken in college including those to be completed this academic year.

It is with great pleasure that we are looking forward to having you with us at the School of Medicine.

Sincerely yours,
Committee on Admission

My own personal story is relevant, too, and should be somewhat inspiring to those of you who have been advised to plan for alternative careers following medical school rejection. For I still believe that if you are aggressive, persevering, and a little bit lucky, you can gain admission to a medical school.

When I decided that I wanted to become a physician, I had just graduated from college. I had been an English major and had taken not one premed course. Naturally, I hadn't taken the MCAT—I hadn't even heard of it. I didn't know any science professors I could ask for recommendations. My undergraduate GPA was 2.96. I had no experience working in a medical environment. Is it any wonder that when I finally found the premedical adviser, he told me to forget it? I would have, too, if I hadn't been obsessed. That was fall 1968. Less than one year later, I began my freshman year of medical school.

In retrospect, it seems incredible even to me. Yet, when I think about it, my approach to the problem of how to convince a medical school to accept me was perfectly sensible. My success at it was in part a tribute to my rationality and in part a tribute to my good luck. The luck I didn't worry about; it was beyond my control. However, I took a lot of care to be rational.

In 1968, I was a totally unqualified college graduate wanting to go to medical school. Well, perhaps I wasn't totally unqualified. It's true I didn't have any premedical coursework or experience, but I did have confidence. Why? Because I had edited my college literary magazine my senior year and almost singlehandedly put all 128 pages of it together. To me it was a monumental achievement, and, although it didn't satisfy any premedical requirements, it showed me that I had the tenacity to complete a task. And getting into medical school was going to be one gargantuan task.

That summer, I decided that it was important to work in a medical environment. I didn't want to do it to impress a medical school of my sincerity;

I wanted to do it to convince myself that I was on the right track. Deciding to become a physician was a bit of an epiphany for me and I wanted to be sure I could trust my revelations. Luckily I had a friend who worked as an assistant administrator at a large metropolitan hospital. I called him to ask if there was anything that I could do to gain medical experience. I was ready to be an orderly, a lab-runner, anything. My friend had an idea. Knowing I had been an English major, he asked me if I would like to write a health publication on lead poisoning for their outpatient clinics. Childhood lead poisoning was becoming epidemic and there was then no preventive information for parents. I said, "When can I start?"

I was hired with the undistinguished title of clerk, paid $2 an hour, and left to my own devices. Six weeks later, I had managed to complete my project and, in the process, was able to check out most of the hospital, which was so large that they had separate emergency facilities for men and women. I met physicians, medical students, and patients. I observed clinics and wards. I made home visits with medical personnel. It all served to strengthen my resolve; I made plans to return to school in the fall to begin premedical coursework.

In the meantime, the cartoon coloring book on lead poisoning I had written and designed and a friend had illustrated was becoming popular in the clinics. The finished product was somewhat primitive; text was typed onto the illustrated pages and then photocopied and stapled. It was a low-budget operation from beginning to end, but it worked. It even received some media coverage in the local papers. Later, it would accompany my applications to medical school to give credibility to my attempt to project myself as a different type of applicant. Medical schools, I came to learn, welcome the nontraditional applicant to add depth and diversity to the incoming class. However, admissions committees must be convinced of that applicant's ability to survive the basic medical sciences. They pay careful attention to performance in premedical courses and on the Medical College Admission Test. Here was my next challenge.

Doing well in premedical courses was somewhat worrisome for me. After all, I had majored in the humanities. I had met only my university's minimal science requirement for graduation—one year. I had taken oceanography and astronomy, neither of which gave me any premedical credits. They were known as science courses for nonscience majors—mickey-mouse but interesting, and nonintimidating. Fortunately, they were offered by the physics and biology departments as well. Naturally, I signed up. As far as I and medical schools were concerned, mickey-mouse biology was Bio 101-102, period. Grades were all.

Chemistry was a different kettle of fish. There was no chemistry for non-chemistry majors. Chem 101 included biology majors, budding chemists, engineers, and premeds. It had the reputation of being absurdly difficult, for its purpose was to separate science majors from the chaff. Realizing that anything less than a grade of B would effectively eliminate me as a contender for medical school, I enrolled in introductory chemistry in night school at a local community college. Even that wasn't easy, but at least I had a fair chance.

While waiting for my premedical courses to start, I made a trip to the local hospital to seek part-time employment. By this time I was coming to enjoy the hospital environment. Again, I was ready to accept any kind of work. Luckily, I was hired by the department of social services, which consisted of one full-time worker, to do part-time medical social work. My lack of experience was no obstacle; she was willing to train me. She wanted a student and I wanted a job. It worked out perfectly.

I divided my time between the department of physical rehabilitation and the cerebral palsy clinic, and I came to see patients differently. Rather than focusing on disease, as I was later taught to do in medical school, I was made to appreciate the impact the disease had on patient and family. Initially, I would do the intake interview and then discuss my impressions with my supervisor. Invariably she would show me how unaware I was of what was really going on. It was humbling. But, eventually, I began to get better at it. I also learned how to do direct service, finding my way through the bureaucracy to get canes, wheelchairs, braces, home health care, educational instruction, and other concrete things that patients required.

Meanwhile, I decided to apply to medical schools for the following fall. I admit I really did this just to energize my interest in my premedical activities. I had no expectations of being considered a serious candidate anywhere. After all, I still had not even completed my first-semester sciences. I had taken the old MCAT and done well on the general information and verbal sections. I was in the 50th percentile in mathematics and the 25th percentile in science. But I considered this a surprising score, since I was competing with science majors. With two months of introductory biology I had outdone 25 percent of them. I was impressed. Yet I had no illusions about medical schools. As far as they were concerned, I had nothing academic to show. Nevertheless, all they could do was say no, and at least I would have had the experience of applying.

I applied to seven medical schools, most of which were in my home state. I was rejected by five of them quickly, including the one attached to the hospital where I had done my health education project. The sixth school waited a little longer to reject me. The seventh requested an interview.

Sometime in February 1969 I boarded an airplane and flew to Milwaukee, Wisconsin, to be interviewed at what was then the Marquette University School of Medicine (now the Medical College of Wisconsin). Little did I know then that my extracurricular work had impressed a member of the admissions committee and he wanted to know me better. I had two interviews; one was perfunctory, the other more interesting and intimate. It went overtime, and when we were done I believed I had an advocate on the committee. God knows, I needed one.

The next three months went by without any response from Marquette. What was up? I had no idea, except that I felt I was fast becoming a mailbox junkie. In the meantime I had completed first-semester biology, chemistry, and physics, earning all B's, and started the second semester of the same. By the end of the second semester (again, straight B's) I had heard nothing more than that my application was being processed and they would notify me as soon as possible. I hadn't been accepted, I hadn't been rejected, and I hadn't been put on a waiting list. Now I had a decision to make: whether to take the masochistic organic chemistry course that summer and be done with it or postpone it for the fall. I opted for the summer. That way I wouldn't be tying up the whole next year and, if Marquette was still considering me for the September class, I would have fulfilled all requirements.

My next decision was where to take it. Being keenly aware of my aversion for cutthroat competition, I avoided the course at Columbia, Harvard, and Berkeley. I selected the University of Minnesota, and on the way out to Minneapolis I conveniently revisited Milwaukee. There I learned, from my advocate, that the admissions committee was still not convinced that I could do medical school work. They were holding a place, waiting to see what grade I earned in organic. That was it. Do or die.

Minneapolis was delightful that summer and the course was civilized. There were five morning lectures and three morning labs. We were out by noon every day. I was competing with premeds, but also with prepharmacy and prenursing and chem majors. On the great bell curve I made another B, proving at least my consistency in science. Fortunately this was sufficient to allay the fears of the other committee members and on July 26, 1969, I received notification that I had been accepted into the freshman class at Marquette. Of course I had to complete the second semester of organic, which I did, earning another B. Medical school began four days after my course ended.

I do not mean to suggest that it was all downhill from there. Now I was forced to compete with all those premedical science majors that I had so assiduously avoided during my college career. These characters had already been exposed to many of the first-year medical school courses in college—anatomy, histology, and physiology, for instance. All I had done was run the obstacle course of the basic premedical requirements. These, it turned out, had minimal relevance to first-year medical school. How I survived that, however, makes for another story.

Where my sympathies lie must be obvious. They're with students, like myself, who have taken a nontraditional route to medicine. Medical schools still accept a preponderance of science majors with high GPAs and MCAT scores. But they accept people like me, too. And if me, why not you?

CHAPTER 8

The Future of Medicine

For the past 35 years I have been in the unique position of being both a family physician and an adviser to premedical students. My advice was solicited mostly through the mail and e-mail by readers of books that I wrote to encourage the nontraditional applicant, having been a bit atypical myself. And for most of the 35 or so years that my books have been in print, I have been able to advise my readers that what awaited them at the end of their arduous endeavors was worth the effort. This was necessary because even in its halcyon days, going into medicine still entailed more postgraduate education than any other professional training and required more sacrifice. Premeds and medical students, who spent most of their lives studying and delaying gratification, realized this. But the good news was that, after much time and expense, they became highly trained and well-paid professionals with limitless possibilities for employment. I could and did say that it did get better and it was worth it. Today, I am not as optimistic.

During the last 20 years, there have been cataclysmic changes in the way medicine is practiced in this country and in the way health care is being delivered. In retrospect, it was predictable. The now almost passé fee-for-service system of reimbursement had a faulty foundation; it was based on what you did to the patient and therefore encouraged doing more. Furthermore, in the old days, physicians were paid what they billed. Although this system nurtured the doctor-patient relationship, it did nothing to contain costs or foster wellness. There was no incentive to do either, and the health care budget rose at double-digit rates, easily tripling the yearly rate of inflation. It was clearly a process that could not go on indefinitely. It was also significant that, over the past 40 or 50 years, most Americans got health insurance to pay their medical bills, and mostly through their workplace. This served to consolidate the payers for health care into large insurance companies, which then became even larger, were able to amass the necessary actuarial data, and continue making the insuring of people's health profitable.

There were some early attempts at reform. Kaiser, the nation's first major HMO, started enrolling patients after the Second World War and was predicated on correct principles. They offered people low-cost health insurance at fixed rates and took care of them in their own hospitals with their own doctors. Physicians were salaried, so there was no incentive for them to do more than what was necessary, as any additional procedures or care would not benefit either them or their organization financially. Criticism of this type of plan is that it is often difficult to get to see your physician, or any physician, and that patients may be undertreated. But the cost of care is hard to beat and, in recent times, patient satisfaction has generally been high.

The government also has been pruning the Medicare program. Initially strongly opposed by organized medicine as socialistic, it was subsequently embraced as it paid physician bills in toto and became an important source of operating revenues for hospitals, medical schools, and residency training programs. However, politicians and health-care administrators, aware that the well could run dry, began instituting reforms in the 1980s, beginning with the relative value system. Under this plan, hospitals were paid a flat rate per diagnosis, regardless of how long it took the patient to get well and be discharged. Reform of physician fees soon followed. Other insurance companies soon began to emulate these models and produced their own fee schedules for doctors and hospitals. The days of *carte blanche* billing were over; the people who paid the bills were now calling the shots. The payers had become the players, and physicians and hospitals had become minor characters in the unfolding drama.

It doesn't take an economist to realize that not only can health care costs be contained but that health care can, in and of itself, be profitable. Indeed, to a businessman, health care is just another industry to be micromanaged, and the potential for profits are enormous. All the elements were in place for a corporate takeover of the profession; excess waste and tremendous possibilities for cost savings; many years' worth of actuarial data on which to base pricing; an abundance of workers, including physicians, from which to draw a relatively cheap labor pool; and industry with the dollars to spend to ensure that their employees received adequate health care. The era of managed care had arrived.

The spate of acquisitions of hospitals, medical practices, medical supply services, computerized billing services, and pharmaceutical drug services by parvenu health care conglomerates is testimony to the exponential rate of change in the profession. There is no going back. The old paradigms are dead; new models are forming at an accelerating rate. The actual practice of medicine, which remained unchanged for generations, is now changing so rapidly that it would be hard to hazard a guess what it might be like to practice in the next 20 years.

What I find of great interest and concern is that through all the ferment, the selection and training of physicians has not changed very much at all. Premeds still take the same required courses and the medical school curriculum remains immutably intact. Furthermore, the factors that once motivated the best and brightest students to go into medicine are still operational—the need for prestige, independence, high remuneration, security, mobility, intellectual challenge, and service. But the playing field has been leveled by managed care and now, by the new health care reform legislation. The times call for different motivations for entering medicine if our premeds are to be happy and successful. The fact that many premeds have not given credence to this is explained by what the great economist Thorstein Veblen described as "habits of thought," or the persistence of beliefs that are no longer useful after the institutions that fostered those beliefs die.

Let me use myself as an example to demonstrate how much medicine has changed over the past 35 years—in practice, although not necessarily in perception. First off, when I was a medical student, medical school was cheap; it cost me only $2,000 per year for tuition. I didn't have to borrow money and I graduated from medical school with only a small debt accrued from some college loans. A rotating internship, completed in 1974, was all I needed to work, and I was able to find employment in emergency rooms, clinics, and even doing some epidemiological research. Private practice was also an option, and I could have hung out my shingle just about anywhere and been busy.

As things turned out, I did part-time work for several years in the city and then relocated to the country, where I found employment in a rural hospital emergency room, and I did open a private practice. Without board certification, I was given hospital staff privileges in all services and continue to hold them today in medicine. I voluntarily stopped doing obstetrics many years ago when the price of insurance became too high. I remain self-employed and have been able to set my own working hours—three days a week in the office. I own the building I practice in and, as the managed care revolution has not yet reached us, still have the ability to choose my private patients, just as they have the option of whether or not to select me as their physician. The result has been that I enjoy my work and believe that, in my case, the doctor-patient relationship is alive and well.

How would my style of practice fare today? In the first place, I could not have afforded medical school without taking out a large loan. If my debt had been typical, I would have graduated owing $150,000–$200,000. This would have dampened my enthusiasm about taking time off for personal growth and I probably would have opted for a residency; the rotating internship has been long defunct and one year of postgraduate medical education is no longer the union card necessary for employment. Nowadays, three to five years of residency training is one of the prerequisites for going to work.

Another prerequisite is board certification. Because board eligibility in many areas requires not only the completion of a residency but a certain number of years in practice as well, it has become a problematic Catch-22 for many doctors looking for their first job. How can they get hired if they don't have their boards? How can they get their boards if they don't practice? The places where I cut my teeth are no longer options for new graduates unless they have board certification in emergency medicine or family practice. Although one year of postgraduate education still qualifies for licensure, the only place I can imagine such an individual could find work would be as a doc-in-the-box in an ambulatory care clinic.

My community, once in need of practitioners, has become saturated and I would be unable to find work here today. Even were I fully "papered," I would still have to look for another location to ply my skills. Probably it would not be where I wanted to live, but where there was a job. And, in all likelihood, I would be an employee, not self-employed. I would be on salary with prescribed work hours and vacation time. My income would be limited by contractual arrangement. My performance would be monitored with careful attention to the bottom line—costs. With a plethora of doctors, I would be a surplus commodity, easily replaced and able to count on little or no patient loyalty. Just another cog in the machine.

Nothing is intrinsically wrong with physicians being treated like any other kind of worker. Indeed, that is the pattern in most of the world.

However, there grew up an entirely different tradition in this country with entirely different expectations. Until relatively recently, most doctors were self-employed and independent. They were able to earn more by working more, could do what they felt was best for the patient without worrying about getting prior authorization for medications and procedures, and could see as many or as few patients as they were comfortable seeing without worrying about whether they were meeting their assigned quota. They were able to practice medicine the way they felt was best. People who selected medical careers treasured their autonomy, were self-directed, and tended to like to have things their way. They liked to give orders, not get them. They liked to be in control.

Current applicants are a lot like this, but the medical world they will be preparing to enter has changed. It will now reward the team player, not the entrepreneur. It will favor people who can play by the rules and not question them. It will no longer represent job security but will be a more and more insecure livelihood as American and international medical schools continue to crank out graduates to fill residency positions. It will favor people of independent wealth because of the high costs of medical education and the projected shrinking salaries of physicians. (Thus, we will see the reemergence of the gentleman doctor who doesn't have to work for money but just wants to work to be of service.) The need to serve, to be useful, to make a difference in other people's lives, will still be a prime motivation, but there will be many more constraints on the way health care is delivered, which will prove to be frustrating to people who will wonder why, after seven to 10 years of postgraduate education to get their MDs, they are having to take orders from people who spent two years after college getting their MBAs.

The crux of the problem is, simply, that there is no mechanism other than the market to regulate physician supply in the face of changing demand for physician services. Managed care is extremely efficient and tolerates no waste. Already many established physicians have been given notice and have either moved to other locales to practice, retired early, dropped out, or retooled into another specialty. It's no secret that physician dissatisfaction is high, and many say they would not do it over again if they could. Many are discouraging to premeds, who are almost universally idealistic. But it may not be registering; more students are applying to medical schools today than ever have before.

The job of the premedical adviser is not only to assist students in their quest to gain admission to a medical school, but also to describe what the actual practice of medicine is like. Because advisers are almost never physicians, they too may labor under many of the same myths as their students. Medicine is just not their workaday world. Even the proverbial soldier in the trenches, such as myself, would have a hard time hazarding a guess about what medicine will be like in 10 to 15 years, about the time it will take my readers, most of whom are high school and university students, to pass through college, medical school, residency training, and be ready to enter the job market.

What will the medical marketplace you are about to enter be like in the next decade or two? The newly enacted health care legislation requires that everyone carry health insurance by 2014. This will add about 35 to 40 million new people to the ranks of those seeking medical care and guarantee a surfeit of work for physicians. The only real question is whether these newly insured individuals will have access to health care, given the limitation in turning out more MDs to meet the increased need. Medical schools are under constraints when it comes to expansion, and there are few new schools slated for construction. The physician workforce will be stretched to the limit and may be inadequate to meet the rising demand for health care services.

Into the breach will jump more midlevels: family nurse practitioners and physician assistants. These jobs, which didn't even exist when I started out in practice, will confound the role of primary care physicians (family medicine practitioners, internists, and pediatricians) and will eventually replace them in the clinical setting, leaving these MDs to more supervisory roles. The difficulty of recruiting young physicians into these specialties will be somewhat ameliorated by loan forgiveness and by new Medicare fee schedules that will award bonuses to primary care providers while keeping fees for specialists static. Still, there will be shortages in M.D. primary care providers for the foreseeable future.

The face of the medical workplace will change radically in the next few decades. The independent practitioner will go the way of the dinosaur, as will small group practices. The economic forces put into play the new Affordable Care Act are likely to accelerate physician employment by hospitals and large groups, as they are the organizations with the financial clout to implement all the requirements of the new legislation. Physicians of the future will be required to use EMRs (electronic medical records), track quality measures and outcomes, meet performance standards, and use other expensive forms of information technology—which will simply not be affordable to small practices—in order to be reimbursed by insurers. The medical landscape will be bereft of "mom and pop" stores in favor of "big box" stores, where physicians are employees and have no control over the way medicine is practiced.

Physician remuneration will no longer be based on volume and intensity parameters but will shift to outcome measurements, with payers demanding better quality at lower costs. Reimbursements will require accountability with payment based on value. "Pay for performance" is the current lingo, reflecting the requirement of physicians to demonstrate that their patient populations remain healthy and have less need for expensive procedures. In this era of biomedical innovation, preventive and personalized care based on evidence-based medicine will be key. In addition, there will be experiments with approaches that could improve the delivery system, including patient-centered medical homes, accountable care organizations, and health care innovation zones. In short—unlike medicine up to this point—the future is in flux, and medical students cannot be sure what awaits them after years spent in college, medical school, and residency training programs.

Should you be a premed? Should you go to medical school? Yes, if you're truly fascinated by medicine, if you really want to make sick people well or prevent disease and disability, if your true mission is service, if you want a job with a fair amount of prestige, decent income, and regular hours (worka-holics beware—you will not be allowed to put in 80- to 100-hour work weeks and will have to spend more time with your family or develop other interests). Yes, if you want a challenging career, crave opportunities for intel-lectual growth and diversity, and prefer working with a group of peers. And, of course, yes, if nothing else will do. But no, if you treasure your indepen-dence, if you want to be your own boss, need to do it your way, or prefer working alone unless you plan on taking courses in practice management during medical school and residency. No, if you have zero tolerance for bureaucracies and red tape. No, if income is of primary importance, or if the ability to choose what you will do and where you will do it is. No, if you can't live with having an education loan as large as your house mortgage. And especially no if you are counting on medicine to be a secure profession.

There will always be sick people, and we will always need physicians to care for them. But let's have physicians who are happy and satisfied in their work and not physicians who feel trapped in a job that they have too much time, energy, and money invested in to leave, although it may not suit their temperament.

Internet Advising: Sara's Story

S ince the initial publication of *Getting into Medical School* in 1975, I have undertaken to advise my readers through personal communications. In the beginning, the task was usually limited to answering a question or two from readers interested enough to write. The inquiries, usually written in longhand or sometimes typed, were received in the mail and were answered in kind. I had no idea if my input actually helped, but occasionally I would get letters of thanks from premeds who were successful in their admissions quest. More often, I heard nothing and wondered if my efforts had been for naught. Still, I answered all queries. If a reader was concerned enough to put in the time to write, I would respond.

With the advent of the Internet and e-mail, my focus changed. Now I had a way to file each letter, respond electronically, and carry on a dialogue with readers and potential advisees on a day-to-day basis. Besides, I could send them relevant materials instantaneously. The process of advising became accelerated and much more convenient. I now had an ongoing relationship with some premeds and a way to offer advice more quickly than they might get it from their college premedical advisors. In the case of nontraditional students, I could now serve as their primary advisor and give them my counsel in a timely fashion. This proved to be immensely more satisfying than giving episodic advice and having no sense of continuity with my advisees.

The result was that I wound up with a relatively small number of advisees who were extremely motivated to succeed and willing to compensate me in some small fashion for my time. I am pleased to say that of the dozen or so students who have entered into my advisory service since 1997, all have ultimately been successful in getting into an allopathic or osteopathic medical school. It wasn't always easy, but they were doggedly determined and persevered. Today, I am proud to call them "doctors."

These e-mailing made, in some cases, for fascinating reading and laid out blueprints for success. One lengthy correspondence, in particular, stands out. Sara Denning-Bolle was a 44-year-old university professor from Reed College who wrote to me when beginning her premedical endeavors. Our Internet advising relationship lasted over three years and comprised over 250,000 words! It appears here in edited form and stands, I believe, as a tribute to this premed's journey—from doctor (PhD) to physician (MD). Today, Dr. Denning-Bolle is completing an internal medicine residency in Portland, Maine. She is 52 years old!

Dear Dr. Brown,

I've been reading with great pleasure the latest edition of Getting into Medical School *and I was particularly intrigued by your own route into medicine as you described it in the chapter entitled "Amazing Success Stories." I was also encouraged by your invitation to the "nontraditional student" to contact you and I decided to take you up on it; I would very much appreciate your reactions and suggestions.*

I decided to go into medicine when I was a freshman in high school. It was all I thought about all through high school, and working and volunteering in hospitals during summers fired my zeal. By the time I started college, however, I had begun to wonder if I had romanticized medicine; unfortunately, I didn't really have anyone to advise me. By the time I got seriously into college work, I had switched my major to history and became fascinated by ancient literatures and languages. I eventually received my PhD in the history of the Ancient Near East and, later, a postdoctoral MA in Biblical Studies in seminary. I have been teaching for 14 years (Loyola University, UCLA, and I just finished a five-year contract at Reed College). Last year I came to a crossroads in my career and I had some serious decisions to make.

My husband (a scholar and retired UCLA professor) encouraged me to give my old passion of medicine a renewed try. It is true that the medical field has continued to gnaw at me for the past quarter-century. My love of history has led me to view medicine in terms similar to history: both require a passionate commitment to the interactions of human beings. One requires a careful and compassionate reading of ancient documents; the other requires a careful and compassionate reading of the human body. One requires a physician of the soul, the other of the body.

I am currently enrolled in a post-baccalaureate program in premed here at Portland State University. Like yourself, the only science courses I took in college were a couple of courses for liberal arts majors. I never even took Chemistry in high school! It has been an enormous challenge and I am doing reasonably well so far (I even managed to get an "A" in my second term of Chemistry!). My greatest fear is the MCAT as I have never done well on standardized tests, although my college and various graduate school GPAs average to a bit over 3.8. I plan to take the MCAT in August to give me time to absorb the requisite amount of science materials. I have had nothing but enthusiastic support from professional colleagues and physicians. I have also read isolated comments about the increase of much older applicants considering medicine as a second career and that medical schools have not been particularly adverse to the new trend. But I will be turning 44 in a couple of weeks. The idea of many more years of training does not deter me. As a scholar in the humanities, my work habits and concentration are excellent. There will always be people who need help and I am eager to go into primary care. I certainly have no mercenary ambitions: scholars in the humanities and liberal arts are used to working in exploitative situations, without decent remuneration.

You sound like one person in the medical field who might give me some honest reactions about such a non-traditional applicant. Perhaps my situation is not quite so bizarre as it appears to me. After all, I am surrounded by fellow students who could be my sons and daughters (there are several students in my courses, including my Chemistry lab partner, who were students of mine at Reed College a few years ago). It's virtually impossible to find anyone in medicine who has addressed the sort of route I am pursuing. While I half-fear your honesty, the tone of your writing encourages me write to you. Am I insane? Would medical school boards take me seriously? If I can maintain a decent science GPA and "make the first cut" would some schools give an old lady a chance? I am in excellent physical condition, having been a long-distance runner for close to 25 years. I can play a mean trumpet. But I would prefer to face squarely this race I've set before myself.

At your convenience, Dr. Brown, I would greatly value your opinions. I apologize if I have been rather loquacious, but it seemed the only way to provide a proper context—and historians love contexts. Let me thank you in any event for making readers feel welcome in turning to you with their various conundrums.

Dear Sara,

Thanks for a great letter. You sound fascinating. I would like to work with you in your quest to get into medical school.

I thought you might like to see that you are not alone. I've enclosed some reading material by a person just like you—a university professor who wanted to go to medical school, and did. She was a bit younger but not so much as to make a difference. I know of older women who get admitted to US medical schools in their forties.

You should know that I offer a proprietary service which is described at my Internet web site **www.mcn.org/b/mfhe**. Check it out and if you would like me to be your premedical advisor, e-mail me through the web site and I'll send you a contract to peruse. If you only want specific questions answered, let me know and we can arrange for that instead.

I hope we can work together to make you a content physician.

Dear Dr. Brown,

I was rather astounded at the speed with which you answered my letter of inquiry! Thank you very much for your suggestions and general tone of encouragement. And many thanks for the marvelous article by Prof. Klaiman! So much of what she described about the academic world at present sounds distressingly familiar and I was amazed at the similarities of our respective situations.

I would very much like to be advised by you. I trust your experience and I feel that you can offer substantive suggestions regarding, for instance, what courses to pursue after this year. My heartfelt thanks for your interest and help. You can't imagine how comforting a simple gesture like your letter has been. I am eager to work with you over the next couple of years.

Dear Sara,

I have received your packet and am tremendously impressed. I have no doubt that, were it not for your age, you would be a shoo-in for medical school (of course, your resume would not be quite so long either). Like myself, you took absolutely no premedical courses as an undergraduate, so you really are starting from scratch. I appreciate what you're going through.

Looking forward to talking with you.

Dear Dr. Brown,

After speaking with you last night, I thought a great deal about your suggestion that I take an accelerated course in Physics and try the MCAT this summer, much earlier than I expected. I am not nearly so optimistic about being able to absorb all this material so quickly, especially as I am amazingly non-quantitative both by nature and training. I would like to propose an alternative plan. I am already committed to teaching Hebrew this summer to a student and I would like very much to go ahead with hospital volunteering. I have one more course in General Biology that I plan to take this coming fall. For the entire academic year, I'll take Physics and Organic Chemistry and begin to study for the MCAT in April, rather than August. You don't seem to think that taking the MCAT a second time, if necessary, is to one's detriment. Any additional science courses (like Biochemistry and Genetics) could be taken the year thereafter.

What do you think?

Dear Sara,

We both had the same idea at the same time—that you should take the April MCAT and apply to medical schools the following fall for the next year's class. That would put your matriculation a little over two years from now. A reasonable plan.

I agree that you don't need additional courses. It's much more important for you to regard the MCAT as a premedical course and spend just as much time studying for it as you would physics or chemistry. We can talk seriously about successful MCAT strategies later, but if you do really well on the MCAT it will be hard to turn you down. Taking the extra science courses (biochemistry, physiology, microbiology, etc.) just isn't worth it. It might make your first year in medical school harder, but at least you'll have a first year.

You really must get on the Net and have a home e-mail address. It will make communicating so much simpler. When I was creating my web site with a friend we wrote back and forth four or five times a day. It's quick, efficient, and cheap.

Dear Dr. Brown,

The school year ended and came out better than I expected. I was so disheartened by the end of May that I fully expected that my pre-med career was fast dissolving. But training as a long distance runner has its advantages: it never occurs to me to stop. I got a B in Chemistry, an A– in Biology, and an A in a Chemical Analysis lab.

The summer goes well. I began my volunteer job at Good Samaritan Hospital here in Portland and I work there three days a week in the cardiology wing. I love it! Most of the work involves patients and I truly feel I have found my calling. I hope to start attending some open-heart surgeries in the next few weeks. As for academics, I'm reading the material for my fall biology course as well as reviewing math and trig for physics. I am amazed at how often I have to go over and over the same mathematical problems. This past year was the first time in my life that I ever had to deal with quantitative exams. Why can't math and algebra tests be essay exams?

The other day in the hospital, I saw in the distance a young boy paging through a patient's chart and it puzzled me what he'd be doing there. When I came abreast of him, I discovered it was a new intern, a young woman with a crewcut. It was then that I thought to myself, "Surely I can do this."

Dear Dr. Brown,

I begin to understand now that the "hands on" work at the hospital reminds one of why one is slogging through redox reactions. I began one day a week in the ER along with the work I do in cardiology and it is truly addictive work.

Dear Sara,

Congratulations. You're online.

Now I can begin to send you pertinent information through e-mail. You'll be amazed at what a resource it is. I belong to a health professions advisory newsgroup that sends me mail daily. I then forward what might be relevant to each of my advisees. For instance, there has been a lot of talk on there lately about osteopathy and the new osteopathic schools. I have two advisees I am pushing in this direction. The information is golden, but some of it is confidential and meant for advisors' eyes only. I don't pass on the really sensitive stuff but don't mind sharing things they tell their advisees anyway. I also pass along information I find on the Net. I'm always keeping my advisees in mind when I Netsurf.

Hi Sandy—

Thanks for the encouraging words. Let me reconstruct what I did this year academically:

Fall:　　　　Calculus (community college): A
　　　　　　General Chemistry: B

Winter:　　　Chemistry: A
　　　　　　General Biology: B

Spring:　　　Chemistry: B
　　　　　　Biology: A–
　　　　　　Chemical Analysis Lab: A

Also calculated into the GPA at this point are two math courses I took last summer, also at a community college, College Algebra: A, and Trigonometry: A. I think all this comes out to something like a 3.66 or so. This coming year I'll have Physics and Organic Chemistry (three terms) and one remaining Biology course to complete the three-course sequence.

At the hospital where I volunteer, many folks are curious why a volunteer "of my age" is there three days a week. None of the doctors I've met in the ER or the OR have exhibited the least surprise at my goal; they are far more mystified by a PhD in ancient history.

Sara,

Did you take a full year of calculus at community college? I'm not sure the other math courses count as part of your premedical GPA. But the A's don't hurt, either. Nevertheless, since calculus is a requirement at some medical schools, the question might arise about finishing up the year.

Organic chemistry is the most important premedical course you will take, but physics is more important for the MCAT. So you are taking your most important courses right now. I assume you are taking no others except biology for one term.

You might think about cutting back on your volunteer time, if it will leave you needed time to get A's in your courses and prepare for the MCAT next August. You'll have plenty of time to volunteer next year. Just do enough to keep your interest up.

You need to start studying for the MCAT now and approach it as a year-long premedical course. That means putting in time each day. Start with the MCAT prep books and the AAMC sample

MCATs. You will want to take an MCAT prep course, too, if only to bolster your confidence. You'll do great in the verbal section; biology and physics are where you need to excel. The writing sample really doesn't carry much weight. I think you need a 30 because then there will be no reason to exclude you from medical school except your age, which would be discriminatory. Eights are average, nines better, but tens or better will get you in—no questions asked.

Keep me posted.

Dear Sandy,

Following OHSU's "highly recommended courses" list, I took a one-term Calculus course; I even took the exact course number they recommended. I asked my professor what the difference is between this one course and the year-long sequence (which he also teaches). He says that the year-long course is designed for engineering students and that it covers every conceivable topic, many of which no engineer is ever likely to encounter. The one-term course is designed for folks in the Health Sciences and Social Sciences; it's a survey course in calculus that covers everything one is likely to need. The other math courses I took (algebra and trigonometry) are listed by OHSU as "required" and of course they are prerequisites to the science courses. My Portland State University (PSU) science GPA, without the three math courses I took at a community college (which don't appear on the PSU tran-script), comes to 3.48. I started listing all of my post-secondary courses and grades on the AMCAS application this summer (since I don't want to waste time next summer recording all 18 years of schooling past high school) and my overall science undergraduate GPA comes to just under a 3.7.

I had already arranged to cut back my volunteer work from three shifts a week (12 hours) to one shift. I am a bit compulsive but not always insane.

When we communicated earlier, you had suggested I not wait until August for the MCAT but take it next April; I could always retake it in August if need be. I had planned to get all the appli-cations out anyway next July at the latest, no matter when I take it. I intend to enroll in a prep course. Do you think I should skip the April test and gamble on August, or try in April, in any event? With Organic Chemistry and Physics all year, I'm not sure I'll have suffi-cient time to prepare for the MCAT, even with a prep course.

Sara,

The math courses sound fine. Don't worry about them.

Glad you already cut your hours back.

About the MCAT. Let's play it by ear for now. You may be ready for the April MCAT if you start studying for it now. After all, biology and chemistry are fresh and physics will be current. If you don't have the MCAT hanging over your head, you can do something else with your summer. Get the AAMC MCAT materials and an MCAT review book. Look at the practice exams. Start putting in an hour a day for MCAT review (remember to treat it like a premedical required course—only it's much more important than any of them). Take a prep course in the winter. If you feel ready by April, go for it. If not, take it in August. Give it your best shot.

My Health Professions Advisor Forum is currently discussing committee letters of recommendation. Your premed advisor at PSU will need to draft this letter based on letters from your professors. It is important, so get to know her well and your professors, too.

Best regards.

Dear Sandy,

I can finally provide you with the early update you requested early last month. I just finished final exams; I know nothing other than I seem to have gotten an A in Physics. The separate lab course that accompanied Organic Chemistry was a killer. It was only a two-unit course but I spent more time on it than for all my Physics material. As far as the rest of Organic Chemistry is concerned: you might recall that I elected to take a no-grade for the first term of Organic last fall after I had stupidly agreed to attend an ill-timed conference in my former field of history, which resulted in my missing an essential final part of the first course. That missed material has proved to be nearly fatal for me this year; fortunately, this professor has been quite kind to me and he suggested I take a no-grade and make up the course later on. He had also said I could continue through the year with the rest of Organic although I am truly suffering for having attended that conference. My grade for the second term was a C (the professor had told me at the beginning of the year, long before I realized how ferocious a reputation he has, that to him a "C" in Organic Chemistry meant that a student had "gotten it." At the time, I recall being alarmed at such news but apparently he is serious about that assessment. So, I guess I do "get it"—but can I convince a medical school of that?!). This professor also delivers a national standardized exam that covers the entire year's material, in lieu of a final exam for the third term.

Since I am planning to re-take the first term this summer, he suggested I wait until after that to take this national exam.

It was a mistake to try to take a review course in the winter with a full science/lab load. I am enrolled in a new review course that begins this week. For the MCAT, I will mostly have to review General Chemistry and Biology. The Verbal Reasoning part of the MCAT has been killing me and I finally discovered why. Having taught 5,000 years' worth of history for 14 years means that for almost any MCAT reading passage, I have taught on some aspect of the topic. The part that I invariably get "wrong" is the "author's implication"—but if I'm dealing with a topic I've actually written articles or a book on, how can the authors of the MCAT passages (who could hardly be expected to know most of these topics the way I have had to) be "right" for "author's implication" while I am "wrong"? Students without a scrap of knowledge about any of these topics usually score well above me. I can only hope that I can learn a test strategy to bypass this because I can't figure out any other way to overcome it. Pretending I've never heard anything about a particular topic doesn't work—I tried that.

As for next academic year, I will be taking courses like Biochemistry, Genetics, and a variety of interesting Biology courses while I wait to see if I'd better start considering PA (Physician Assistant) programs.

Sara,

It has been a year for you! But you survived and did well. You are to be congratulated. I am a little confused about what's going on in Organic Chemistry. You have to retake one term in that and will you be doing that this summer, along with taking a review course in preparation for the August MCAT? Am a bit surprised that the verbal is throwing you but I can see your point. You're too analytical and reading too much into the questions. Don't know a fix for that, although you might query John Hackett at the AAMC about your concerns, with specific examples. I can send you his e-mail, if you like.

I agree with less hospital time this summer. Grades and MCAT are all. I think that a strong showing on the MCAT will overcome a less than perfect grade in Organic, so that is where you need to put your efforts right now.

Where are you in the application process? What schools are you thinking about? Don't begin to think about being a PA yet. Remember, you're the most qualified applicant for your age that I've ever seen. Someone over 45 is going to get into OHSU's class, and it should be you.

Which brings me to a tactic for you; one that should abet your cause and is right up your alley. You need to write an article for a medical magazine about your situation. In your line of work you say "publish or perish." Well, publish something about being a forty-plus-year-old history and religion professor at Reed College who gave it all up to become a premedical student. Your story is magazine-worthy and, when published in a suitable place, should accompany your applications to medical school. You are not as familiar with the medical trade magazines as I am but I can suggest some you might look at for the human interest pieces they print. Then we can conceive of how it might work. I've been published twice this year in Physicians Management *and* Patient Care *and have four more articles in queue. Some of these magazines are desperate for good copy. Remember, I got into medical school with a coloring book. Surely you can find an angle here, and I can help.*

Let me know what you think, and keep in touch.

Greetings, Sandy!

Just today I inquired into grades and things did not turn out too badly: A in Physics and A– in the Organic Chemistry lab that nearly sucked the lifeblood out of me. And yes, I am repeating the first term of Organic Chemistry this summer while preparing for the MCAT and taking a prep course. I also discovered that my Biology grade was changed for the fall term from a B+ to A–. I did it without an inch of groveling.

I would be happy to write for a journal. True, "publish or perish" is well known in academia. Unfortunately for me, publishing actually contributed to my perishing. I wrote "too much" for an academic market that sought unskilled laborers. Actually, a few months ago, I wrote a piece I plan to submit to JAMA's (Journal of the American Medical Association) "A Piece of My Mind" rubric. As soon as my husband finishes his critique, I'll send it to them. Certainly I remember with great delight your lead poisoning coloring book episode, though you are rather modest in saying that that's what got you into medical school. I suspect a few other things were also considered....

Sara,

I like your AMCAS essay. I like its brevity and terseness. I don't know if you need to be so blatant about your age. You have stated it subtly and indirectly earlier on. They can figure out how old you are by themselves, without you drawing attention to it. By downplaying it, you're showing that you're not self-conscious about it. You will have to deal with it at your interviews, but let's not put the cart before the horse.

By the way, what do you know about the history of science and medicine? Or rather, is there an article in it for you? The magazines you should look to publish in are Patient Care (essay section), Postgraduate Medicine ("Physician at Large"), Journal of the American Medical Association (JAMA; "A Piece of My Mind"), The New Physician, Western Journal of Medicine (human interest and history of medicine pieces accepted), and perhaps, Physician's Management. I know some of the editors, having written for these magazines, so maybe we can put something together. Remember, virtually no premed publishes.

Hi Sandy,

Thanks for the feedback on the personal statement. Your criticisms are well taken and I agree completely with you on them. I'll edit accordingly. I'll finish up the essay for JAMA and restart the personal statement. Thanks for your thoughts.

Sara,

How are you preparing for the August MCAT? I believe it is an important test for you, but not absolutely critical, i.e., great scores will get you in (32+), good scores (27–30) won't keep you out. Would like to see you do 30 or better.

We need to talk soon about the schools you'll be applying to. Send me your list as soon as possible.

As for the essay you're writing—send it on to me. It would be great if you could be published in JAMA, but it's tough to get in there and even if you do, it could be six months to a year's wait for them even to make a decision about it. You need something that can accompany your application, or at least to be able to say that your essay was accepted for publication in such and such a journal. The journals I write for usually publish me in one to three months. That timeline would work better for you in applying for the entering class.

Let's hear from you soon. Time is of the essence.

Hello Sandy,

Here are the schools I've begun to zero in on. My preliminary decisions are based on the comments that people in your Forum made regarding older applicants, schools that had reasonable numbers of out-of-state residents, and schools that indicated reasonable GPA and MCAT scores. If you have any further suggestions or criticisms, please let me know. I included two California schools even though I am no longer a resident there, because we still own our house in Santa Monica and my husband is Professor Emeritus at UCLA.

Most definite:	OHSU (Oregon)
	UCLA
	USC
	University of Vermont

Interesting Possibilities:	U. of Connecticut
	Pritzker
	Northwestern
	Tufts
	Mt. Sinai
	Albert Einstein
	Meharry Medical
	Jefferson
	Penn State
	Temple
	Medical College of Wisconsin (Madison)

I'll finish up the Organic Chemistry retake course in about a week and a half; it's going much better and I should be able to get something in the B range. I am rather desperate over the lack of time invested in the MCATs. I gave my all this past year to coursework and now I have to atone for my sin of going to that conference last fall by having to retake this Organic Chemistry course. I can only hope that things can get pulled together in the final 5–6 weeks before the MCAT. I'm usually good at that.

Thanks for the feedback.

Sara,

Just received your essay today that you want to submit to "A Piece of My Mind" in JAMA. I like it but it needs a different perspective. As I read and reread it, one idea came to me. You actually mentioned it at the bottom of page 3: the different kind of time you were able to spend with your patient as a volunteer than you would as a medical student or resident (or professor!), yet how, *being even on the fringes of the medical fraternity had allowed you the privilege of being close to a patient and her family and how that had, perhaps, strengthened your own resolve to pursue a medical career. I think you need another paragraph on page 3, on where you are as a 44-year-old volunteer/premedical student. Ask yourself: how am I different from all these other volunteers putting in their "medical experience" time, in the context of this woman whom you drew so close to. Or maybe another focus could be how the professor-student relationship contrasts to the (student) physician-patient one. Remember, you already are a doctor; you want to become a physician. There's a title for you: "Doctor to Physician."*

I'm not sure I'm making any sense, but I think that the patient should not be the focus but more your relationship in the context of your own background. Also, take a look at Patient Care Magazine. I've written for them before. They have an essay in the back of each issue entitled "Reflections," and usually are receptive to good copy. I might even be able to ask the editor if they would consider a piece written by a premedical student.

Keep plugging away for the MCATs and let me know about refocusing the article.

Hi Sandy,

Thanks for such a speedy reply to the essay. Of course, I'm perfectly willing to try to refocus the essay but only with great difficulty. I can't help but submerge myself in the wider and, to me, more significant context. What I love so much about volunteering is that I get to have the close contact with patients that I enjoyed as a professor. Students were always telling me things about themselves I know they would never confess to other professors. So I was accustomed to very personal relationships with students. But to focus on me in my essay is virtually impossible. I'll try rewriting some parts and see what you think.

Last weekend, I took the first full-length MCAT-style exam—the midterm, as Kaplan calls it. I felt dreadfully unprepared since I had only been studying for this O. Chem class. The results were much more encouraging than I expected. The Physical Science section was abysmal—a 6—but I hadn't yet started the review. The Biological Science section was a 9 as was Verbal Reasoning. I was truly expecting little more than 6s on any of the sciences. The nicest part was that the actual length of the exam never bothered me; all those years as a scholar and marathon runner are finally paying off. In any event, now that I can fully concentrate on this mass of material (after my Chemistry final in a few days), I trust I can bring up those scores. Amazingly, in spite of the difficulty I've had all year with Organic Chemistry, I did quite well on those passages in the MCAT.

Let me know what you think about the list of medical schools I sent you.

Many thanks.

Dear Sandy,

I did manage to get a B in Organic Chemistry to take the place of that missing grade last fall....

Sara,

Looking forward to reading your rewritten essay. It's ok to send it to three or four places simultaneously, I believe. You need to get it published somewhere within the next five or six months.

Your medical school list has some problems. For one, I believe that Penn State only takes in-staters, it being state-supported. I think Meharry takes mostly blacks. Sinai and Einstein are very competitive, and Sinai's class is small. The Medical School of Wisconsin is in Milwaukee (it's my alma mater). Do not apply to University of Wisconsin Medical School in Madison. Your first four schools are good choices. Of course, Oregon is a must and your best chance.

Only a couple of weeks until the MCAT? How's it going, champ?

Sara,

Here is my list of schools for you to apply to:

Most definite (schools who accept your age): OHSU, Tulane, Tufts, University of Michigan, St. Louis U., Creighton U., North Dakota, Case Western, Jefferson, Vermont.

Other possibilities, for one reason or another: George Washington, Howard, Emory, Northwestern, Albany, Hopkins.

Dark Horses: Loma Linda, Mt. Sinai, NY Medical College, Rochester.

Now for the Osteopathic Medical Schools:

COMP (Pomona), San Francisco, COMS (Iowa), UHS (Kansas City, MO). Osteopathic medical schools accept proportionately more students your age.

Apply to 15 or so allopathic and four or five osteopathic schools. Some of the allopathic schools who do accept students your age still place a great deal of importance on the MCATs, so don't rest on your laurels yet.

Sara,
    The schools I suggested came out of the *Premedical Advisors' Handbook* and not the official AAMC guide. For the most part, they were kind to the older applicant. Howard takes minorities; you're a minority. Hopkins is secure enough to take chances. Most of the schools I listed accept at least 50% out of state. Use what you like; it's just my intuition.
    The AMCAS essay looks great. The only line I don't like is "medicine is my home." I know what you mean (i.e., "I know that when I begin my study of medicine, it will feel like coming home") but it just doesn't sound quite right here.
    Regards.

Sandy,
    I just picked up the results of my last full-length MCAT-style Kaplan tests. Amazingly enough, my overall scores are as dismal as when I started, perhaps a tiny bit better: 24–25. Never mind that I have studied endlessly and know the material better than a few weeks ago. For some reason, the Kaplan strategies have not worked for me. I think the problem keeps coming down to the same simple dilemma: never having had any exposure to standardized, multiple-choice exams up until two years ago. And working as a history scholar has not at all prepared me for these kinds of exams. I am coming from a discipline that is just too far afield from all this. Nor can I make up for it by learning "strategies" or "test-taking skills." I feel as if I am letting you down in all this...
    I'll give it my very best shot this next weekend; if the scores are still as desultory as these, I'll simply plan to retake the exam in April.
    Disheartened, Sara

Sara,
    Relax about the MCATs. You'll do fine. Just make sure you don't stay up all night the night before.

Hi Sandy,

I don't think the MCAT went very well. It has been hellishly hot in Oregon all summer, with temperatures in the mid-90s the final weeks before the exam. I couldn't sleep most of the summer and the two nights before the exam I barely slept at all. It was difficult even to focus on the passages. Fortunately, I don't have to face the results for another six weeks.

Actually, my greatest sense of relief came only a few days ago when I finally mailed off the application for Johns Hopkins and, at the same time, the page proofs of my swan-song manuscript in academia. It is a volume I co-authored with a Dutch colleague; we translated and discussed a hitherto untranslated 14th-century dialogue written by an Orthodox theologian-monk. What a different universe I inhabited!

Frankly, I am not anxious to fill out the application for the osteopathic medical schools. I confess my reasons are lamentably trivial. Filling out the AMCAS application was a small nightmare because I have to record 18 years' worth of post-secondary school and graduate courses (about 99% of which haven't a thing to do with science). I just don't have the energy to repeat the entire process for osteopathic medicine.

I hope I haven't let you down completely, Sandy, especially since you've been such a relentless advocate for me. I fully expect to have to retake the MCAT in April and try all over again. It was just too much to do in one summer. Classes start up again in a few weeks and, old scholar that I continue to be, I eagerly look forward to the new material as if I were facing a new group of students. My enthusiasm is not diminished even if I have buried all hope for the coming year.

Sara,

Let's wait and see how you did before writing the post-mortems. In the meantime, get those applications out to osteopathic schools. And keep the faith.

Regards.

Sandy,

Ok, no post-mortems yet...As far as osteopathic schools are concerned: My heart is just not in it, Sandy. I would rather have to reapply and retake the MCAT next spring rather than not get accepted anywhere and have to go to osteopathic medical school. It's also clear from reading the material that osteopathic schools seem to want to "tighten up" the application process so *that it isn't just a safety valve for applicants. Most schools either require a letter from a DO or strongly recommend it. I still have some time to consider this; applicants are advised not to send in their application until the MCAT scores are available.*

Admit it: it's hard to deal with an old scholar who has a few opinions and strong feelings. I really don't mean to be cantankerous.

Sara,

What allopathic schools did you wind up applying to? I can understand your not wanting to go the osteopathic route. So be it. Let me know your scores as soon as you get them. We still have work to do.

Sandy,

Regarding medical schools: I basically combined most of your suggestions with a few of mine: OHSU, UCLA, USC, George Washington, Howard, Chicago Medical, Penn State, Northwestern, Tufts, Michigan, Albany, Case Western, Oklahoma, Vermont, Medical College of Wisconsin. My greatest headache at the moment is gathering transcripts from seven different institutions and to continually encounter bureaucratic foul-ups; as if the rest of this hellish process isn't enough to crack the firmest resolve.

Sandy,

The scores are even worse than I could have imagined:

> *Physical Sciences: 6*
> *Biological Sciences: 8*
> *Verbal Reasoning: 7*
> *Writing Sample: T*

T???? I never heard of anyone scoring T before! How can a scholar of history get below average on the Verbal, yet score perfectly on the Writing? I can only hope that these scores are so dismal as to astonish folks with the discrepancy between the rest of my record and these numbers. Obviously, this is not a test one can take with several days of no sleep.

I assume I retake this hideous exam next April? Please Sandy, what is your assessment of all this? I cannot describe my mortification.

Sara,

You've really got to get more sleep before exams! Next time, I'll prescribe a soporific.

Your scores are quite interesting and remind me of mine on the older MCAT (two versions back). I scored in the 99th percentile on general information, 90th in verbal, 50th in math, and 25th in science—and I got into medical school! So, let's see what happens.

Now you can only wait for interviews and hope someone will see past your scores to what an unusual person you are and how much you would bring to the field of medicine. Should you not get invited for an interview, you will need to retake the MCAT and, I predict, you will blow them away this next time, because all you will really have to do until next April is study for it. No more Organic Chemistry to get in the way.

So take heart and expect the best.

Sandy,

I am forever amused by your certainty that I could score well on these kinds of exams, even with a few hours of decent sleep. My next nightmare is that I take it with plenty of sleep, time, etc., and still don't improve. I am presently taking the first term of an Anatomy course (the bones and muscles term) and I plan to take Introduction to Genetics in the winter; I can retake a prep course in the winter as well.

Many thanks.

Sandy,

In looking over secondary applications, occasionally a school refers to the applicant sending a resume, if he wishes to do so. Should I send any of these places my resume? You have one, so you know it's pretty long; I don't want to overload schools with more paperwork. I was amused to read in Vermont's catalogue that they welcomed the "nontraditional" applicant which they defined as people who waited "a year or two" after graduating from college before applying to medical school!

Sara,

I don't think the AMCAS application shows schools who you really are or what you're capable of. I think you should show off your resume. Remember, you're an oddball. Schools like taking in one or two of these types yearly. The transcript doesn't show your publications, academic positions, etc. I would think a medical school might boast about having a professor from Reed College in the freshman class. What have you got to lose (except secondary application money)? Strut your stuff!

Sandy,

Though my news remains desultory, I thought I should at least bring you up to date.

My little essay "From Dr. to Physician" was promptly returned by New Physician (my article didn't "suit their needs" at present) and just yesterday by JAMA (it is "intriguing" but doesn't fit their criteria—though even that sentence sounds like part of the form letter, I'm afraid). I'll try the Western Journal of Medicine.

Both Northwestern and Case Western immediately rejected me, obviously upon espying my MCAT scores. My husband was greatly relieved.

I sent in all the secondaries but heard nary a word from OHSU. I called a few days ago to see if one should expect some sort of confirmation of application receipt. The news was worse than I expected. They don't send out secondaries unless the applicant has an MCAT total of 24 and a GPA of 2.8. It didn't matter that my GPA is 3.6. I am below 24 so that is the end of the application process. The secretary said I could appeal the decision but that the decision had never been reversed. So, one day of rotten testing outweighs 20 years of consistently good academic work plus a career. I'll write a letter of appeal once I receive the official axe. I had never expected OHSU to be so slavishly dedicated to numbers.

I'll plan to take the MCAT again, in any event. I couldn't possibly feel worse physically than I did the day I took it. I just finished two courses that I enjoyed immensely and will miss a great deal.

Sara,

Besides taking the MCAT again you can think about foreign medical schools. They still work and it's not so bad living in the Caribbean for awhile.

Sandy,

While attending school in the Caribbean is a seductive idea, I have been reading several disturbing articles about the difficulty foreign-schooled students are having getting residencies in the States—whether or not they are US citizens. Are you familiar with that new test, only administered in Philadelphia once a year, which all foreign-trained students have to take? I've also talked to a number of young doctors from various countries who are working as volunteers in hospitals, sometimes full-time, because they can't even get hospitals to send them the proper applications for residency programs and they want to prove how serious they are about practicing medicine in this country. It's a prejudice of a horrific sort that has only just surfaced in this virulent form in the last few years.

In my more optimistic moments, fleeting as they are these days, I feel certain that someone's curiosity will be piqued somewhere. My advisor at school said that I may actually have more of a chance with a place like Johns Hopkins because they can afford to take risks. Besides, Johns Hopkins makes it very clear that they have no interest in MCAT or GPA cutoffs.

Sandy, I am an old and persistent dog—they'll have to shoot me in the head before I let go.

Dear Sandy,

I had mailed my letter of appeal to OHSU last week; it was one of the most eloquent and reasonable letters I had ever composed. In reply, I just received a memo from the woman in Admissions. Actually, it was more of a form memo. There wasn't a single reference in it to anything in my letter; in fact, there wasn't a hint of humanity in it. Rules are rules, she replied, and nothing can alter that. The rigidity of bureaucracy is astounding. The only detail missing was a line wishing the recipient a pleasant holiday season. What a process.

Sara,

Let me tell you a story. Many years ago, when I was going through what you're going through, I wrote a cartoon coloring book on lead poisoning for Downstate Medical Center. It was a huge success—even had some press coverage. So, when I was ready I applied there for medical school. I received a letter much the same as yours. The head of the admissions committee had his name stamped on it. I was furious. So I wrote him back saying something like "since this does not bear your handwritten signature I have reason to doubt its authenticity." He wrote back saying it was authentic, with his signature again stamped on the letter. Luckily, Marquette noticed the coloring book and invited me for an interview. That got my foot in the door and the rest was history.

You need to get invited for an interview. But your MCAT scores are working against you. You have to write a coloring book (only kidding). You have to get lucky, as I did. Or change your strategy.

One of my advisees scored a 23 on the MCAT and got asked to interview at two osteopathic medical schools. You asked about St. George's. Several years ago they invited premedical advisors down, all expenses paid, for a five-day junket. I took my son and we had a ball. They do a good job preparing their students for the USMLE and have good clinical clerkships in the US and UK. Also, there is a new proprietary medical school in Cambridge, which I may have some information on. Don't forget Guadalajara; and Ross medical schools for foreign students.

Let me know what you're thinking of doing and have a great year.

Sandy,

I'm still convinced that I could get a more passable score on the MCAT with a few extra nights' sleep and actual preparation, so I'd prefer not to go the osteopathic or foreign medical school route. My cardiologist from OHSU (who wrote such a great letter for my file) told me last night at supper that medicine is filled to the brim with stodgy physicians who harbor specific, closed ideas about what a doctor should look like—and I obviously don't fit any preconceived model. I simply need to have the luck to run into a more imaginative fellow who likes coloring books and isn't put off by my route into medicine or my degrees. I'm convinced that there must be at least one such person somewhere.

In the meantime, I'm steeling myself for more bad news in the weeks to come. I know one shouldn't take these rejections personally but they sure feel like a horrific kick in the gut.

Thanks for the words of encouragement.

Hi Sandy,

I've not heard from any medical school; a classmate of mine who took the April MCAT and finished all his applications in mid-summer has only just been getting interviews, including Yale. I just restarted an MCAT review course.

I was in touch with a man from OHSU who had interviewed a fellow student of mine (who really shouldn't be going to medical school); she had asked me to write her a letter for her pre-med committee file and, since she had helped me with Organic Chemistry, I complied with her request. She got an interview at OHSU (she had the right numbers, except for a "6" on Verbal Reasoning) and one of her interviewers was fascinated that a fellow student would write a letter for her. So he gave her his number to give to me, asking me to call him should I also get an interview. It turned out that he is a close friend of my cardiologist from OHSU. Anyway, I got in touch with the doctor and he was quite kind and sympathetic about my predicament. But he also said that, as far as he was aware, the cutoffs for OHSU were non-negotiable and that outside reviews of the application process prevented the school from going around those cutoffs. He said that about one-third of OHSU's entering class, at any one time, were reapplicants, and he thought that that was fairly standard around the country. He also told me that the oldest member of this year's freshman class is a man of 47. Good sign.

I am plowing through Genetics and loving it as well as studiously following the review course. I'm really quite calm about the idea of reapplication but perhaps that's because I haven't gotten any outright rejections for the past four weeks. Actually, George Washington only just sent me a postcard telling me that my file is complete—although I sent everything in a few months ago. So things are taking their time.

Sara,

Not having heard from other schools is an encouraging sign. Maybe they're reading the applications.

Dear Sandy,

No news is probably disastrous news at this point. There are still a number of schools who have not responded (including Hopkins) but I assume it's getting rather late for hope. I admit I felt a bit dashed upon receiving my rejection from Marquette. Some months ago the dean actually wrote me a personal letter telling me I didn't need an extra letter from my PhD chairman (some schools want a letter from your graduate advisor); I was impressed by the personal approach of the school and harbored foolish dreams that they might look beyond the MCAT scores. Oh, well. I've been studying faithfully for April's MCAT and working on my Genetics course, which has gone surprisingly well. Finals are next week; for the moment I have an A in the course but the professor has no curve in the class and his exams are jam-packed, covering everything in creation. If this next MCAT does not improve as well as it should, I'll look more closely at DO. There seems to be less prejudice towards DOs than towards FMGs.

Sara,
Probably no news is good news. How many schools are you still waiting to hear from and which ones are they? I would imagine that by virtue of your numbers alone, if you hadn't made the cut you would have heard by now. Maybe they're actually reading your application, looking for that one 45-year-old they're going to allow into the freshman class. I'll bet they don't have too many PhDs in languages with a six-page resume applying. Might there be an interview in your future?

I didn't realize that the April MCATs are almost upon us. You had better get a good night's sleep this time. A substantial boost in your scores will make a big difference. Also, should you need to reapply, your applications can go out sooner.

Hello Sandy,
The remaining schools are: Hopkins, Tufts, USC, Howard (they never sent word that the application was complete though it was all sent in about four months ago; I don't trust them), Jefferson (who didn't ask a single question on their secondary application; it was mostly geared to kids from peripheral areas in Pennsylvania who were planning to apply to their Physician Shortage Area Program), and Chicago Medical (Finch). I didn't think much interviewing was going on after March. I'll wait until I get the MCAT scores (mid-June) before sending in the AMCAS application. Everything should be in well before July this time. And now I have all those personal relationships with the AMCAS assistants since the foul-up, so perhaps things will go more smoothly this time. How much bad luck is still out there, anyway?

Sara,

There's an interesting article in this issue of the Advisor that I'm going to copy and send to you. It's about humanism in medicine. By the way, did you know that 50% of English majors get accepted, as opposed to 33% of Biology majors. I'll bet PhDs in arcane languages have the highest acceptance rate of all.

Keep the faith.

Dear Sandy—

Well, I almost felt encouraged that I hadn't yet heard from all those schools. Then, the other night, I arrived home from an 11-hour day, including three excruciating hours at the review course with General Chemistry, and was greeted by two rejection letters (Jefferson and Tufts). The next day I called USC and Chicago, to inquire whether I should begin to despair. Both schools are fairly late wrapping up their application process; USC interviews through April and Chicago, through May. The mean GPA at Chicago is only 3.2—way below mine—so if I get no interest out of them, it must only be due to those abominable MCAT scores. I'm going to look into volunteer work at a hospital near my old employer (Reed College) which is an osteopathic hospital. That way, I can more realistically apply to osteopathic schools if I really don't do well on the MCAT.

Sandy,

The MCAT is in a week and I am not feeling greatly encouraged by my progress. Though the absolute score on my practice exams go up, the scaled score doesn't, since the test is scored relative to all other test takers. I fear I am really a hopeless cause. I simply cannot think in quantitative terms. My training in history completely militated against that. How can I possibly start now when I've never done it and have no wish to do so? At least I am sleeping better now but I have little hope that I will significantly improve my score. And now when I see who among my friends is getting into medical school for this next year, I am appalled. I am just too old to be competing with 22-year-olds who haven't any idea how to talk to a patient.

Genetics went well and I thoroughly enjoyed the course. I even got a 97 on my final exam. The professor has been a jewel and a real paragon of understanding. I am working on an independent studies course with him this term on the genetics of Type 1 diabetes and he told me not to even think about the course until after the MCAT. I also started biochemistry with a wonderful man who is a researcher up at the Portland VA next to OHSU. I am desperately hoping he is older than I am. The first exam is next week, a few days before the MCAT.

Despondent but realistic, Sara.

Sara,

Can you say...Grenada? A few weeks ago I met a young woman who was doing a residency in NYC who had graduated from there. The door is far from shut on the international medical school graduate. Remember, you only have to spend two years there. The clinical years are back in the States. Also, Ross is apparently moving ahead with plans to open a school in Wyoming ($36,000 for tuition but heck, it's only money) and the Kigezi International School of Medicine may be opening a campus in Bellingham, WA (a missionary school that would send you to Ugandan villages for a while). By the way, Ross does not require the MCAT. Their average GPA is 3.2. However, the plans for Kigezi are on hold since they got a chilly reception from the University of Washington. I know you want to remain in the USA but I want you to keep this as an option after the next round of MCATs. Or osteopathic medical school, which might be even better. I think I told you that one of my advisees just got into the Florida school with a 23 on the MCATs.

Hang in there.

Hi Sandy,

Grenada begins to sound increasingly appealing...Yesterday was the MCAT. I still had trouble sleeping but not because of nervousness. It suddenly turned hot and dry here (the first time since last September!) and I suffered from merciless allergies that kept me awake at night no matter how many allergy pills I ingested. The exam seemed to go a bit better and I did not have that awful impending sense of horror upon emerging from it that I had last August. Still, what I really need is an MCAT that starts about 1:00 p.m. and is a 7-hour essay exam. This week I'm going over to the osteopathic hospital and inquire into volunteer work.

I am thoroughly enjoying the biochemistry class and I'll begin work on the Genetics project on diabetes. I also have a genetics fly lab in which we cross all sorts of flies with each other, none of whom seem to mind much. I'm the only one in the lab who trudges down several flights of stairs each week to let loose the unwanted generations rather than consign them to the jar of motor oil. Fortunately, my professor is quite indulgent with me and *doesn't object. So, I am unleashing all sorts of mutant flies into the Portland area, many of which can barely fly beyond the borders of the campus before their little lifespans run out.*

Thanks for the updates, Sandy, and for keeping the faith.

Sandy,

I've been in contact with an osteopathic physician here in Portland who has worked closely with pre-meds. He even has a group that meets one evening a month to discuss a variety of topics. Next week I'm going to spend a morning with him and his patients in the hospital where his office is based. He wants to get to know me well enough so he can add a letter to my file (I didn't even bring up the subject!). He seems eminently normal. One of the first things he told me was how one of his best friends entered medical school at age 50 after having been a professor at Purdue, with a PhD in horticulture. Still, that's a long way from ancient history. I'm becoming convinced that when medical schools say they want diverse students, they really mean kids either in college or not long out of it who took a lot of history or English literature courses in college, not adults who taught the stuff. But then, maybe I'm becoming cynical.

I finally got the address for the Western Journal of Medicine *and will send off that essay. Do you have any other suggestions for possible journals to send that piece to?*

The biochemistry exam I took right before the MCAT went better than I thought; I got a 97 on it. I do fine when I have tests with questions that require answers in real sentences.

Your faithful advisee.

Sara,

I think the osteopathic connection is a good one. They tend to take more older applicants, especially in your age group. In case you're interested, I've just received the latest edition of the pre-medical advisors' reference manual with lots of good information on minimal MCAT scores accepted by individual schools and average age and spread of applicants. Ask away about any schools you like.

Better let me see that essay again so I can give you more ideas about where you might send it. And let me know your MCAT scores as soon as you get them.

Warm regards.

Sandy,

May I ask about Howard and Finch (in Chicago)? I've not gotten my rejections from them; although both interview through May, I assume they are both lost causes. But since Finch's average GPA is 3.2 and Howard's MCAT averages are 7s, I'm still mystified as to what is turning folks off regarding my application. What are the age spreads for these schools and how low an MCAT score do they consider? Finch, I noticed, has an easy way to reactivate applications the second time around, so I thought I'd reapply to them. I'll wait until I get the MCAT scores before deciding where to apply.

I'll also let you know if Dr. Turner, the osteopathic physician, is truly normal or not and how the morning goes with him and his patients.

Sara,

Finch interviews until the end of May. They do not use numerical cutoffs and accept ten students a year over the age of 35. Howard also interviews into May but doesn't send rejection letters until then either. 20% of accepted applicants are "non-traditional," whatever that means. Their mean MCATs are lower, with a minimum of 7 required on all three sections. USC interviews until the end of April and you need a 30 on the MCAT to be viable, although they claim to take students in their 40s.

Finch sounds like your best hope. I'm crossing my fingers for you to get an interview.

Sandy,

I received the most amazing form of a rejection from Howard. They sent back my entire secondary application, complete with the uncancelled check, but with no indication of why they sent it or what it all meant. I called them to ask and the woman actually giggled nervously and first said that my reapplying wouldn't be affected by this. By what? Finally, she admitted that perhaps an explanatory note would have helped. But helped what? It finally dawned on me that this is how Howard sends out a rejection letter without having to even send one (hence, not wasting a single piece of paper). It was the most astonishing piece of non-human communication I've yet received in this entire vile process. Shortly thereafter, I received my latest biochemistry exam back and got 100% on it! The professor announced that it is the most difficult of all his exams. So much for Howard.

I had an absolutely marvelous morning with Dr. Turner, the osteopathic physician, last week and I was amazed at how instantly comfortable I felt! This man practices medicine the way I thought it was supposed to be practiced, with a real holistic and sympathetic bent. The way he handles his patients is fantastic and they obviously revere him. I will definitely put much more energy into osteopathic medical schools this time around. They do not seem to require the cookie-cutter sort of applicant I've witnessed so far. It was an incredible breath of fresh air. What took me so long to find this?!
    Uplifted, Sara

Sara,
    Glad to hear about your biochemistry test and positive experiences with the osteopathic physician. If the allopathic schools don't want you, the osteopathic ones will be lucky to get you. Read up on the tenets of osteopathy.

Sandy,
    I finally received my rejection from Chicago. It reminded me of your stamped signature letters. Only this was completely xeroxed, down to the signature. It is curious that your source of advising information states that they have no cutoffs but the official brochure does not blush at saying that the average MCAT scores are 9s and 10s—even with the average GPA of 3.2 and their age range of 20–56 (they claim). I'll go ahead and apply to them but, as time goes on, I'm convinced that I am not destined to get a hearing at allopathic schools. In fact, the more time I spend shadowing Dr. Turner, the osteopathic physician, the more I get the feeling that that is the direction that is more suited to my interests and orientation. I'll probably apply about half to osteopathic and half to allopathic schools. School ends in a few days. I actually scored another 100% on a biochemistry exam! There were only two in the entire class (of 80)! I no longer blush when I brag, considering that I seem to have paid my dues to every conceivable disaster. It appears that I'll finally pull a 4.0 this year. Of course, someone will not fail to point out that, after all, I didn't carry a full load, etc.

Sara,

Depending on your MCAT scores this time around you may be best advised to apply to osteopathic schools; osteopathic physicians don't like knowing they're playing second fiddle to the allopaths. It makes a big difference. I've known students accepted over students with better credentials just because osteopathy was their first choice. Get cracking on the works of Dr. Still, the founder of osteopathy.

Hi Sandy—

The longer I am with my osteopathic physician, the more I am drawn to osteopathic medicine. I think that if OHSU falls through again this year, I may well choose osteopathic schools over allopathic ones (assuming I have a choice—which is a bit cheeky given my record). I had already looked into the works of A.T. Still and the osteopathic movement. I'm going to look for more of his writings. The old life of the scholar does come in handy at times.

Well, Sandy, I'm obviously not a good test-taker. The scores inched up a few notches: Verbal Reasoning: 9; Physical Sciences: 7; Biological Sciences: 8; Writing Sample: S. I think that if the combined scores were a single point lower, I'd be in a complete tizzy about whether or not to retake the exam but with a 24 I think I'll let it go. I was surprised that Biology didn't go up considering how much better I was with the material but I think it was due to Organic Chemistry taking up about 50% of the test and it just wasn't as fresh this year as last August. Ironically, after having an entire course in Genetics in the winter, in which I did really well, there wasn't one single genetics question, much less a passage on my MCAT version. What are the chances for that? This 24 will at least allow me a secondary to OHSU but the less-than-8 on the Physical Sciences will probably be the end of it.

I'll send off the AACOMAS application in the morning; I've applied to ten schools. I'll await whatever information you can come up with before sending off the AMCAS. There may be a big difference between 21 and 24 for some schools. It's ironic that my science GPA went up this year to, I think, over a 3.6. Please tell me not to despair.

Sara,

Congrats on your improved MCATs. You're now in the acceptable DO range but still a little shy for the allopathic schools.

I sent the information you requested out today. You can apply to Oregon but the DO schools will ask you if you applied to any allopathic schools and you won't be able to tell them "No," because you really want to be an osteopathic doctor! They feel that any student who applied to both will accept the allopathic school if they have a choice. These people (understandably) love being first choice and not playing second fiddle.

What osteopathic schools are you considering?

Hi Sandy,

Many thanks for the information which arrived today. It was extremely useful for eliminating several schools. I see that even your alma mater has gone the stingy route and no longer seems to have the same spirit of adventure when they took the risk of admitting someone who had barely finished his science prerequisites and was most famous for his artwork. I'll apply to OHSU, Chicago Medical, Albany, and Boston University. I'll get around the osteopathic question regarding other applications to allopathic schools somehow. I suspect that the 7 on one of the science sections will still be my undoing. Looks like I had my conversion experience to osteopathy just in time! Dr. Turner, the DO, just handed me a lengthy letter of recommendation he wrote for me, asking me to "edit" it. I was surprised because I hadn't even asked him for a letter. He's been a real blessing and reminds me of what I think you might be like. I can be very honest with him; I'll ask his opinion about applying to allopathic schools. The schools I applied to are the osteopathic schools in Philadelphia, Chicago, Kansas City, MO., Des Moines, Michigan State, New York (Long Island), New England (Maine), Kirksville, Pomona, and New Jersey.

Also—you had asked me to send another copy of that essay I had submitted to various journals about my volunteer experiences. I edited it a bit, following suggestions by the JAMA reader. I'll send it on to you.

Sandy, thanks for your help and good cheer. Let's hope it goes better this time.

Sara,

Nice piece but too long. Most medical magazines will give it a page—so it needs to be pared down to about 1,200 words. I would second your idea about looking into osteopathic journals. I don't know of any, but I'm sure they exist. Check them out at the medical school library and mail off your article to a few. If you're going to go the osteopathic route, this will be a plus on your application.

Your time is coming.

Sara,

I don't know if they gave you your percentile scores on the April MCATs with your raw scores, but here they are:

Writing Sample: S: top 5%

P: 7—24–36%

B: 8—28–44%

VR: 9—54–70%

MCAT says that medical schools shouldn't add up the scores, but look at each score individually. Of course, they do add them up and everyone talks about their composite score. Your raw score of 24 is in the osteopathic ballpark. I think we both know that and I'm glad you're looking into those schools. I'll bet you get a few bites and requests for interviews, too. I'll let you know more soon about the schools you applied to.

Keep trying to get your article published and shadow that osteopathic physician!

Sandy,

I haven't had a chance to write since returning from an exhausting and depressing trip overseas. I managed to get, just barely, all the secondaries off to osteopathic schools before leaving in August. OHSU's didn't arrive until I returned home. A number of surprises awaited me. While in Holland, the medical school in Pomona got in touch with me and requested an interview. In the huge pile of mail when we got home was also an interview invitation to Kansas City. And last week I received invitations from Chicago (the osteopathic school) and the New England school, which looks especially intriguing. I just returned from the interview in Pomona (southern California). I've always detested Pomona; I've driven through the area (about 40 miles inland from Los Angeles, in the desert) dozens of times on my way to somewhere else and I never failed from offering thanks to God that I didn't live there. It's even at the foot of a mountain range—which you can't see most of the year because of the crud in the air. The school has an excellent curriculum that helped offset the striking lack of appeal in its physical layout. The school accounts for about 20% of osteopathic primary care physicians so there are positive aspects to the school. But I never felt comfortable in the interview and I doubt severely I impressed them. They were not at all friendly and seemed almost hostile to my collection of degrees. The last week of September I interview in Kansas City and go directly to Chicago (both osteopathic). Chicago is looking increasingly interesting from the package I just received today. In mid-October I have an interview at the University of New England, located just south of Portland, Maine. That school so far is my first choice for osteopathic schools, but they take extremely few folks from outside the New England area, so I was ecstatic to get an interview (my Connecticut passport must have helped). In any event, things are certainly much brighter already than a year ago. I'm only taking one course this term, Microbiology, which apparently has a killer lab, so the course is worth one and a half courses rather than just one.

I'll also forward an e-mail I received from a British physician who is an editor with the Western Journal of Medicine. I had sent them my essay and this was her response. That particular essay they liked but not enough to print it. Instead, she inquired into whether I would write them an essay on why a 46-year-old woman, who was firmly entrenched in a scholarly career, would turn to medicine. I was quite taken aback—but flattered!

Sara,

Congratulations on all your interviews. Things are looking up from last year. Not only are you going to get into school this year, but I believe you may have a choice among several. Trust me.

The word from the Western Journal of Medicine is definitely encouraging. Don't be miffed. Just write the story they want you to and they'll publish it and it may get you into an allopathic school. Since you're only in one science class this semester, you should have the time. Get on it, as there is some lag between acceptance and publication and it would be nice to be able to use it this year.

Let me know how the interviews are going.

Best regards.

Sandy,

I was not in the slightest miffed by Western Journal of Medicine not wanting my original essay. I'm an old academic who has suffered from the publication route like any other academic. I have already written the new essay; I just need to type it up and send it to them this week. The editor wants it as close to September 20th as possible.

Thanks for the encouragement!

Dear Sandy,

I just returned a few days ago from the interviews in Kansas City and Chicago (actually, in Downers Grove, about 25 miles west of the city in a beautiful rural-like suburb). Both schools are extremely impressive and I think the interviews went reasonably well. I'm too seasoned an academic to put much stock in one's private impressions on one's own interviews. While in KC I heard from my husband that I was only put in the "hold" category in Pomona. What a relief. If I had been rejected outright I would have been crushed, of course; but if I had been accepted, I would have had to cough up a $1,000 deposit and then try to convince myself the place was livable—which I'm convinced it's not. Apparently I overwhelmed them about as much as they did me. This interview racket is quite amusing because a number of kids who were with me in Pomona were also in KC and Chicago (and they were accepted at Pomona). Chicago was so impressive that several of them had already changed their minds about Pomona after a few hours at the Chicago school. I should hear something from both places in a couple of weeks. I have my New England interview in two weeks; I'm particularly anxious about that one because I still think it's going to be my first choice.

The article for WJM is on its way. Frankly, I don't hold any illusions that it will admit me to an allopathic school; I've gotten awfully spoiled by the reception and warmth of the osteopathic folks and I'm no longer sure I can "go back." Funny how that works.

I'll let you know as soon as I hear more.

Sara,

I also suspect you will hear within two to three weeks from both schools. Let me know as soon as you get your first acceptance and we'll celebrate over the Internet! The allopaths' loss will be the osteopaths' gain.

Would like to see a copy of your latest article.

Hi Sandy,

On my way to my microbiology lab today to attend to my E. coli colonies, I received word of acceptance from the school in Kansas City! Gosh. And to think that you have had a major hand in goading me on. KC isn't quite my first choice (I think it vies with Chicago for 2nd place) but what a wonderful school to "have" to go to if New England comes to naught! It is truly a most welcome school, on every account. And their first-time pass rate on the boards is phenomenal (95–97%). Perhaps I'll be so relaxed now for New England that I won't be such a doggone intellectual. You never know—even stuffy New Englanders can be won over.

I'll send you a copy of the unedited version of the essay I sent to WJM (that is, before they object to the length).

Thanks so much, Sandy! I'll be in touch as soon as I hear anything from Chicago and Maine.

Sara,

You made me proud.

I am curious how you heard "on your way" to microbiology class. Was it as exciting as your husband having a plane fly overhead and drop leaflets or do some skywriting, or do you have a cellular phone?

Do we have to start calling you doctor now or can we wait until you start medical school?

CONGRATULATIONS!!!

Sandy,

No, receiving the news was not quite as dramatic as you suggested, but we have certainly celebrated with some wonderful Veuve Cliquot champagne that we picked up in Holland.

And no, you needn't call me "Dr." just yet; "Professor" still suffices.

Many, many thanks!

Hi Sandy,

In haste—

While in Boston a few days ago about to drive up to Maine for my interview, my husband called to tell me that the admissions woman from Chicago left me a message. She said that the admissions committee had just met and she wanted to be the first to tell me that I had been accepted! What a personal touch. And she so sounded genuinely excited, I felt terrifically guilty for my Yankee leanings toward Maine. In any event, the Maine school is great but the interview was extremely hard to read. They promised us an answer by week's end. If Maine accepts me, we'll probably go there; if not, probably Chicago. I've heard increasingly disturbing details about OHSU now that I have unwitting informants (i.e., my own former students, now OHSU medical students, God wring their souls). I have so enjoyed the terrific camaraderie among students at all three schools I've liked (Pomona being an exception) and the true joy of students who love being where they are is intoxicating. The excitement and passion of the DO students are really hard to pass up.

So, your guidance seems to have worked its miracle. I doubt whether I'll even consider any more interviews. I'm pooped and everything from Portland requires an act of God to get to.

More when I hear—

Sandy!

MAINE SAID YES!

And to make matters more complicated, I just got a call from OHSU and they want to interview me this coming week. They are beginning their own interview cycle then and I'm scheduled for the second day of interviewing. I couldn't feel more ambiguous about it. I no longer know if I even want to go the allopathic route, given a choice, especially after the fantastic experiences and staff/students I met at KC, Chicago, and Maine. Maine remains my top choice. The school is superb and the facilities amazing. It is the only school I applied to that appeared on US News & World Report's list a few months ago of the top fifty primary care medical schools. Of course, I'll try to keep an open mind and at least see what the alternatives are. The osteopathic interviews are panel-style, which are usually harder and more difficult to assess. OHSU simply has two interviews, both one-on-one, and I generally do well talking to strange people. It's hard to imagine, though, that OHSU can out-impress Maine. What a conversion I must have had.

Your grateful advisee,

Sara,

    Sounds like your dance card is full. Too bad you can't auction off those acceptances you won't be using. Three schools! Most pre-meds are lucky to get into one.

    You don't have to travel for your next interview. That's good. If they accept you it will pose a dilemma. Going to OHSU would certainly be convenient; you won't have to uproot and move across the country. But maybe your heart's in Maine with the osteopathic physicians.

Sandy,

    The OHSU interview day was not particularly impressive. The interviews themselves were the most pleasant part of the day. Each interview was supposed to be 30–40 minutes; one doctor kept me 50 minutes and the other 90 minutes. Both went well and felt like comfortable discussions. But the students were not at all winsome like the osteopathic students. The OHSU students decided to forego the campus tour "because it's raining"—but this is Oregon and the rainy season won't let up until next June! As a result, I still haven't the faintest idea what the medical school is like. And although the students were quite nice, there was not the overpowering passion, enthusiasm, and general heartwarming reception I felt at the osteopathic schools. OHSU made no effort to "sell" itself or make you feel particularly welcome. Most of us there felt like we should feel lucky to have been granted an interview. Allopathic schools generally interview a larger percentage of the applicant pool—about 15–20%; osteopathic schools interview about 10–13%. That means it's more selective to get the interview invitation itself at the osteopathic schools but if you do get the interview you have a greater chance of being accepted. So the schools go out of their way to wine and dine you. Every interviewee I spoke to at all the osteopathic schools felt exactly the same way. OHSU was quite a letdown and it was only their second day of interviewing so their lackluster reception could not be due to interview burn-out.

    There are DO residents at OHSU and Good Samaritan (the large hospital where I've been volunteering the last three years). I also found out that, if as a DO you elect to take the allopathic boards, in addition to the osteopathic boards, the pass rate on the allopathic exam is over 90%. I think that there isn't the separation between the two fields as even twenty years ago. I applied to Maine, for one reason, because they are extremely regionally-preferential and they'd like their graduates to want to stay in New England. Those are my roots, after all, and I've no problem with the idea of settling in New England—on the contrary, it's quite appealing! At any rate, OHSU will let us know their decision in four to five weeks. I think I have an excellent chance but I doubt I've been inspired sufficiently by them to be lured away from the osteopathic schools. I surely never expected such riches to choose from...

Considering the misery of last year, this year's events are overwhelming to my modest mind. Thanks for never losing faith in me.

Sara,

Sounds like your mind is made up, but let me know when you hear from Oregon.

Hi Sandy,

I didn't expect to hear from OHSU for at least another two weeks but today I got their answer—they said yes. I knew the interviews went okay but I was sure the less-than-stellar MCAT scores (especially the 7 on the Physical Sciences) would, at best, earn me a place on the wait list. And what about those two C's and a B in Organic Chemistry? What happened to the myth that one must get A's in Organic? The school's proximity is distressingly seductive...but if that's the major selling point, it isn't enough. Besides, I didn't like the tone of the letter which said that I should be "commended" for having been accepted into medical school, given the highly competitive market.

I received an e-mail from Western Journal of Medicine; *they had wanted my article to be 800–1,000 words and I knew it was way over the limit though I wasn't sure how much over. I decided to leave it up to them. To my amazement they liked it a lot and decided that even though it turned out to be 1,600 words, they would only shorten it a bit and "work the other articles around it." Neat!*

What follows is Sara's essay, "From 'Doctor' to Physician," which appeared in the *Western Journal of Medicine*.

"If you could be anything you wanted to be, what would you be?" My father's query startled me. A year before, I had decided on a career in the Peace Corps and had dreamed of working long and harsh hours in remote lands with like-minded souls. I had just learned that Peace Corps stints (at that time) were of 2 years' duration, with one or two possible renewals. I had become morbidly depressed as only a 13-year-old can become at shattered dreams. Still, my response was quick, as if by instinct, "If I was a guy, I'd be a doctor. An orthopedic surgeon." If the reply surprised my father, he never let on. "So you're not a guy. So what?"

From that day on, I planned for a medical career. I would have all the bones in the body memorized before beginning college courses in biology. Summer volunteer work and hospital employment only furthered my zeal. I graduated from high school in 3 years so as to get going on the goal I had set before me.

Thirty-two years after that brief conversation with my father, I am applying to medical schools. Despite my best-laid plans, bone memorization schedules, and unabashed enthusiasm, my academic life took a different direction. I became a "Dr," but one of philosophy. I received a PhD in the field of ancient Near Eastern history and culture, tackling, instead of bones, Sumerian and Akkadian, our first written languages dating from 3000 to 500 B.C. Rather than tending to people's bodies, I worked with the intellect, teaching for 14 years as a university professor. For many years, I taught night courses at the University of California at Los Angeles, where several of my students were physicians who eagerly read ancient history—stories written by Egyptians, Greeks, and Romans and the philosophical treatises of the Stoics. Many expressed their "envy" that I earned my keep by reading and writing. It was clear that these physicians yearned for an intellectual dimension their medical lives lacked, just as surely as I slowly sensed the absence of science in my own life. I never regretted my decision to become a scholar of ancient languages and history, but medicine continued to beckon me.

So it was, at age 43, I decided once again on a career in medicine. I had to start from scratch, teaching myself elementary algebra during my final semester of teaching at Reed College, Portland, Oregon, in preparation for the science program I had enrolled in. Finally, I was studying the college courses, I had missed 25 years previously. A number of my classmates were former Reed students of mine. Students whose essays on the Old Testament, Homer, and Plato I had critically evaluated were now laboratory partners in physics and tutored me in organic chemistry. Science students tend to be more technicians than intellectuals, and I would notice that whenever my organic chemistry professor provided a brief historical excursion on a topic, pens suddenly ceased their furious note-taking. When studying for exams, I often heard comments like, "He just told us that stuff to give us a break." On those occasions, I was not always successful at holding my tongue. But I had the zeal of a convert. I needed it. To maintain the grades to remain a viable medical school applicant, I needed to call on all the mental reserves I could muster.

But had I simply romanticized medicine? I needed to find out, so I began a volunteer job in a cardiology wing at a sizable Portland hospital 3 days a week, apprehensive of what I would discover both there and within myself. To my surprise, within a few days, I felt completely at home. Many years of speaking with students and colleagues made conversing with patients and their families natural and easy.

My volunteer coat, I found, signals my volunteer status only to nurses and physicians. Often when I have been assisting younger nurses, a distressed patient has turned to me, obviously seeking refuge in the "medic" with silver streaks in her hair, asking me if everything would be all right, or, in a couple of cases, if the nurse was doing the right thing. One of my greatest weaknesses, in fact, is to befriend patients. A cardiologist, a close friend of mine, has warned me about getting too involved with patients, knowing the difficulty such friendships might cause later on when my time is no longer my own.

I tend to think too much. But my life as a historian had made me sensitive to relations between people, and I have instinctively paused to observe how nurses, physicians, and residents react to each other and to patients. Physicians who have been on the ward for a long time often enjoy a warm relationship with staff. But I am amazed and occasionally appalled by the immaturity of some interns and residents. They show the same fear I remember so well of college students who desperately tried to appear at home in their new intellectual environment. In trying to shrug off their discomfort, they will assume a diffidence, an unconscious striving to look "cool" and "in charge"—even when it is neither called for nor possible. It has been painful at times to see the dismissive manner some residents display toward seasoned nurses and volunteers. I have often wondered if I am simply envious that such distressingly young looking men and women, some of who could be my sons and daughters, have completed a medical education I covet. But I have also had the experience of a number of patients who, again not recognizing the volunteer jacket, have turned to me for an explanation—as if I could give one—of medical jargon an intern has just used in conversation with them.

I have been generally gratified by the warm reception by physicians, nurses, and staff if they know my plans. One cardiologist, whose research project I had been asked to assist with and who had been told of my career change, exclaimed with a wide grin on meeting me, "I don't know whether to admire you or revile you!" The words were ambiguous, but the grin was obvious encouragement. Of course, it is easy to champion the underdog, but the sincere enthusiasm I have received augurs well.

I admit to envying my younger premed cohorts their stronger science backgrounds and, for many, their having grown up in an environment where science is bred in the bone. But, on the eve of several medical school interviews, I am confident that my years spent wrangling with ancient and arcane languages have brought many advantages. *Exempli gratia*, I already know that Latin bone terms are no obstacle.

Sara,

I'm so excited for you!

I know what I would do, if I had your choices, but I will not attempt to influence you, except to suggest that you go to OHSU and talk to some students and call students at Maine and sound them out. Get more information and opinions, since you're afforded the luxury of a choice.

Let WJM know that you were accepted to medical school. I'm so happy you're going to be published there. I feel they have an obligation to literary medical types to encourage them to keep up their writing. The kind of thing I'm doing for Family Practice Management you can do for the New Physician—a diary of your experiences as a medical student, for example.

Sandy,

I took your advice even before I got it by e-mail. Not trusting first impressions, I had talked to as many OHSU and Maine students as I could. I'm afraid that those first impressions have only been confirmed for OHSU—but strengthened for Maine. I hear a lot about the cut-throat sense of competition at OHSU and that students there tend to mostly fend for themselves. Since I also know a good many of my classmates who are now first year students there, I can also understand how many of them fit very well into that sort of environment. But at Maine (as well as KC and Chicago), the students have an incredible network for study groups, taping lectures and transcribing the notes for everyone, etc. I've already told you how enthusiastic the official student guides at the osteopathic schools were; this was confirmed by the barrage of students who came to talk to us interviewees (easily perceived since we mostly looked like undertakers) and students who immediately sat with interviewees in the cafeteria at lunch. I heard from one of my former Reed students, now in the MD-PhD program at OHSU, that the school has had a hard time just trying to get first and second year students to volunteer to be student guides for this year's interviewees. These little hints tell me a lot about a school. I couldn't help but notice the great discrepancy between the students at the osteopathic schools who showed us interviewees every nook and cranny of their schools, regardless of the weather—and the OHSU students who didn't want to trudge through the rain. This happened not just on my day but also on another (sunny!) day when a fellow student had his OHSU interview. (Maine's curriculum also includes, in the second year, several required seminar-like courses that show medicine's interwovenness with other disciplines, e.g., medicine and the arts; medicine and religion, etc.). Chicago and KC also included similar courses. OHSU, by contrast, has nothing remotely similar. I sat down with my husband and we combed through all the literature of the various schools who accepted me and compared and contrasted every aspect that was important to us. I am not at all surprised that you would still opt for an allopathic school but I know that, especially as a family practitioner, you yourself cannot help but have a good deal of sympathy with osteopathic principles. But I am also a historian; one of the reasons I love being one is because it requires looking at human cultures from a wide variety of disciplines in order to be just to the people one studies. Since last spring, I've read a number of volumes written by A.T. Still (the founder of osteopathic medicine who started out as an "allopathic" physician) and I love the interdisciplinary method of the osteopathic schools. Remember too that DOs are not nearly as visible on the West

Coast as they are in the Midwest and on the East Coast. I would not have nearly the problem identifying myself back East as out here.

Well, this was a lengthy apology (i.e., self-defense). Be assured that I've done my homework well and that I feel confident that I'm heading in the right direction. I've studied the works of the ancient Stoics far too long not to think that there was a good reason for the hardships of last year. I've been bestowed with a remarkable chance to compare what was my dream for years (going to OHSU) with what is, in fact, far more amenable to my intellectual orientation. It's much easier, ironically, to be able to leave Portland voluntarily than to think that my home school didn't even want to consider me. Besides, I'll still be heading to another Portland, one that's virtually on the same latitude.

Hi Sandy—

I'm re-auditing the second term of anatomy; I had sat in on the class last winter but could do little other than listen since I was preparing AGAIN for the MCAT. This time I can actually read the textbook. Plus, I had found a great textbook last summer in Leiden, Holland, on Medical Biochemistry, used in the medical school there. It turns out also to be used at OHSU. I'm reading through two chapters a week for the next few months. Maybe something will stick.

I think we move to Maine in June or so. Excited????

Sara,

Glad to hear you're finally relaxing. Wait till next year. Better make a big deposit in the sleep bank now.

APPENDIX II

Summer Programs for the Premed

Now that you've read the entire book and are a step ahead of the other students who haven't, there is one final important area to discuss. It has already been stated that candidates who have worked in a medical environment are judged to be motivated and thought to make capable future physicians by admissions committee members. How then can you gain this valuable experience?

You have to go where the action is—to hospitals, laboratories, and research institutions. Summer employment at a medical center is fun, exciting, and educationally beneficial because it gives you a chance to see physicians and scientists at work. In addition, it may help to strengthen your career choices and better define your own personal goals. This, in turn, will enable you to speak with some degree of authority about what medicine means to you and why you are contemplating such a career.

There are two ways in which you can become involved with a program that will introduce you to the medical field. The first is by getting a job or volunteering at your local hospital. Most hospitals in the United States have some sort of volunteer program that you can join. As a hospital volunteer, you will be able to see and interact with patients as well as the medical staff. A second option is to apply for a summer position with an institution that provides summer work experience for students.

What follows is a listing of summer programs for premeds that have had particular appeal for me. These were culled from the Web site of the Health

169

Professions Advisory Program at Syracuse University, a wonderful resource for summer opportunities. For brevity, I have purposely left out all enrichment programs for underrepresented minorities and most summer research programs, with the exception of several outstanding ones. Dates listed are approximate and may vary from year to year. The full current listing can be found at **hpap.syr.edu/spstate.htm.**

ARIZONA HEART INSTITUTE FOUNDATION
Colonel Alexander W. Gentleman
Cardiovascular Summer Student Program
(6 weeks: Early June–mid-July)
Arizona Heart Institute Foundation
Cardiovascular Summer Student Program
2601 E. Thomas Road, Suite 225
Phoenix, AZ 85016
(602) 200-0437
E-mail: foundation@azheart.com
Web site: **www.azheartfoundation.org/database.asp?id=14**

Eligibility: Full-time college student interested in pursuing a medical career.

Application Deadline: Mid-March.

Features/Benefits: The program exposes students to all aspects of cardiovascular medicine: cardiovascular surgery, cardiac catheterization laboratory, preventive medicine/conditioning, non-invasive screening laboratory, and cardiology rounds. There is no tuition for the program, but students are responsible for their own living expenses and transportation.

Commitment: As a result of limited positions, each student must commit to the following requirements: full six-week commitment, 8 to 10 hours per day, participation and presentation of a group research project.

(**See also:** California, American Heart Association, Student Research Program)

BRIDGEPORT HOSPITAL
Yale University School of Medicine and Fairfield University
Research Associates Program
Medical Decision-Making and Clinical Research Course
(Early June–mid-August)
Research Associates Program
Department of Emergency Medicine
Bridgeport Hospital
66 Lilalyn Drive
Fairfield, CT 06825
(203) 384-4610
E-mail: ChiefRA@RAProgram.org
Web (application): **www.RAProgram.org**

Eligibility: Open to all college students and graduates who are interested in a career in the health professions.

Application Deadline: Spring: mid-January; Summer: early June; Fall: mid-September; Application fees are $185.

Features/Benefits: Research Associates (RAs) identify and enroll eligible patients into studies being conducted in the emergency department of a Level-2 trauma center. Additional opportunities to participate in other components of clinical research are available. The companion three-credit course at Fairfield University, Medical Decision-Making and Clinical Research, explores the academic questions related to service in the ED and other specialties of medicine. Room in the student residence and meals in the university cafeteria are available as part of a package to students who are taking the Fairfield University course.

Commitment: Maximum of one 4-hour shift in the ED during school semesters. Additional shifts are available during the summer.

HARTFORD HOSPITAL
Summer Student Fellowship Program
(10 weeks: Early June–mid-August)
Rosemarie Portal
Program Director, Summer Student Research Fellowship
Medical Education Department
Hartford Hospital
80 Seymour Street
Hartford, CT 06102-5037
E-mail: Rportal@harthosp.org
OR
Janet Hegeman
Summer Student Fellowship Coordinator
Medical Education Programs
Hartford Hospital
80 Seymour Street
Hartford, CT 06102-5037
E-mail: Jhegema@harthosp.org
Web site: **www.harthosp.org/ResidenciesFellowships/**
        SummerStudentResearchFellowship/default.aspx
(on-line application)

Eligibility: Open to all premedical students who have completed the junior or senior year by May 30.

Application Deadline: Mid-February. Following submission of the completed application the applicant should schedule the *required* interview. Interviews are held through March 1. All decisions will be announced by April 1.

Features/Benefits: Introduction to research methodology, patient treatment, and ethical issues. Students engage in an assigned clinically-related investigative project within a department division suited to their medical and scientific interests and educational qualifications. Research investigations are conducted under the guidance of full-time physicians. $1,500 stipend for the 10-week period.

Expenses including travel and meals in the hospital cafeteria are met by the student. Dormitory housing is available and may be partially or wholly subsidized.

NATIONAL INSTITUTES OF HEALTH
Summer Internship Program in Biomedical Research (SIP)
(Minimum commitment is eight weeks; no official start/end date)

Summer Internship Program Coordinator (contact names, e-mail addresses, phone numbers and institutes or centers offering programs are available at the NIH Web site listed below; approximately 1,000 students are selected, including those returning from previous summers).

Research and Training Opportunities at NIH
Summer Internship Program in Biomedical Research (SIP)
National Institutes of Health
Building 7, Room 300
Bethesda, MD 20892-0760
(301) 469-1409
Web site: (online application) **www.training.nih.gov/student/**

Eligibility: This program is designed for students (college juniors, graduating seniors planning to attend graduate or professional school in the fall, and first-year graduate or medical school students) who are enrolled at least half-time, with an interest in biomedical research. Must be enrolled in degree-granting programs, with a GPA of 3.0 or better, and must have expressed strong interest in or be pursuing studies in disciplines related to biomedical research. Candidates must be U.S. citizens or permanent residents.

Application Deadline: March 1. Some of the programs, including NCI, do not have a deadline. **Late applications will not be accepted.** Application is available online and is open mid-November through March 1.

Features/Benefits: The program provides students with biomedical research training in one of the highly productive intramural research laboratories of the Institute (each applicant may apply to three institutes or centers). The mentor system is used. Summer fellowships will be paid once a month in accordance with current stipend rates. Support amounts vary from $990 for high school students before graduation to $2,200 per month for those students with three or more years of graduate school. Students are responsible for their own travel and housing expenses.

MAYO GRADUATE SCHOOL
(10 weeks: June–early August)
Glenda Mueller
SURF Program Coordinator
Mayo Graduate School
200 First Street SW
Rochester, MN 55905
(507) 284-3862
Fax: (507) 293-0838
E-mail: gmueller@mayo.edu
Web site (online application): **www.mayo.edu/mgs/surf.html**

Eligibility: Must be a student currently in their sophomore or junior year of college with a GPA of 3.0 and seriously considering a biomedical research career as a PhD or MD/PhD

Application Deadline: February 1.

Features/Benefits: The Program gives students the opportunity to preview the dynamic research opportunities available to PhD and MD/PhD students. Fellowship recipients can choose from a wide variety of areas in the biomedical sciences. Mayo laboratories have state-of-the-art facilities and create a rich academic environment for students with interests in basic science research. Appointees receive a fellowship award of $5,000 before tax. Students are responsible for their own travel, housing, and meals. Convenient housing costs approximately $150/week.

UMDNJ-ROBERT WOOD JOHNSON MEDICAL SCHOOL
Summer Clinical Internship Program
(2 weeks: Early–mid-June)
Carol Terregino, M.D., Assistant Dean for Admissions,
UMDNJ-RWJMS, TC118
675 Hoes Lane
Piscataway, NJ 08854
(732) 235-4577

Eligibility: For undergraduates interested in careers in medicine.

Application Deadline: Early March. Application consists of college transcript, one letter of recommendation, and online application.
Accepted applicants will be notified by April of acceptance.

Features/Benefits: Students will have the opportunity to shadow clinical
faculty members in specialty areas at the medical facilities in New
Brunswick, New Jersey. Lunchtime seminar series will complement
the clinical experiences. Students will also take part in presentations
of clinical topics selected and researched at the end of the two
weeks. Transportation and lodging are the participant's responsibility.

BROOKHAVEN NATIONAL LABORATORY
Science Undergraduate Laboratory Internships (SULI)
(10 weeks: May–August)
Mel Morris
Brookhaven National Laboratory
Building 438, P.O. Box 5000
Upton, NY 11973-5000
(631) 344-5963
Fax: (631) 344-5832
Web site: www.bnl.gov/education/programs/suli.asp

Eligibility: Must be a U.S. citizen or permanent resident and 18 years of age or older. Must have completed at least junior year with a B average or better.

Application Deadline: February 1.

Features/Benefits: The program offers cutting-edge research under the direction of Brookhaven National Laboratory (BNL) staff. Students will attend scientific seminars, visit major BNL facilities, and interact with fellow undergraduates, graduates, post-doctoral fellows, technical staff, as well as their immediate research group. Opportunities to present research verbally and/or in writing are available and may appear in a scientific journal or BNL report. Students will receive a $425 per week stipend. Details regarding transportation and housing will be arranged with students' prospective research labs.

NEW YORK CITY DEPARTMENT OF HEALTH AND MENTAL HYGIENE
Health Research Training Program (HRTP)
(Summer Session: June–August [full-time, maximum
35 hours/week for 10–12 weeks and part-time, minimum
20 hours/week for 10–12 weeks])
Health Research Training Program
NYC Department of Health and Mental Hygiene
2 Lafayette Street, 20th Floor, CN65
New York, NY 10007
Fax: (212) 676-2172
E-mail: hrtp@health.nyc.gov
Web site: **www.nyc.gov/health/hrtp**

Eligibility: Open to all college undergraduate, graduate, or professional school students. Recent graduates are ineligible to apply. A minimum GPA of 3.0 is required.

Application Deadline: Mid-February. Completed application comprises HRTP student application, resume, personal statement, official transcript, one academic reference, and pre-employment form.

Features/Benefits: The HRTP of the New York City Department of Health and Mental Hygiene is one of the oldest and largest public health traineeships in the country. Students will work under close supervision and mentorship of experienced professionals and learn the principles and practises of pubic health planning, research, and administration evaluation. Interns are also exposed to a rigorous curriculum of seminars and workshops geared to understand how to promote the well-being of New York residents. Financial support is available depending upon the accepted program.

NEW YORK PRESBYTERIAN HOSPITAL
Westchester Campus
Summer Pre-Career Practicum
(8 weeks, Early June–Late July)
Laurel A. Torres, Volunteer Coordinator
E-mail: lat9002@nyp.org
Volunteer Services Office
New York-Presbyterian Hospital
21 Bloomingdale Road
White Plains, NY 10605
(914) 997-5780
Fax: (914) 682-6909
Web site: **www.nyp.org/volunteer/westchester-location.html**

Eligibility: College students interested in social work, psychiatry, medicine, recreational therapy, nursing, research, psychology, and hospital administration. Eligibility determined by demonstrated academic ability and a required personal interview. Volunteers must commit 30 hours per week.

Application Deadline: March 15.

Features/Benefits: The intensive volunteer opportunity allows students to assist nursing staff in daily activities that include, but are not limited to, room checks, escort, sitting in on small group activities and/or groups, interacting with patient populations, attending case conferences, etc. Patients' disorders come from a variety of backgrounds including geriatrics, schizophrenia, borderline personality disorders, eating disorders, and substance abuse.

SYRACUSE UNIVERSITY
Division of International Programs Abroad (DIPA)
Comparative Health Policy & Law
(Late May–Late June)
Syracuse University
Division of International Programs Abroad (DIPA)
Summer Programs Office
119 Euclid Avenue
Syracuse, NY 13244-4170
(800) 251-9674
E-mail: DIPAsum@summail.syr.edu
Web site: **summerabroad.syr.edu**

Eligibility: Applications are especially encouraged from students study-ing or intending to study medicine, health policy, the sociology of medicine, health economics, public administration, health law, health communication, or other related fields. Program fees and tuition are estimated at $7,163 for undergraduate students and $7,589 for graduate students.

Application Deadline: March 15. There is a $55 application fee.

Features/Benefits: Students are required to register for six credits. This will be a traveling course studying various issues in health policy and law in London, Amsterdam, and Geneva. The class will examine—in dialogue with distinguished guest faculty—such matters as the care and treatment of the dying, the rationing of health care resources, the care and treatment of the elderly, the arguments for and against physician-assisted suicide and euthanasia, and cultural differences in the understanding of illness, diagnosis, and treat-ment. Classes begin in London, with extended visits to a variety of locations, and the final stop will be the World Health Organization in Geneva.

AMERICAN SOCIETY FOR MICROBIOLOGY

ASM/AAAS Mass Media Science and Engineering Fellows Program (10 weeks: Early June–mid-August)

AAAS Mass Media Science and Engineering Fellows Program
1200 New York Avenue, NW
Washington, DC 20005
(202) 326-6760
Carrie Patterson, ASM
E-mail: cpatterson@asmusa.org
Web site: www.aicgs.org/gardinet/prog085.shtml

Eligibility: Eligible individuals are students in the natural or social sciences or engineering. Applicants must demonstrate a commitment to the public understanding of science and technology. English, journalism, and other nontechnical majors are not eligible.

Application Deadline: Early February. Notifications will be sent out mid-April.

Features/Benefits: The program is designed to strengthen the relationship between science and technology and the media. Participants strengthen their communication skills by learning to describe complex technical subjects to nonspecialists and increase their understanding of editorial decisionmaking. AAAS selects 20 to 30 Mass Media Fellows each summer. Fellows are provided a weekly stipend up to $4,000, up to $1,000 in travel expenses, and a one-year ASM student membership.

Amigos de las Américas
5618 Star Lane
Houston, Texas 77057
Tel: (713) 782-5290/(800) 231-7796
Fax: (713) 782-9267
E-mail: info@amigoslink.org
Web site: **www.amigoslink.org**

This is a grassroots, nonprofit organization that trains and sends high school and college students on 3–8 week volunteer excursions to Latin America, namely Mexico, Paraguay, Central America, and Dominican Republic (as of 2005). During the summer, ADLA sends students on a variety of programs, all of which aim to enhance their respective communities through service. Some programs help the lives of locals by constructing various necessities (i.e., grain storage sheds, latrines) while other programs are geared toward interaction with locals (e.g., teaching youths about proper nutrition). Those who want to increase their fluency in Spanish and provide service to enchanting communities, all while immersing themselves in a new culture, should consider this program. The experiences and stories are very charming and quite positive; participants seem to gain a deep sense of satisfaction from working in culturally intriguing localities. The ADLA program was established in 1965.

Hugh Edmondson Research Internship
Jiunn Huang, PhD, CLS
Pathology Education, UCDHS
4625 Second Avenue, CLB, Room 1001c
Sacramento, CA 95817
Tel: (916) 734-0231
Fax: (916)734-0320
E-mail: jiunn.huang@ucdmc.ucdavis.edu
Web site: **som.ucdavis.edu/departments/pathology/education/
fellowships/edmondson/**

This eight-week program is for talented students interested in serious biochemical/biomedical research. The program requires a Monday–Friday, eight-hour-a-day commitment at the UC Davis pathology lab or Sacramento medical center/health sciences campus. Housing and transportation must be arranged by the student, but assistance finding a residence is provided for students who do not live in the Sacramento/Davis area. The program gives the participant a $2,000 stipend. They also offer students supplementary lectures and classes aimed to develop critical thinking skills. Please see the Web site for updated requirements and an application.

Summer Opportunities in Bio-ethics
Contact Information for Ms. Karen Augustine
NINDS Assistant Summer Program Coordinator
10 Center Drive
Building 10/Room 3B14
Bethesda, MD 20892-1296
Tel: (301) 594-6270
Fax: (301) 594-5799
E-mail: augustink@ninds.nih.gov
Web site: **www.princeton.edu/~bioethic/resources/post-bac/
summer.html**

National Institute of Neurological Disorders and Stroke (NINDS)
Mr. Tony Casco
10 Center Drive, Room 5S208
Bethesda, MD 20892
Tel: (301) 443-1910
E-mail: cascod@ninds.nih.gov
OR
Dr. Rita Devine-Ward
10 Center Drive, Room 5S208
Bethesda, MD 20892
Tel: (301) 594-9562
Fax: (301) 402-2871
E-mail: wardr@ninds.nih.gov
Web site: **www.ninds.nih.gov/jobs_and_training/summer/**

The Summer Program in the Neurological Sciences offers a unique opportunity for academically talented high school, undergraduate, graduate, and medical students to receive first-rate training in neuroscience research. Students get hands-on experience working with leading scientists in the Institute's Division of Intramural Research, the "in-house" research component of the NINDS. Students will attend lectures dealing with the newest advancements in health research. To finish the summer program, students will participate in the NIH Summer Research Program Poster Day. This gives students experience with presenting scientific work before a scientific community.

Undergraduate Student Research Program
American Heart Association and Western States Affiliate
Summer Research Program with Stipend
(10 weeks: Early June–Late August)
1710 Gilbreth Road
Burlingame, CA 94010-1317
Tel: (650) 259-6700
Fax: (650) 259-6891
E-mail: research@heart.org
Web site: **www.americanheart.org/
presenter.jhtml?identifier=3013196**

Eligibility: Applicant must (1) be enrolled full-time in an undergraduate degree program, (2) attend an institution in or be a resident of California, Nevada, or Utah, (3) be either a United States citizen or possess a student, exchange, or permanent resident visa, (4) have junior or senior academic status in the fall following the summer program, (5) have completed four semesters or six quarters of any combination of courses in the biological sciences, physics, or chemistry by May, and (6) have completed at least one quarter of college level calculus, statistics, computational methods, or computer science before May. In addition, two faculty recommendations are required, so prospective students should keep a lookout for potential letter writers that can attest to their work ethic and passion for research. While these may seem like extensive requirements, it is entirely possible to apply and receive this fellowship as a first-year college student. In many of these cases, Advanced Placement classes can substitute for the course requirements. Also, while past research experience is desirable, it is by no means required.

Application: A complete application consists of an application form, visa verification, two faculty recommendations, official transcripts, and an optional personal data form. The deadline for the application is usually in early December, at which point all required documents must be received by the application office.

Features/Benefits: This program encourages students from all disciplines to consider careers related to research that is broadly related to the cardiovascular and cerebrovascular areas. Accepted students have the option of working with a faculty member they already know or being assigned to one of AHA's faculty supervisors. Projects can range from basic molecular research to direct physiological studies. There is a $4,000 stipend for the 10-week period. Students are responsible for their own travel and housing expenses. For a more detailed description of the program, visit the "Program Description" document on the Web site.

Other Web Resources

cirrus.chem.plu.edu/cirrus.php?action=1
CIRRUS: a searchable database of summer programs for undergraduates in chemistry provided by Pacific Lutheran University

Princeton Post-College Opportunities
www.princeton.edu/ghp/resources/post-college-opportunitie/
    index.xml
A thorough list of available post-baccalaureate opportunities.

Family Medicine Interest Group
fmignet.aafp.org/online/fmig/index/getinvolved.html
Resource for clinical volunteer work.

explorehealthcareers.org
www.explorehealthcareers.org/10_13_2_index.html
Great search engine for clinical and academic opportunities. Just use "summer" as keyword!

Association of American Medical Colleges (AAMC)
aamc.org/members/great/summerlinks.htm
List of summer undergraduate research programs by school.

The American Academy of Family Physicians (AAFP) has compiled a directory of preceptorship opportunities for premedical students. It lists over 80 programs in 34 states that offer premeds the chance to observe patient care in family practice residency programs. These shadow programs allow premeds to work with physicians, residents, medical students, and other premeds for upward of eight weeks throughout the year. Many include seminars, assigned readings, research, group participation, and supervised patient management. Some offer stipends, lodging, and a food allowance. Many are open to high school students as well as college premeds and accept students from out of state. A complete listing can be had by requesting the entire directory from the AAFP at 8880 Ward Parkway, Kansas City, MO 64114-2797, c/o the Student Interest Department.

These summer programs should interest many premedical students from numerous colleges and universities. If you are unsuccessful in obtaining entrance to these programs, as they are becoming more competitive, here are some other words of advice from the Career Planning Offices of Bryn Mawr and Haverford colleges:

"Look in the phone book for a list of hospitals and then send away for information from those hospitals which interest you. Ask them if they sponsor internships, research-oriented or otherwise, for undergraduates, or if they are willing to hire you, or accept you as a volunteer, for some position in their hospital. It may not be an internship, but it is an excellent way to become familiar with hospitals, medicine, and what the discipline of medicine requires from those who practice it.

"Another worthwhile reference source is the journals of the various health professions. Thumb through these journals, looking specifically for articles describing an ongoing research program that might be of interest to you. Write down the names of the people conducting the research and the address of the institution sponsoring the research project; mail them a letter stating your interest in their program, telling how you heard about it and asking whether they sponsor internships or would like to hire someone with your qualifications."

Remember to point out that you are interested in a medical career and hope to gain something out of the classroom or real-world experiences. Be honest and you'll be surprised at the warmth of the reactions you'll receive.

APPENDIX III

Directory of American Medical Schools

The following directory of American medical schools provides a beginning for your search for a medical school. These schools are all accredited by the Liaison Committee on Medical Education (LCME), an accrediting agency sponsored by the Association of American Medical Colleges and the American Medical Association.

For additional information on admissions policies and programs of study at these schools, you should check *Medical School Admission Requirements,* 2010–2011 edition, published by the Association of American Medical Colleges, Washington, D.C., and the *AAMC Curriculum Directory* and the *AAMC Directory of Medical Education,* also published annually by the AAMC.

For the most current information on each school, you should contact the school directly. Schools are designated by their membership in AMCAS (see pages 37–39 for complete explanation).

Each profile in the directory includes the following data:
- The correct name and address of the medical school; whether the MCAT is required for admission.
- Both the overall GPA and the science GPA, if available.
- Information about the medical school: the founding date; under public or private control; special programs.
- Enrollment data and costs, in approximate figures.

- Information about the application, notification, and response dates; amount of deposit; early decision plan; state residency preference; admissions criteria; and the person or office to whom admissions correspondence should be sent.
- Information about minority students, including percentage of the total and first-year student classes, percentage receiving aid, special programs, aid application deadlines, and the person or office to whom aid inquiries may be addressed; the application fee.

Important Note:

All information regarding tuition and fees on the following pages was updated in 2010. For more current information, be sure to contact individual schools directly.

Albany Medical College*
Office of Admissions
47 New Scotland Avenue
Albany, NY 12208
Tel: (518) 262-5521
E-mail: admissions@mail.amc.edu
www.amc.edu

MCAT: required

GPA: 3.6

FOUNDED: 1839; *private.* The Medical College has joint programs with undergraduate schools at Rensselaer Polytechnic Institute, Union College, and Sienna College, sponsors the Accelerated Biomedical Program, a six-year program leading to the BS and MD degrees.

ENROLLMENT: 71 men, 73 women (first-year).

TUITION & FEES: Resident, $43,008; Nonresident, $43,008.

APPLICATIONS: Should be submitted between June 1 and November 15; the application fee is $105. Notification begins October 15; response must be received within two weeks. A deposit is required to reserve place in class. In recent years, approximately 47% of entering students have been state residents. Admission factors include academic record, MCAT scores, and personal qualifications as evaluated from letters of recommendation and a personal interview. *Correspondence to:* Office of Admissions.

MINORITY STUDENTS: Comprise 3% of the first-year class; most of these students receive aid. The Medical College offers a special orientation program and introduction to the basic medical sciences for entering students who exhibit special academic needs. Tutorial assistance is available during the academic year. *For additional information:* Office of Minority Affairs. Information regarding application for financial assistance is made available in mid-November.

----
*member AMCAS

Albert Einstein College of Medicine of Yeshiva University*

1300 Morris Park Avenue
Bronx, NY 10461
Tel: (718) 430-2106
E-mail: admissions@aecom.yu.edu
www.aecom.yu.edu

MCAT: required

GPA: 3.7

FOUNDED: 1955; *private.*

ENROLLMENT: 88 men, 92 women (first-year).

TUITION & FEES: Resident, $42,364; Nonresident, $42,364.

APPLICATIONS: Should be submitted between June 1 and March 15; the application fee is $115. Notification begins January 15; response must be received within 2 weeks until May 1, within one week thereafter; a deposit is needed to hold place in class. Early Decision plan is available. While no strict preference is given to state residents, about 42% of the entering class have been New York residents in recent years. Admission criteria include academic performance, MCAT results, letters of recommendation, and personal qualifications as judged by the Committee on Admissions. *Correspondence to:* Office of Admissions.

MINORITY STUDENTS: 13% of the first-year class; most of these students receive aid. *For additional information:* Office of Minority Student Affairs. Applications for aid are available from the Student Financial Officer.

----

*member AMCAS

Baylor College of Medicine

One Baylor Plaza
Houston, TX 77030
Tel: (713) 798-4842
E-mail: admission@bcm.tmc.edu
www.bcm.edu

MCAT: required

GPA: 3.9

FOUNDED: 1900, moved to Houston in 1943; *private.* An MD/PhD program is offered with the Graduate School of Biomedical Sciences. A biomedical engineering program with Rice University and a structural and computational biology program with Rice University and the University of Houston are also available.

ENROLLMENT: 90 men, 86 women (first-year).

TUITION & FEES: Resident, $6,550; Nonresident, $19,650.

APPLICATIONS: Should be submitted between June 1 and November 1; the application fee is $80. Notification begins October 15, response must be received within two weeks; a deposit is needed to secure a position in the class. Early Decision plan is available. Some preference is given to state residents; 78% of a recent freshman class were residents of Texas. Admission factors include collegiate curriculum and performance, MCAT scores, and personal qualifications as evaluated in letters of recommendation and the personal interview. *Correspondence to:* Office of Admissions.

MINORITY STUDENTS: Comprise 22% of the first-year class; most of these students receive aid. The application fee may be waived. The College of Medicine also sponsors a summer work-study program for minority premedical students. *For additional information:* Associate Dean. Applications for aid should be requested within two weeks of submission of application.

Boston University*
School of Medicine
715 Albany Street
Boston, MA 02118
Tel: (617) 638-4630
E-mail: medadms@bu.edu
www.bumc.bu.edu

MCAT: required

GPA: 3.6

FOUNDED: 1848 as the New England Female Medical College; *private.* Special programs include a seven-year Liberal Arts–Medical Education Program that admits students after the senior year of high school.

ENROLLMENT: 87 men, 90 women (first-year).

TUITION & FEES: Resident, $44,786; Nonresident, $44,786.

APPLICATIONS: Should be submitted between June 1 and November 1; the application fee is $100. Notification begins in February; response must be received within two weeks. A deposit is needed to hold place in class. Early Decision plan is available. Selection factors include scholastic record, college recommendations, involvement in college and community activities, as well as personal qualifications. *Correspondence to:* Admissions Office.

MINORITY STUDENTS: Comprise 85% of the first-year class; most of these students are receiving aid. The Office of Minority Affairs organizes programs for the recruitment and support of minority students. These include a special prematriculation summer program in the medical sciences. *For additional information:* Associate Dean for Student and Minority Affairs.

---

*member AMCAS

Brody School of Medicine at East Carolina University*

Greenville, NC 27834
Tel: (252) 744-2202
E-mail: somadmissions@ecu.edu
www.ecu.edu/admissions

MCAT: required

GPA: 3.6

FOUNDED: 1977; *publicly controlled.*

ENROLLMENT: 37 men, 39 women (first-year).

TUITION & FEES: Resident, $9,034; Nonresident, $34,024.

APPLICATIONS: Should be submitted between June 1 and November 15; the application fee is $60. Notification begins October 15; response must be received within three weeks; $100 deposit needed to hold place in class. Early Decision plan is available. Preference is given to state residents. Admission factors include academic record, MCAT scores, and personal qualifications as evaluated in letters of recommendation and two personal interviews. *Correspondence to:* Associate Dean, Office of Admissions.

MINORITY STUDENTS: Comprise 32% of the first-year class. *For additional information:* Assistant Dean for Student Affairs.

---

*member AMCAS

Case Western Reserve University*

School of Medicine
10900 Euclid Avenue
Cleveland, OH 44106-4920
Tel: (216) 368-3450
E-mail: casemedadmissions@case.edu
medisnew.cwru.edu/

MCAT: required

GPA: 3.7

FOUNDED: 1943; *private.*

ENROLLMENT: 101 men, 84 women (first-year).

TUITION & FEES: Resident, $41,966; Nonresident, $41,966.

APPLICATIONS: Should be submitted between June 1 and November 1; the application fee is $85. Early Decision plan is available. Preference is given to state residents. Admission factors include academic performance, MCAT results, verbal skills, letters of recommendation, and the personal interview. *Correspondence to:* Associate Dean for Admissions and Student Affairs.

MINORITY STUDENTS: Comprise 10% of the first-year class; most students receive aid. *For additional information:* Office of Minority Programs.

---

*member AMCAS

Chicago Medical School*

Rosalind Franklin University of Medicine and Science
3333 Green Bay Road
North Chicago, IL 60064
Tel: (847) 578-3204
E-mail: cms.admissions@rosalindfranklin.edu
www.rosalindfranklin.edu.cms

MCAT: required

GPA: 3.7

FOUNDED: 1912

ENROLLMENT: 100 men, 90 women (first-year).

TUITION & FEES: Resident, $39,472; Nonresident, $39,472.

APPLICATIONS: Should be submitted between June 1 and November 1; the application fee is $100. Admission factors include academic achievement, MCAT scores, appraisals received, and personal itnerviews (when granted).

MINORITY STUDENTS: Comprise 5% of the first-year class.

----

*member AMCAS

Columbia University*
College of Physicians and Surgeons
630 West 168th Street
New York, NY 10032
Tel: (212) 305-3595
E-mail: psadmissions@columbia.edu
www.cumc.columbia.edu/dept/ps

MCAT: required

GPA: 3.8

FOUNDED: 1767; *private.*

ENROLLMENT: 78 men, 77 women (first-year).

TUITION & FEES: Resident, $42,848; Nonresident, $42,848.

APPLICATIONS: Should be submitted between June 1 and October 15; application fee is $85. Notification begins February 1; response must be received within three weeks; no deposit required to hold place in class. Admission factors include academic record, letters of recommendation, the personal interview, nonacademic achievements and activities, and personal qualifications. *Correspondence to:* Admissions Office.

MINORITY STUDENTS: Comprise 9% of the first-year class. Tutorial assistance is available to all students who require such help. *For additional information:* Associate Dean for Minority Affairs.

---

*member AMCAS

The Commonwealth Medical College

150 N Washington Avenue
Scranton, PA 18503
Tel: (570) 504-7000
www.thecommonwealthmedical.com

MCAT: required

GPA: 3.0

FOUNDED: 2009; *private.*

ENROLLMENT: 65 students (first-year).

TUITION & FEES: Resident, $35,750; Nonresident, $42,000.

APPLICATIONS: Should be submitted between June 1 and December 15. Admission criteria include MCAT scores, GPA, general academic background, letters of recommendation, and personal qualifications as judged by the admissions committee.

MINORITY STUDENTS: The school has an active minority recruitment program.

Creighton University*
School of Medicine
2500 California Plaza
Omaha, NE 68178
Tel: (402) 280-2799
E-mail: medschadm@creighton.edu
www.medicine.creighton.edu

MCAT: required

GPA: 3.72

FOUNDED: 1892; *private.*

ENROLLMENT: 63 men, 63 women (first-year).

TUITION & FEES: Resident, $42,612; Nonresident, $42,612.

APPLICATIONS: Should be submitted between July 1 and November 1; application fee is $95. Notification begins October 1; response must be received within two weeks; a deposit is needed to hold place in class. Early Decision plan is available. Some preference is given to residents of those states without medical schools and to Creighton University graduates. Admission factors counted heavily include GPA, MCAT, and recommendations from academic professors or premedical committee. *Correspondence to:* Office of Admissions.

MINORITY STUDENTS: Comprise 8% of the first-year class; most of these students receive aid. The application fee may be waived. *For additional information:* Director of Minority Affairs for Health Sciences. Submit application for financial aid after acceptance.

---

*member AMCAS

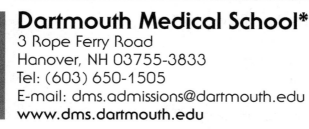

Dartmouth Medical School*
3 Rope Ferry Road
Hanover, NH 03755-3833
Tel: (603) 650-1505
E-mail: dms.admissions@dartmouth.edu
www.dms.dartmouth.edu

MCAT: required

GPA: 3.7

FOUNDED: 1797; *private*. Students in a special program spend the first two years at Dartmouth and then transfer to Brown University for the last two years.

ENROLLMENT: 44 men, 34 women (first-year).

TUITION & FEES: Resident, $40,120; Nonresident, $40,120.

APPLICATIONS: Should be submitted between July 1 and January 2; the application fee is $75. Some preference is given to state residents and applicants from northern New England. Admission factors include consideration of both academic and personal qualifications. *Correspondence to:* Office of Admissions.

MINORITY STUDENTS: Comprise 22% of the first-year class. The application fee may be waived. The Committee on Equal Opportunity, which includes minority students and faculty members, is involved in the evaluation and selection of minority applicants. *For additional information:* Assistant Dean, Minority Affairs. Application for aid should be made upon acceptance.

----

*member AMCAS

Drexel University*
College of Medicine
2900 Queen Lane
Philadelphia, PA 19129
Tel: (215) 991-8202
E-mail: medadmis@drexel.edu
www.drexelmed.edu

MCAT: required

GPA: 3.5

FOUNDED: Drexel University College of Medicine is the consolidation of two venerable medical schools with rich and international histories: Hahnemann Medical College and Woman's Medical College of Pennsylvania. Established in 1848 and 1850, respectively, they were two of the earliest medical colleges in the United States, and Woman's was the very first medical school for women in the nation.

ENROLLMENT: 127 men, 128 women.

TUITION & FEES: Resident, $42,480; Nonresident, $42,480.

APPLICATIONS: Should be submitted between June 1 and December 1; the application fee is $75.

MINORITY STUDENTS: Comprise 19% of the first-year class.

*member AMCAS

Duke University*
School of Medicine
P.O. Box 3710
Durham, NC 27710
Tel: (919) 684-2985
E-mail: medadm@mc.duke.edu
www.dukemed.duke.edu

MCAT: required

GPA: 3.8

FOUNDED: 1930; *private.*

ENROLLMENT: 51 men, 50 women (first-year).

TUITION & FEES: Resident, $41,839; Nonresident, $41,839.

APPLICATIONS: Should be submitted between June 1 and November 15; the application fee is $80. Notification begins February 28; response must be received by school within three weeks; $100 deposit needed to hold place in class. In-state students receive special consideration. Admission factors include academic record, MCAT results, extracurricular activities, faculty evaluations, and the personal interview. *Correspondence to:* Committee on Admissions.

MINORITY STUDENTS: Comprise 22% of the first-year class; almost all of these students receive aid. *For additional information:* Associate Dean, Medical Education. Application materials for financial aid are available upon acceptance.

---

*member AMCAS

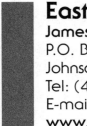

East Tennessee State University*
James H. Quillen College of Medicine
P.O. Box 70580
Johnson City, TN 37614
Tel: (423) 439-2033
E-mail: sacom@etsu.edu
www.com.etsu.edu

MCAT: required

GPA: 3.73

FOUNDED: 1978.

ENROLLMENT: 27 men, 33 women.

TUITION & FEES: Resident, $21,043; Nonresident, $41,993.

APPLICATIONS: Should be submitted between June 1 and November 15; the application fee is $50. Admission factors include academic achievement, MCAT scores, recommendations, extracurricular activities, and work experience.

MINORITY STUDENTS: Comprise 5% of the first-year class.

---

*member AMCAS

Eastern Virginia Medical School*

700 W. Olney Road
Norfolk, VA 23507
Tel: (757) 446-5812
E-mail: nanczki@evms.edu
www.evms.edu

MCAT: required

GPA: 3.6

FOUNDED: 1973; *private.*

ENROLLMENT: 53 men, 62 women (first-year).

TUITION & FEES: Resident, $24,204; Nonresident, $43,400.

APPLICATIONS: Should be submitted between June 1 and November 15; the application fee is $100. Notification begins October 15; response must be received within two weeks; a deposit is needed to hold place in class. Early Decision plan is available. Preference given to state residents. Admission criteria include academic achievement, MCAT results, written evaluation, personal interview, and evidence of sustained motivation. *Correspondence to:* Office of Admissions.

MINORITY STUDENTS: Comprise 5% of the first-year class; almost all of these students receive aid. The Medical School sponsors a remedial assistance program for students requiring such help during the academic year. *For additional information:* Assistant Dean, Minority Affairs.

---

*member AMCAS

Emory University*
School of Medicine
1440 Clifton Road, NE
Atlanta, GA 30322
Tel: (404) 727-5655
E-mail: medadmiss@emory.edu
www.med.emory.edu

MCAT: required

GPA: 3.7

FOUNDED: 1915; *private.*

ENROLLMENT: 62 men, 70 women (first-year).

TUITION & FEES: Resident, $40,700; Nonresident, $40,700.

APPLICATIONS: Should be submitted between June 1 and October 15; the application fee is $100. Notification begins October 15; response must be received within three weeks; no deposit is needed to hold place in class. Preference given to state residents; approximately three quarters of the entering students are Georgia residents. The remaining positions are filled by out-of-state applicants, with some preference for residents of the southeastern states. Selection factors include academic performance, fitness and aptitude for the study of medicine, and personal qualifications. *Correspondence to:* Medical School Admissions, Room 303, Woodruff Health Sciences Center Administration Building.

MINORITY STUDENTS: Comprise 63% of the first-year class; most of these students receive aid. The application fee may be waived. *For additional information:* Director, Office of Minority Affairs. Applications for aid should be submitted upon acceptance.

----
*member AMCAS

Florida International University*
College of Medicine
1200 SW 8th Street
Miami, FL 33199
Tel: (305) 348-0644
E-mail: med.admission@fiu.edu
www.medicine.fiu.edu/admissions

MCAT: required

GPA: no data available.

FOUNDED: 2009; *private.*

ENROLLMENT: 40 (first-year).

TUITION & FEES: Resident, $41,360; Nonresident, $70,786.

APPLICATIONS: Should be submitted between June 1 and October 15; the application fee is $30. Admission criteria include academic background, letters of recommendation, and personal qualifications as judged by an interview and the admissions committee.

MINORITY STUDENTS: no data available.

*member AMCAS

The Florida State University*
College of Medicine
1115 West Call Street
Tallahassee, FL 32306
Tel: (850) 644-1855
E-mail: medinformation@med.fsu.edu
www.med.fsu.edu

MCAT: required

GPA: 3.7

FOUNDED: 2000; *publicly controlled.*

ENROLLMENT: no data available.

TUITION & FEES: no data available.

APPLICATIONS: Should be submitted between July 1 and April 30; the application fee is $30. Admission criteria include MCAT scores, GPA, general academic background, letters of recommendation, and personal qualifications as judged by the admissions committee.

MINORITY STUDENTS: The school has an active minority recruitment program.

----
*member AMCAS

Georgetown University*

School of Medicine
Box 571421
Washington, D.C. 20057
Tel: (202) 687-1154
E-mail: medicaladmissions@georgetown.edu
www.sow.georgetown.edu

MCAT: required

GPA: 3.67

FOUNDED: 1851; *private.*

ENROLLMENT: 101 men, 93 women (first-year).

TUITION & FEES: Resident, $41,356; Nonresident, $41,356.

APPLICATIONS: Should be submitted between June 1 and October 31; the application fee is $130. Notification begins October 15; response must be received within three weeks; a deposit is required to hold place in class. Admission factors include scholastic record, MCAT scores, personal qualifications, letters of recommendation, and the personal interview. *Correspondence to:* Office of Admissions.

MINORITY STUDENTS: Comprise 7% of the first-year class; most of these students receive aid. A year-long prematriculation program is available to qualified students; priority is given to residents of the District. *For additional information:* Director, Office of Minority Affairs. Application for aid should be made upon acceptance.

*member AMCAS

The George Washington University*
School of Medicine and Health Sciences
2300 Eye Street, NW
Washington, D.C. 20037
Tel: (202) 994-3506
E-mail: medadmit@gwu.edu
www.gwumc.edu/admis

MCAT: required

GPA: 3.6

FOUNDED: 1825; *private.*

ENROLLMENT: 77 men, 100 women (first-year).

TUITION & FEES: Resident, $45,892; Nonresident, $45,892.

APPLICATIONS: Should be submitted between July 1 and January 1; the application fee is $125. Notification begins October 15; response must be received within two weeks; no deposit is needed to hold place in class. Early Decision plan is available. Some preference is given to residents of the District of Columbia and the surrounding metropolitan area. Admission factors include academic record, trends in performance, MCAT scores, extracurricular activities and work experiences, letters of recommendation, the personal interview, and the essay portion of the application. *Correspondence to:* Office of Admissions.

MINORITY STUDENTS: Comprise 19% of the first-year class; more than half of these students are receiving aid. Tutorial assistance is available to all students who require help. Minority students and faculty members serve on the Committee on Admissions. *For additional information:* Associate Vice President for Graduate Medical Education. Financial aid information and applications are available upon acceptance.

---

*member AMCAS

Harvard Medical School*

25 Shattuck Street
Boston, MA 02115
Tel: (617) 432-1550
E-mail: admissions-office@hms.harvard.edu
www.hms.harvard.edu/hms/hms.asp

MCAT: required

GPA: 3.8

FOUNDED: 1782; *private.*

ENROLLMENT: 88 men, 77 women (first-year).

TUITION & FEES: Resident, $40,499; Nonresident, $40,499.

APPLICATIONS: Should be submitted between June 1 and October 15; the application fee, due with request for application, is $85. Response after notification must be received within three weeks; no deposit needed to hold place in class. Admission criteria include the MCAT, extracurricular activities, summer occupations, and letters of recommendation. Also considered are personal integrity, judgment, maturity, and aptitude. *Correspondence to:* Office of the Committee on Admissions.

MINORITY STUDENTS: Comprise 11% of the first-year class. Some tutorial assistance is available to those in need of such help. *For additional information:* Associate Dean for Student Affairs. Application for aid should be made upon acceptance.

*member AMCAS

Hofstra North Shore—LIJ*
School of Medicine
Hempstead, NY 11549-1000
Tel: (516) 463-7516
E-mail: medicine@hofstra.edu
www.medicine.hofstra.edu

MCAT: required

GPA: 3.0

FOUNDED: 2009; *private.*

ENROLLMENT: 40 students (first-year).

TUITION & FEES: Resident, $53,000; Nonresident, $53,000.

APPLICATIONS: Should be submitted between July 1 and December 1. Admission criteria include MCAT scores, GPA, general academic background, letters of recommendation, and personal qualifications as judged by the admissions committee.

MINORITY STUDENTS: The school has an active minority recruitment program.

---

*member AMCAS

Howard University*
College of Medicine
520 W Street, NW
Washington, D.C. 20059
Tel: (202) 806-6270
E-mail: hucmadmissions@howard.edu
www.med.howard.edu

MCAT: required

GPA: 3.4

FOUNDED: 1868; *private (federal government supported).* Special programs include the Early Entry Medical Education Program, which admits students after two or three years of college work; a six-year combined BS-MD program; and a five-year curriculum schedule for students who need extra time to complete the requirements.

ENROLLMENT: 66 men, 64 women (first-year).

TUITION & FEES: Resident, $29,846; Nonresident, $29,846.

APPLICATIONS: Should be submitted between June 1 and December 15; the application fee is $45. Notification begins October 15; response must be received within one month; a deposit is needed to reserve place in class. Admission factors include academic record, MCAT scores, motivation and personal qualifications, letters of recommendation, and an interview. *Correspondence to:* Admissions Office.

MINORITY STUDENTS: Comprise 49% of the first-year class. Most receive aid. *For additional information:* Assistant Dean, Student Affairs.

---

*member AMCAS

Indiana University*
School of Medicine
1120 South Drive, Fesler Hall 213
Indianapolis, IN 46202-5113
Tel: (317) 274-3772
E-mail: kabaxter@iupui.edu
www.medicine.iu.edu

MCAT: required

GPA: 3.7

FOUNDED: 1907; *publicly controlled.* The University School of Medicine has first- and second-year medical programs on seven college campuses in the state.

ENROLLMENT: 173 men, 135 women (first-year).

TUITION & FEES: Resident, $27,151; Nonresident, $42,130.

APPLICATIONS: Should be submitted between June 1 and December 15; the application fee is $50. Notification begins October 15, response must be received within three weeks; no deposit needed to hold place in class. Early Decision plan is available. Strong preference is given to state residents. Admission criteria include the MCAT, scholarship, character, and residence. *Correspondence to:* Medical School Admissions Office, Fesler Hall 213.

MINORITY STUDENTS: Comprise 10% of the first-year class; tutorial and financial assistance are available, as is a 2-week prematriculation program. *For additional information:* Admissions Office.

---

*member AMCAS

Jefferson Medical College of Thomas Jefferson University*

1015 Walnut Street
Philadelphia, PA 19107
Tel: (215) 955-6983
E-mail: jmc.admissions@jefferson.edu
www.jefferson.edu/jmc/admissions

MCAT: required

GPA: 3.63 science

FOUNDED: 1824; *private.* A cooperative program with the Pennsylvania State University leads to a combined BS-MD degree; the Physician Shortage Area Program is designed to recruit and educate medical students to enter family medicine and practice in rural communities and inner cities of Pennsylvania (physician-shortage areas).

ENROLLMENT: 132 men, 123 women (first-year). Up to 40 places in each class may be filled from the cooperative program; 20 more places are usually set aside for Delaware residents through a special program with the state.

TUITION & FEES: Resident, $43,033; Nonresident, $43,033.

APPLICATIONS: Should be submitted between June 1 and November 15; the application fee is $80. Notification begins October 15; response must be received within two weeks; a deposit is needed to hold place in class. Early Decision plan is available. Preference may be given to state residents. Admission factors include consideration of undergraduate college attended, academic performance, MCAT scores, letters of recommendation, and a personal interview. *Correspondence to:* Associate Dean for Admissions.

MINORITY STUDENTS: Comprise 11% of the first-year class; most of these students receive aid. Application for aid should be made by April 1. *For additional information:* Assistant Dean for Student Affairs.

----

*member AMCAS

The Johns Hopkins University*
School of Medicine
733 North Broadway
Baltimore, MD 21205
Tel: (410) 955-3182
E-mail: somadmission.jhmi.edu
www.hopkinsmedicine.org/som

MCAT: required

GPA: 3.9

FOUNDED: 1893; *private.* In addition to the four-year program, an optional three-year program is offered. A combined MD/PhD program in all disciplines and master's and doctoral programs in public health are available.

ENROLLMENT: 59 men, 59 women (first-year).

TUITION & FEES: Resident, $37,579; Nonresident, $37,579.

APPLICATIONS: Should be submitted between June 1 and October 15; the application fee is $75. Notification begins November 1, response must be received within three weeks; no deposit needed to hold place in class. Early Decision plan is available. Admission factors include academic record, MCAT scores, extracurricular activities, and personal qualifications. *Correspondence to:* Committee on Admission.

MINORITY STUDENTS: Comprise 11% of the first-year class. An advising system is available to students that permits the selection of both preclinical and clinical faculty advisers. A faculty member is also designated as minority student adviser. *For additional information:* Assistant Dean for Student Affairs.

----

*member AMCAS

Keck School of Medicine*
University of Southern California
1975 Zonal Avenue
Los Angeles, CA 90089
Tel: (323) 442-2552
E-mail: winikows@hsc.usc.edu
www.usc.edu/keck

MCAT: required

GPA: 3.61

FOUNDED: 1885, *private.*

ENROLLMENT: 86 men, 73 women (first-year).

TUITION & FEES: Resident, $43,536; Nonresident, $43,536.

APPLICATIONS: Should be submitted between July 1 and November 1; the application fee is $90. Notification begins January 1; response must be received within two weeks; a deposit is needed to hold place in class. Early Decision plan is available. Admission factors weighted most heavily include GPA, MCAT results, extracurricular activities, the personal statement, letters of recommendation, and the interview. *Correspondence to:* Office of Admissions.

MINORITY STUDENTS: Comprise 25% of the first-year class. The application fee may be waived. The School of Medicine sponsors a Summer Workshop for minority and disadvantaged students, including both academic and hospital orientation programs. Tutorial assistance is available during the academic year. *For additional information:* Assistant Dean, Minority Affairs. Application for aid should be made upon acceptance.

---

*member AMCAS

Loma Linda University*

School of Medicine
Loma Linda, CA 92350
Tel: (909) 558-4467
E-mail: admissions@sm.llu.edu
www.llu.edu/medicine

MCAT: required

GPA: 3.72

FOUNDED: 1909; *private*. Seventh-Day Adventist Church.

ENROLLMENT: 97 men, 75 women (first-year).

TUITION & FEES: Resident, $35,506; Nonresident, $35,506.

APPLICATIONS: Should be submitted between June 1 and November 1; the application fee is $75. Notification begins December 1; response must be received within 30 days; a deposit is needed to hold place in class. Preference is given to Seventh-Day Adventists. Admission factors include GPA, MCAT scores, letters of recommendation, and the personal interview. *Correspondence to:* Associate Dean for Admissions.

MINORITY STUDENTS: Comprise 6% of first-year class. *For additional information:* Assistant Dean for Clinical Affairs.

---

*member AMCAS

Louisiana State University*

School of Medicine in New Orleans
1901 Perdido Street
New Orleans, LA 70112
Tel: (504) 568-6262
E-mail: ms-admissions@suhsc.edu
www.medschool.suhsc.edu

MCAT: required

GPA: 3.7 science

FOUNDED: 1931; *publicly controlled.*

ENROLLMENT: 98 men, 81 women (first-year).

TUITION & FEES: Resident, $12,866; Nonresident, $27,014.

APPLICATIONS: Should be submitted between June 1 and November 30; the application fee is $50. Notification begins October 15; response must be received within two weeks; a deposit is needed to hold place in class. Strong preference is given to state residents; recently 96% of the entering class were Louisiana residents. Admission factors include the MCAT, scholastic performance, extracurricular activities, character, attitude, and interest. *Correspondence to:* Admissions Office.

MINORITY STUDENTS: Comprise 6% of the first-year class. A broad program of student aid is administered by the Student Financial Aid Office to help students financially through awards, scholarships, and loans. *For additional information:* Assistant Dean, Minority Affairs.

---

*member AMCAS

Louisiana State University*
School of Medicine in Shreveport
1501 Kings Highway, P.O. Box 33932
Shreveport, LA 71130
Tel: (318) 675-5190
E-mail: shvadm@lsumc.edu
www.shlsuhsc.edu/medschool/index/html

MCAT: required

GPA: 3.8

FOUNDED: 1966, admitted first class in 1969; *publicly controlled.*

ENROLLMENT: 71 men, 46 women (first-year).

TUITION & FEES: Resident, $10,458; Nonresident, $24,606.

APPLICATIONS: Should be submitted between June 1 and November 1; the application fee is $50. Notification begins October 15; response must be received within two weeks; a deposit is needed to hold place in class. Strong preference given to state residents. Selection factors include academic record, MCAT scores, recommendations, and personal interviews. *Correspondence to:* Office of Student Admissions, LSU Medical Center.

MINORITY STUDENTS: Comprise 6% of the first-year class; most of these students receive aid. The application fee may be waived. *For additional information:* Director, Multicultural Affairs. Applications for aid are available after acceptance.

----
*member AMCAS

Loyola University of Chicago*

Stritch School of Medicine
2160 South First Avenue
Maywood, IL 60153
Tel: (708) 216-3229
www.meddean.luc.edu/

MCAT: required

GPA: 3.7

FOUNDED: 1870; *private.*

ENROLLMENT: 70 men, 76 women (first-year).

TUITION & FEES: Resident, $37,620; Nonresident, $37,620.

APPLICATIONS: Should be submitted between June 1 and November 15, the application fee is $70. Notification begins October 15; response must be received within two weeks; no deposit is needed to hold place in class. Early Decision Plan is available. Some preference is given to state residents and to applicants committed to the needs of the Illinois health care system. Admission factors weighted most heavily are the MCAT, GPA, character, evidence of community service, and motivation. *Correspondence to:* Office of Admissions.

MINORITY STUDENTS: Comprise 3% of the first-year class. The application fee may be waived. *For additional information:* Associate Dean for Student Affairs. Applications for aid should be made upon acceptance.

---

*member AMCAS

Marshall University*
Joan Edwards School of Medicine
1600 Medical Center Drive
Huntington, WV 25701
Tel: (304) 691-1738
E-mail: warren@marshall.edu
www.musom.marshall.edu/

MCAT: required

GPA: 3.5

FOUNDED: 1978; *publicly controlled.*

ENROLLMENT: 35 men, 43 women (first-year).

TUITION & FEES: Resident, $16,738; Nonresident, $42,328.

APPLICATIONS: Should be submitted between June 1 and November 15; the application fee is $50 for residents, $100 for nonresidents. Notification begins October 15; response must be received within two weeks of notification; no deposit needed to hold place in class. Preference is given to state residents. Selection factors include academic records, MCAT scores, and personal qualifications. *Correspondence to:* Admissions Office.

MINORITY STUDENTS: Comprise 27% of the first-year class. *For additional information:* Associate Dean for Student Affairs.

---

*member AMCAS

Mayo Clinic College of Medicine*

Mayo Medical School
200 First Street, SW
Rochester, MN 55905
Tel: (507) 284-3671
E-mail: MedSchoolAdmissions@mayo.edu
www.mayo.edu/mms

MCAT: required

GPA: 3.9

FOUNDED: 1972; *private,* academic affiliation with University of Minnesota, associated with the Mayo Clinic.

ENROLLMENT: 23 men, 19 women (first-year).

TUITION & FEES: Resident, $29,700; Nonresident, $29,700.

APPLICATIONS: Should be submitted between June 1 and November 1; the application fee is $85. Notification begins October 15; response must be received within two weeks; a deposit is required to hold place in class. Early Decision plan is available. Slight preference is given to state residents. Admission factors counted most heavily include GPA, MCAT, interviews, and letters of recommendation. *Correspondence to:* Admissions Committee.

MINORITY STUDENTS: Comprise 10% of the first-year class. The medical school offers preadmission laboratory experiences and tutoring programs for students of disadvantaged backgrounds. *For additional information:* Associate Dean for Student Affairs. Application for aid should be made upon acceptance.

----

*member AMCAS

Medical College of Georgia*
School of Medicine
1120 Fifteenth Street
Augusta, GA 30912
Tel: (706) 721-3186
E-mail: stdadmin@mail.mcg.edu
www.mcg.edu

MCAT: required

GPA: 3.8

FOUNDED: 1828; *publicly controlled;* a unit of the University System of Georgia.

ENROLLMENT: 110 men, 80 women (first-year).

TUITION & FEES: Resident, $14,237; Nonresident, $31,663.

APPLICATIONS: Should be submitted between June 1 and November 1; no application fee. Notification begins October 15; response must be received within two weeks; a deposit is required to hold place in class. Early Decision plan is available for Georgia residents only. Preference is given to state residents; a maximum of 5% of first-year places is open to nonresidents. Admission factors include academic aptitude and performance, MCAT scores, potential to practice medicine as evaluated by premedical adviser, personal references, and the personal interview. *Correspondence to:* Associate Dean for Admissions.

MINORITY STUDENTS: Comprise 6% of the first-year class; most of these students are receiving aid. The School of Medicine sponsors a summer program for premedical minority students as part of its recruitment program for such students. *For additional information:* Associate Dean, Special Academic Programs.

----

*member AMCAS

Medical College of Wisconsin*

8701 Watertown Plank Road
Milwaukee, WI 53226
Tel: (414) 456-8246
E-mail: mcwms@mcw.edu
www.mcw.edu/acad/admission

MCAT: required

GPA: 3.72

FOUNDED: 1890s; *private.*

ENROLLMENT: 116 men, 96 women (first-year).

TUITION & FEES: Resident, $38,940; Nonresident, $38,940.

APPLICATIONS: Should be submitted between June 1 and November 1; the application fee is $60. Notification begins October 15; response must be received within two weeks; a deposit is needed to hold place in class. Early Decision plan is available. Preference given to state residents; about a third of recent entering classes have been from Wisconsin. Admission criteria include GPA, MCAT, candidate's statement in application, academic recommendations, personal interview, and suitability for the medical profession. *Correspondence to:* Office of Admissions and Registrar.

MINORITY STUDENTS: Comprise 11% of the first-year class. Two students per class from underrepresented minority backgrounds may be eligible for the Tuition Forgiveness Program. *For additional information:* Associate Dean for Academic Affairs. Students may apply for aid as soon as they have been accepted and indicate their intent to enroll.

----

*member AMCAS

Medical University of South Carolina*

College of Medicine
171 Ashley Avenue
Charleston, SC 29464
Tel: (843) 792-3283
E-mail: taylorwl@musc.edu
www.musc.edu/com/com/html

MCAT: required

GPA: 3.63

FOUNDED: 1824; *publicly controlled.*

ENROLLMENT: 70 men, 65 women (first-year).

TUITION & FEES: Resident, $20,566; Nonresident, $56,618.

APPLICATIONS: Should be submitted between June 1 and December 1; the application fee is $75. Notification begins October 15; response must be received by school within two weeks; a deposit is needed to hold place in class. Early Decision plan is available. Strong preference is given to state residents. Admission factors counted most heavily are the MCAT, GPA, recommendations, and personal characteristics. *Correspondence to:* Office of Enrollment Services.

MINORITY STUDENTS: Comprise 10% of the first-year class. The Postbaccalaureate Reapplication Education Program is designed to further prepare South Carolina students interested in MUSC. *For additional information:* Assistant Dean, Minority Affairs.

----

*member AMCAS

Meharry Medical College*
School of Medicine
1005 D. B. Todd Jr. Boulevard
Nashville, TN 37208
Tel: (615) 327-6223
E-mail: admissions@mmc.edu
www.mmc.edu

MCAT: required

GPA: 3.5

FOUNDED: 1876; *private,* with support from states participating in the Southern Regional Educational Board (AL, FL, GA, LA, MD, MS, NC, TN, and VA).

ENROLLMENT: 48 men, 52 women (first-year).

TUITION & FEES: Resident, $32,336; Nonresident, $32,336.

APPLICATIONS: Should be submitted between June 1 and December 15; the application fee is $65. Notification begins October 15; response must be received by school within three weeks; a deposit is needed to hold place in class. Early Decision plan is available. Preference is given to residents of states that are members of the Southern Regional Educational Board. Admission factors weighted most heavily include GPA, MCAT scores, recommendations, and interest in primary health care. *Correspondence to:* Director, Admissions and Records.

MINORITY STUDENTS: Comprise 40% of the first-year class; most of these students receive aid; most remain to graduate. The School of Medicine sponsors recruiting seminars and a Summer Biomedical Science Program for minority and disadvantaged students. Tutorial assistance is available during the academic year. *For additional information:* Associate Dean for Student Affairs. Application for aid should be made after acceptance, prior to July 15.

---

*member AMCAS

Mercer University*
School of Medicine
1550 College Street
Macon, GA 31207
Tel: (478) 301-2542
E-mail: admissions@mercer.edu
www.medicine.mercer.edu

MCAT: required

GPA: 3.6

FOUNDED: 1982; *private.*

ENROLLMENT: 46 men, 40 women (first-year).

TUITION & FEES: Resident, $37,200; Nonresident, $37,200.

APPLICATIONS: Should be submitted between June 1 and November 1; the application fee is $50. Notification begins October 15; response must be received within 10 days; a deposit is needed to reserve place in class. Early Decision plan is available. Admission factors include academic and personal potential, letters of recommendation or premedical committee evaluation, and personal interview. *Correspondence to:* Office of Admissions and Student Affairs.

MINORITY STUDENTS: Comprise 15% of the first-year class. *For additional information:* Associate Dean for Admissions.

----

*member AMCAS

Michigan State University*
College of Human Medicine
East Lansing, MI 48824-1317
Tel: (517) 353-9620
E-mail: mdadmissions@msu.edu
www.MDadmissions.msu.edu

MCAT: required

GPA: 3.6

FOUNDED: 1964; *publicly controlled.*

ENROLLMENT: 73 men, 83 women (first-year).

TUITION & FEES: Resident, $28,010; Nonresident, $60,890.

APPLICATIONS: Should be submitted between June 1 and November 15; the application fee is $60. Notification begins October 15; response must be received within two weeks; a deposit is needed to reserve place in class. Early Decision plan is available. Preference given to state residents; approximately 85% of recent first-year students have been Michigan residents. Admission criteria include academic performance and trends, MCAT scores, letters of recommendation, relevant work experience, suitability for the MSU program, and the personal interview. *Correspondence to:* Office of Admissions, A-239 Life Sciences.

MINORITY STUDENTS: Comprise 5% of the first-year class; many of these students receive aid. *For additional information:* Director of Student Affairs.

----
*member AMCAS

Morehouse School of Medicine*

720 Westview Drive, SW
Atlanta, GA 30310
Tel: (404) 752-1650
E-mail: mdadmissions@msm.edu
www.msm.edu

MCAT: required

GPA: 3.4

FOUNDED: 1978; *private.*

ENROLLMENT: 21 men, 31 women (first-year).

TUITION & FEES: Resident, $29,248; Nonresident, $43,900.

APPLICATIONS: Should be submitted between June 1 and December 1; the application fee is $50. Notification begins December 20; response must be received within two weeks; a deposit is needed to hold place in class. Early Decision plan is available for Georgia residents only. Admission factors are MCAT scores, undergraduate curriculum and record, extent and nature of extracurricular activities, and personal qualifications. Preference given to residents of Georgia, but well-qualified nonresidents are encouraged to apply. *Correspondence to:* Admissions and Student Affairs.

MINORITY STUDENTS: Comprise 75% of the first-year class. *For additional information:* Student Affairs.

---

*member AMCAS

Mount Sinai School of Medicine of New York University*

1 Gustave L. Levy Place
New York, NY 10029
Tel: (212) 241-6696
E-mail: admissions@mssm.edu
www.mssm.edu

MCAT: required

GPA: 3.65

FOUNDED: 1968; *private.*

ENROLLMENT: 72 men, 68 women (first-year).

TUITION & FEES: Resident, $35,250; Nonresident, $35,250.

APPLICATIONS: Should be submitted between June 1 and November 1; the application fee is $105. Notification begins November 15; response must be received within two weeks; no deposit needed to hold place in class. Early Decision plan is available. *Correspondence to:* Director of Admissions, Room 5-04, Annenberg Building.

MINORITY STUDENTS: Comprise 19% of the first-year class. The School of Medicine offers a pre-entrance summer program for accepted students in addition to tutorial assistance during the academic year. *For additional information:* Assistant Dean, Student Affairs. Applications for aid should be made upon acceptance.

---

*member AMCAS

New Jersey Medical School*
University of Medicine and Dentistry of New Jersey
185 South Orange Avenue
Newark, NJ 07109-2714
Tel: (973) 972-4631
E-mail: njmsadmiss@umdnj.edu
www.njms.umdnj.edu

MCAT: required

GPA: 3.7

FOUNDED: 1954, acquired by state in 1965; *publicly controlled.*

ENROLLMENT: 95 men, 83 women (first-year).

TUITION & FEES: Resident, $24,121; Nonresident, $37,188.

APPLICATIONS: Should be submitted between June 1 and December 1; application fee is $75. Notification begins October 15; response must be received within two weeks; a deposit is needed to hold place in class. Early Decision plan is available for state residents only, to whom preference is given. Admission factors weighted most heavily include GPA, MCAT, motivation, determination, recommendations, and extracurricular activities. *Correspondence to:* Director of Admissions.

MINORITY STUDENTS: Comprise 9% of the first-year class; most of these students receive aid. The Medical School sponsors a special summer program for minority and disadvantaged students. *For additional information:* Assistant Dean for Minority Affairs. Application for aid should be made upon acceptance.

----

*member AMCAS

New York Medical College*
Valhalla, NY 10595
Tel: (914) 594-4507
E-mail: mdadmit@nymed.edu
www.nymc.edu

MCAT: required

GPA: 3.5

FOUNDED: 1860; *private.*

ENROLLMENT: 94 men, 94 women (first-year).

TUITION & FEES: Resident, $41,500; Nonresident, $41,500.

APPLICATIONS: Should be submitted between June 1 and December 15; the application fee is $100. Notification begins October 15; response must be received within two weeks; a deposit is needed to hold place in class. Early Decision plan is available. Admission factors include the MCAT, GPA, a premedical curriculum, recommendations, motivation, and integrity. *Correspondence to:* Admissions Office.

MINORITY STUDENTS: Comprise 37% of the first-year students. Financial assistance is available, 85% of the students receive aid. *For additional information:* Associate Dean for Student Affairs. Applications for aid should be made as early as possible.

---

*member AMCAS

New York University
School of Medicine
550 First Avenue
New York, NY 10016
Tel: (212) 263-5290
E-mail: admissions@med.NYU.edu
www.med.nyu.edu

MCAT: required

GPA: 3.7

FOUNDED: 1841; *private.*

ENROLLMENT: 80 men, 80 women (first-year).

TUITION & FEES: Resident, $40,729; Nonresident, $40,729.

APPLICATIONS: Should be submitted between June 1 and October 15; the application fee is $100. Notification begins December 20; response must be received within two weeks; a deposit is needed to secure position in the class. Selection criteria include academic performance, MCAT results, letters of recommendation, the personal interview, aptitude, and motivation. *Correspondence to:* Office of Admissions.

MINORITY STUDENTS: Comprise 5% of the first-year class; most of these students receive aid. The application fee may be waived. *For additional information:* Office of Minority Affairs. Accepted students are eligible to file applications for financial assistance.

Northeastern Ohio Universities*

College of Medicine and Pharmacy
4209 State Route 44
P.O. Box 95
Rootstown, OH 44272
Tel: (330) 325-6270
E-mail: admission@neoucom.edu
www.neoucom.edu

MCAT: required

GPA: 3.73

FOUNDED: 1973: *publicly supported.* Special programs include a combined BS-MD program for high school graduates.

ENROLLMENT: 57 men, 58 women (first-year).

TUITION & FEES: Resident, $27,861; Nonresident, $55,722.

APPLICATIONS: Should be submitted between June 1 and November 1; the application fee is $50. Notification begins October 15; response must be received within two weeks; no deposit needed to hold place in class. Early Decision plan is available. Preference is given to state residents. Selection factors include academic records, MCAT scores, personal qualifications, and demonstration of sincere motivation for the practice of medicine. *Correspondence to:* Office of Admissions.

MINORITY STUDENTS: Comprise 6% of the first-year class. *For additional information:* Special Assistant to the President for Minority Affairs and Affirmative Action.

---

*member AMCAS

Northwestern University*
Feinberg School of Medicine
303 East Chicago Avenue
Chicago, IL 60611
Tel: (312) 503-8206
E-mail: med-admissions@northwestern.edu
www.medschool.northwestern.edu

MCAT: required

GPA: 3.8

FOUNDED: 1859; *private.* Special programs include an Honors Program in Medical Education leading to the MD degree after three years of undergraduate work at the Evanston campus and four years at Northwestern.

ENROLLMENT: 85 men, 84 women (first-year). 60 members of each class are admitted from the Honors Programs.

TUITION & FEES: Resident, $40,313; Nonresident, $40,313.

APPLICATIONS: Should be submitted between June 1 and October 15; the application fee is $75. Notification begins November 15; response must be received within two weeks; no deposit is necessary to hold a place in class. Early Decision plan is available. Preference is given to state residents. Admission factors include academic performance, personal qualifications and achievements, and a personal interview. *Correspondence to:* Associate Dean for Admissions.

MINORITY STUDENTS: Comprise 5% of the first-year class. *For additional information:* Assistant Dean for Minority Affairs. Applications for aid may be submitted only upon acceptance to the school; deadline July 1.

----

*member AMCAS

Oakland University*
William Beaumont School of Medicine
2200 N Squirrel
Rochester, MI 48309
Tel: (248) 370-2769
E-mail: medadmit@oakland.edu
www.oakland.edu/medicine

MCAT: required

GPA: 3.0

FOUNDED: 2008; *private*.

ENROLLMENT: no data available.

TUITION & FEES: Resident, $42,760; Nonresident, $42,760.

APPLICATIONS: Should be submitted between June 1 and November 15. Admission criteria include MCAT scores, GPA, general academic background, letters of recommendation, and personal qualifications as judged by the admissions committee.

MINORITY STUDENTS: The school has an active minority recruitment program.

---

*member AMCAS

Ohio State University*
College of Medicine
370 West Ninth Avenue
Columbus, OH 43210-1200
Tel: (614) 292-7137
E-mail: medicine@osu.edu
medicine.osu.edu

MCAT: required

GPA: 3.7

FOUNDED: 1914; *publicly controlled.* The Independent Study Program provides the option of completing the MD degree requirements within three calendar years.

ENROLLMENT: 120 men, 92 women (first-year).

TUITION & FEES: Resident, $28,809; Nonresident, $44,491.

APPLICATIONS: Should be submitted between June 1 and November 1; the application fee is $60. Notification begins October 7; response must be received within two weeks; no deposit needed to hold place in class. Early Decision plan is available. Preference is given to state residents. Admission criteria include GPA, MCAT, letters of recommendation, the personal interview, and nonacademic achievements. *Correspondence to:* Admissions Office.

MINORITY STUDENTS: Comprise 10% of the first-year class. Academic assistance programs are available to students who exhibit special academic needs. *For additional information:* Office of Minority Affairs.

----
*member AMCAS

Oregon Health and Science University*
School of Medicine
3181 SW Sam Jackson Park Road
Portland, OR 97239
Tel: (503) 494-2998
www.ohsu.edu/som-dean/admit.html

MCAT: required

GPA: 3.8

FOUNDED: 1887; *publicly controlled.*

ENROLLMENT: 56 men, 62 women (first-year).

TUITION & FEES: Resident, $29,665; Nonresident, $40,480.

APPLICATIONS: Should be submitted between June 1 and October 15; the application fee is $100. Notification begins November 1; response must be received by school within two weeks; no deposit needed to hold place in class. Preference is given to state residents, residents of neighboring western states without medical schools (Alaska, Montana, and Wyoming), and underrepresented minorities. Admission factors include preprofessional training, evidence of scholarship, MCAT scores, evaluations from premedical instructors, evidence of good moral character, and the personal interview. *Correspondence to:* Director of Admissions.

MINORITY STUDENTS: Comprise 3% of the first-year class. *For additional information:* Director, Multicultural Affairs. Applications for aid should be submitted upon acceptance, prior to March 1.

---

*member AMCAS

Paul L. Foster School of Medicine at Texas Tech University*
Health Science Center at El Paso
4800 Alberta Avenue
El Paso, TX 79905
Tel: (915) 545-6551
www.ttuhsc.edu

MCAT: required

GPA: no data available.

FOUNDED: 2003; *publicly controlled.*

ENROLLMENT: no data available.

TUITION & FEES: Resident, $11,700; Nonresident, $18,500.

APPLICATIONS: Should be submitted between May 1 and October 1. Admission criteria include MCAT scores, GPA, general academic background, letters of recommendation, and personal qualifications as judged by the admissions committee.

MINORITY STUDENTS: The school has an active minority recruitment program.

---

*member AMCAS

Pennsylvania State University*

College of Medicine
P.O. Box 850, 500 University Drive
Hershey, PA 17033
Tel: (717) 531-8755
E-mail: studentadmissions@hmc.psu.edu
www.hmc.psu.edu/md

MCAT: required

GPA: 3.7

FOUNDED: 1967; *publicly controlled.*

ENROLLMENT: 77 men, 77 women (first-year).

TUITION & FEES: Resident, $33,058; Nonresident, $44,920.

APPLICATIONS: Should be submitted between June 1 and November 15; the application fee is $70. Notification begins October 1; response must be received by school within two weeks; a deposit is needed to hold place in class. Early Decision plan is available. Preference is given to state residents. Selection factors include GPA, MCAT, letters of recommendation, and an interview. *Correspondence to:* Office of Student Affairs.

MINORITY STUDENTS: Comprise 6% of first-year students; most of these students receive aid. The College of Medicine has organized a special recruitment program for minorities and students from disadvantaged backgrounds. *For additional information:* Associate Dean for Student Affairs.

---

*member AMCAS

Ponce School of Medicine*

P.O. Box 7004
Ponce, PR 00752
Tel: (787) 840-2575
E-mail: admissions@psm.edu
www.psm.edu/student_affairs

MCAT: required

GPA: 3.5

FOUNDED: 1977 (originally Catholic University of Puerto Rico School of Medicine);
private.

ENROLLMENT: 34 men, 34 women (first-year).

TUITION & FEES: Resident, $19,352; Nonresident, $28,850.

APPLICATIONS: Should be submitted between June 15 and December 15; the
application fee is $50. Notification begins October 15; response must be
received within four weeks; a deposit is necessary to hold place in class.
Early Decision plan is available. Admission decisions are based on the
MCAT score, GPA, recommendations, and personal interview. Preference is
given to residents of Puerto Rico; because courses are taught in both
English and Spanish, students must have functional knowledge of both
languages. *Correspondence to:* Admissions Office.

*member AMCAS

Robert Wood Johnson Medical School*
University of Medicine and Dentistry of New Jersey
675 Hoes Lane
Piscataway, NJ 08854-5635
Tel: (732) 235-4576
E-mail: rwjapdmterregca@umdnj.edu
www.rwlms.umdnj.edu

MCAT: required

GPA: 3.7

FOUNDED: 1961 as a two-year medical school, introduced clinical program for one half of each class in 1970; in 1974 the school graduated its first class of MDs; formerly known as Rutgers Medical School; *publicly controlled.*

ENROLLMENT: 68 men, 98 women (first-year).

TUITION & FEES: Resident, $24,296; Nonresident, $37,363.

APPLICATIONS: Should be submitted between June 1 and December 1; application fee is $75. Notification begins October 15; response must be received within two weeks; a deposit is needed to hold place in class. Early Decision plan is available. Preference is given to state residents. Selection factors include academic achievement, MCAT scores, faculty recommendation, and the personal interview. *Correspondence to:* Office of Admissions.

MINORITY STUDENTS: Comprise 8% of the first-year class. The Medical School sponsors a prematriculation summer program for accepted minority and disadvantaged students. *For additional information:* Assistant Dean for Special Academic Programs. Financial aid materials are available upon acceptance.

---

*member AMCAS

Rush Medical College of Rush University*

600 South Paulina Street
Chicago, IL 60612
Tel: (312) 942-6913
E-mail: RMC_admissions@rush.edu
www.rushu.rush.edu/medical

MCAT: required

GPA: 3.6

FOUNDED: 1837, closed 1943 and reopened in 1971; *private*.

ENROLLMENT: 60 men, 70 women (first-year).

TUITION & FEES: Resident, $44,928; Nonresident, $44,928.

APPLICATIONS: Should be submitted between June 1 and November 1; the application fee is $75. Notification begins October 15; response must be received within two weeks; a deposit is needed to hold place in class. Early Decision plan is available. Admission criteria include academic performance, MCAT results, letters of recommendation, and the personal interview. *Correspondence to:* Office of Admissions, 524 Academic Facility.

MINORITY STUDENTS: Comprise 12% of the first-year class; most of these students receive aid. The application fee may be waived. *For additional information:* Chairperson, Committee on Admissions. Applications for aid may be made upon acceptance.

----
*member AMCAS

Saint Louis University*

School of Medicine
1402 South Grand Boulevard
St. Louis, MO 63104
Tel: (314) 977-9870
E-mail: slumd@slu.edu
medschool.slu.edu

MCAT: required

GPA: 3.7

FOUNDED: 1836; *private.*

ENROLLMENT: 98 men, 78 women (first-year).

TUITION & FEES: Resident, $43,830; Nonresident, $43,830.

APPLICATIONS: Should be submitted between June 1 and December 15; the application fee is $100. Notification begins October 15; response must be received within two weeks; a deposit is needed to hold place in class. Early Decision plan is available. Admissions qualifications include the MCAT, GPA, demonstrated scientific ability, character, and motivation. *Correspondence to:* Admissions Committee.

MINORITY STUDENTS: Comprise 6% of the first-year class; most of these students receive aid. The application fee may be waived. *For additional information:* Associate Dean, Admissions and Student Affairs.

---

*member AMCAS

San Juan Bautista School of Medicine*
P.O. Box 4968
Caguas, PR 00725
Tel: (787) 743-3083
E-mail: admissions@sanjuanbautista.edu
www.sanjuanbautista.edu/admission.aspx

MCAT: required

GPA: 3.3

FOUNDED: 2009; *private.*

ENROLLMENT: 29 men, 38 women (first-year).

TUITION & FEES: Resident, $17,000; Nonresident, $43,500.

APPLICATIONS: Should be submitted between June 1 and April; the application fee is $75. Admission criteria include MCAT scores, GPA, science background, motivation, and personal qualifications as judged by an interview and the admissions committee.

MINORITY STUDENTS: Comprise 31% of the first-year class.

---

*member AMCAS

Southern Illinois University*
School of Medicine
P.O. Box 19624
Springfield, IL 62794-1226
Tel: (217) 545-6013
E-mail: admissions@siumed.edu
siumed.edu

MCAT: required

GPA: 3.5

FOUNDED: 1969; *publicly controlled.*

ENROLLMENT: 40 men, 32 women (first-year).

TUITION & FEES: Resident, $22,210; Nonresident, $22,210.

APPLICATIONS: Should be submitted between June 1 and November 15; the application fee is $50. Notification begins October 15; response must be received within 15 days; a deposit is required to hold place in class. Early Decision plan is available. Nonresidents must apply EDP. Admission requirements include GPA, MCAT, interviews, and letters of academic recommendation. *Correspondence to:* Office of Student and Alumni Affairs.

MINORITY STUDENTS: Comprise 18% of the first-year class. The School of Medicine sponsors a Medical Education Preparatory Program (MEDPREP) to aid minority students in preparing for medical school. *For additional information:* Director, MEDPREP.

---

*member AMCAS

Stanford University*
School of Medicine
251 Campus Drive
Stanford, CA 94305
Tel: (650) 723-6861
E-mail: admissions@med.stanford.edu
med.stanford.edu

MCAT: required

GPA: 3.75

FOUNDED: 1908; *private;* a flexible curriculum allows completion of the MD program in three to five years.

ENROLLMENT: 40 men, 46 women (first-year).

TUITION & FEES: Resident, $43,389; Nonresident, $43,789.

APPLICATIONS: Should be submitted between June 1 and October 15; the application fee is $80. Notification begins October 15; response must be received within two weeks; no deposit needed to hold place in class. Early Decision plan is available. Selection factors include academic record and demonstrated motivational and personal qualifications for medicine. *Correspondence to:* Office of Admissions.

MINORITY STUDENTS: Comprise 17% of the first-year class; most of these students receive aid. The School of Medicine has a strong commitment to recruit women and minority students. *For additional information:* Associate Dean for Student Affairs. Applications for aid are available after acceptance.

---

*member AMCAS

State University of New York Downstate Medical Center*

College of Medicine
450 Clarkson Avenue
Brooklyn, NY 11203-2098
Tel: (718) 270-2446
E-mail: admission@downstate.edu
www.downstate.edu

MCAT: required

GPA: 3.7

FOUNDED: 1860 (acquired by state system in 1950); *publicly controlled.*

ENROLLMENT: 85 men, 85 women (first-year).

TUITION & FEES: Resident, $19,370; Nonresident, $34,070.

APPLICATIONS: Should be submitted between June 2 and December 15; the application fee is $80. Notification begins October 15; response must be received within two weeks; a deposit is needed to hold place in class. Strong preference given to state residents. Admissions decisions are based on college records, letters of recommendation, MCAT scores, the interview, and community service. *Correspondence to:* Director of Admissions.

MINORITY STUDENTS: Comprise 10% of first-year students. Various scholarships, work-study programs, and loans are available; most students receive assistance. The application fee may be waived. *For additional information:* Associate Dean for Minority Affairs.

---

*member AMCAS

State University of New York*
Upstate Medical University
766 Irving Avenue
Syracuse, NY 13210
Tel: (315) 464-4570
E-mail: admiss@upstate.edu
www.upstate.edu/com

MCAT: required

GPA: 3.8

FOUNDED: 1834 (acquired by state system in 1950); *publicly controlled.*

ENROLLMENT: 83 men, 77 women (first-year).

TUITION & FEES: Resident, $19,596; Nonresident, $34,656.

APPLICATIONS: Should be submitted between June 1 and October 15; the application fee is $100. Notification begins October 15; response must be received within two weeks; no deposit needed to hold place in class. Early Decision plan is available. Strong preference given to state residents. Admission factors include scholastic and scientific aptitude and performance, MCAT scores, letters of recommendation, personal qualifications, and the personal interview. *Correspondence to:* Admissions Committee.

MINORITY STUDENTS: Comprise 26% of the first-year class; most of these students receive aid. *For additional information:* Office of Multicultural Resources. Application for aid should be made upon acceptance.

---

*member AMCAS

Stony Brook University School of Medicine*

Health Sciences Center
Stony Brook, NY 11794-8434
Tel: (631) 444-2113
E-mail: somadmissions@stonybrook.edu
www.stonybrookmedicalcenter.org/som

MCAT: required

GPA: 3.65

FOUNDED: 1971; *publicly controlled.*

ENROLLMENT: 67 men, 59 women (first-year).

TUITION & FEES: Resident, $18,800; Nonresident, $33,500.

APPLICATIONS: Should be submitted between June 1 and December 15; the application fee is $75. Notification begins on October 15; response must be received within 15 days; no deposit needed to reserve place in class. Early Decision plan is available. Strong preference given to state residents. Admission decisions are based on MCAT, GPA, recommendations of premedical adviser, and personal abilities. *Correspondence to:* Committee on Admissions.

MINORITY STUDENTS: Comprise 17% of first-year students. Students may avail themselves of a variety of state, federal, and private programs of financial assistance administered by the Office of Student Services. The application fee may be waived. *For additional information:* Associate Dean.

----

*member AMCAS

Temple University*
School of Medicine
3340 North Broad Street
Philadelphia, PA 19140
Tel: (215) 707-3656
E-mail: medadmission@temple.edu
www.medschool.temple.edu

MCAT: required

GPA: 3.7

FOUNDED: 1901; *state-related.*

ENROLLMENT: 95 men, 83 women (first-year).

TUITION & FEES: Resident, $38,502; Nonresident, $47,004.

APPLICATIONS: Should be submitted between June 1 and December 15; the application fee is $70. Notification begins October 15; response must be received by school within two weeks; a deposit is needed to hold place in class. Early Decision plan is available. Preference is given to state residents. Selection factors include academic performance, extracurricular activities, MCAT scores, recommendations, and the interview. *Correspondence to:* Admissions Office.

MINORITY STUDENTS: Comprise 7% of the first-year class; most of these students receive aid. The School of Medicine operates the Recruitment, Admissions, and Retention (RAR) Program, which actively identifies potential minority applicants and provides special follow-up services and financial aid during the term of their medical education. Matriculation summer program is offered for accepted minority students. *For additional information:* Assistant Dean.

---

*member AMCAS

Texas A&M University*
Health Science Center
College of Medicine
159 Joe Reynolds Medical Building
College Station, TX 77843
Tel: (979) 845-2634
E-mail: watkins.orths@medicine.tamhsc.edu
www.medicine.tamhsc.edu

MCAT: required

GPA: 3.8

FOUNDED: 1973; *publicly controlled.*

ENROLLMENT: 45 men, 60 women (first-year).

TUITION & FEES: Resident, $10,682; Nonresident, $23,782.

APPLICATIONS: Should be submitted between May 1 and October 15; the application fee is $45. Notification begins November 15; response must be received within two weeks; no deposit needed to hold place in class. Preference is given to state residents. Admission factors include academic records, MCAT scores, personal qualifications, and demonstration of motivation. *Correspondence to:* Associate Dean for Student Affairs and Admissions.

MINORITY STUDENTS: Comprise 4% of the first-year class. *For additional information:* Coordinator, Minority Access to Medical Careers.

----

*member AMCAS

Texas Tech University
Health Sciences Center
School of Medicine
3601 4th Street
Lubbock, TX 79430-0001
Tel: (806) 743-2297
E-mail: somadm@ttuhsc.edu
www.ttuhsc.edu

MCAT: required

GPA: 3.57

FOUNDED: 1972; *publicly controlled.*

ENROLLMENT: 75 men, 65 women (first-year).

TUITION & FEES: Resident, $9,762; Nonresident, $22,862.

APPLICATIONS: Should be submitted between May 1 and October 15; the application fee is $50. Notification begins October 15; response must be received by school within two weeks; a deposit is needed to hold place in class. Early Decision plan is available. Strong preference is given to state residents. Admissions decisions are based on MCAT, GPA, breadth and strength of undergraduate curriculum, letters of recommendation, and the personal interview. *Correspondence to:* Office of Admissions.

MINORITY STUDENTS: Comprise 25% of first-year students. Upon acceptance students may apply for aid. *For additional information:* Assistant Dean for Minority Affairs.

Tufts University*
School of Medicine
136 Harrison Avenue
Boston, MA 02111
Tel: (617) 636-6571
E-mail: medadmissions@tufts.edu
www.tufts.edu/med

MCAT: required

GPA: 3.6

FOUNDED: 1893; *private.*

ENROLLMENT: 97 men, 81 women (first-year).

TUITION & FEES: Resident, $47,116; Nonresident, $47,116.

APPLICATIONS: Should be submitted between June 1 and January 15; the application fee is $105. Notification begins December 1; response must be received within two weeks of notification; a deposit is needed to hold place in class. Early Decision plan is available. Admission factors counted most heavily include GPA, MCAT, caliber of college work, personality, and motivation. *Correspondence to:* Office of Admissions.

MINORITY STUDENTS: Comprise 12% of the first-year class. The application fee may be waived. *For additional information:* Assistant Director of Student Services. Applications for aid are available upon acceptance.

---

*member AMCAS

Tulane University*
School of Medicine
1430 Tulane Avenue
New Orleans, LA 70112
Tel: (504) 988-5187
E-mail: medsch@tulane.edu
www.tmc.tulane.edu/departments/admissions/index/html

MCAT: required

GPA: 3.5

FOUNDED: 1834; *private.*

ENROLLMENT: 94 men, 81 women (first-year).

TUITION & FEES: Resident, $45,080; Nonresident, $45,080.

APPLICATIONS: Should be submitted between June 1 and December 15; the application fee is $95. Notification begins October 15; response must be received before May 15; a deposit is required to hold place in class. Admission factors weighted most heavily include GPA (overall and science), MCAT scores, faculty recommendations, special accomplishments and talents, substance of undergraduate programs, and trends in academic performance. *Correspondence to:* Office of Admissions.

MINORITY STUDENTS: Comprise 3% of the first-year students; a majority of these students receive aid. A prematriculation summer enrichment program is available to entering minority and other disadvantaged students, as are tutorial and counseling services. *For additional information:* Associate Dean for Student Services.

----
*member AMCAS

Uniformed Services University of the Health Sciences*

F. Edward Hébert School of Medicine
4301 Jones Bridge Road
Bethesda, MD 20814-4799
Tel: (301) 295-3101
E-mail: admissions@usuhs.mil
www.usuhs.mil

MCAT: required

GPA: 3.5

FOUNDED: 1972; *publicly controlled.* The school aims to prepare men and women for careers as medical corps officers.

ENROLLMENT: 120 men, 51 women (first-year).

TUITION & FEES: There are no tuition charges, and books and supplies are also furnished without charge.

APPLICATIONS: Should be submitted between June 1 and November 15; there is no application fee. Notification begins November 1; response must be received within two weeks; no deposit required to hold place in class. Selection factors include letters of reference, personal statement, and a service preference statement. Transcripts should not be submitted until requested. *Correspondence to:* Admissions Office; Room A-1041.

MINORITY STUDENTS: Comprise 6% of first-year students. The School of Medicine operates the Accession of Qualified Underrepresented Applicants (AQUA) program to increase the number of qualified minority and women applicants. *For additional information:* Director of Admissions/Registrar.

---

*member AMCAS

Universidad Central del Caribe*
School of Medicine
Ramón Rúiz Arnau University Hospital
P.O. Box 60327
Bayamón, PR 00960-6032
E-mail: icordero@uccaribe.edu
www.uccaribe.edu

MCAT: required

GPA: 3.5

FOUNDED: 1976; *private.*

ENROLLMENT: 33 men, 33 women (first-year).

TUITION & FEES: Resident, $24,500; Nonresident, $31,890.

APPLICATIONS: Should be submitted between June 1 and December 15; the application fee is $100. Notification begins in February; response must be received within 10 days. A deposit is needed to hold place in class. Early Decision plan is available. Admission factors include undergraduate academic record, GPA, MCAT, personal interview, and letters of recommendation. *Correspondence to:* Office of Admissions.

----
*member AMCAS

University of Alabama*

School of Medicine
University Station
A-100, Volker Hall
1600 University Boulevard
Birmingham, AL 35294-0019
Tel: (205) 934-2433
E-mail: medschool@uab.edu
www.uab.edu/uasom

MCAT: required

GPA: 3.8

FOUNDED: 1859; *publicly controlled.*

ENROLLMENT: 104 men, 72 women (first-year).

TUITION & FEES: Resident, $16,608; Nonresident, $43,848.

APPLICATIONS: Should be submitted between June 1 and November 1; the application fee is $75. Notification begins October 15; response must be received within two weeks; a deposit is needed to hold place in class. Early Decision plan is available for Alabama residents only. Preference is given to state residents. Admission factors weighted most heavily include GPA, MCAT scores, letters of recommendation, the personal interview, and personal qualifications. *Correspondence to:* Assistant Dean for Student Services for Admissions.

MINORITY STUDENTS: Comprise 6% of the first-year class; most of these students receive aid. The application fee may be waived. The Office of Minority Student Affairs and the Admissions Committee provide counsel to minority students interested in the study of medicine. *For additional information:* Coordinator, Minority Enhancement Program. Applications for aid should be made by March 1.

----
*member AMCAS

University of Arizona*
College of Medicine
P.O. Box 245075
Tucson, AZ 85724
Tel: (520) 626-6214
E-mail: medapp@email.arizona.edu
www.medicine.arizona.edu

MCAT: required

GPA: 3.8

FOUNDED: 1967; *publicly controlled.*

ENROLLMENT: 51 men, 83 women (first-year).

TUITION & FEES: Resident, $17,767; Nonresident,not applicable.

APPLICATIONS: Should be submitted between June 1 and November 1; application fee is $75. Notification begins January 30; response must be received within two weeks; no deposit needed to hold place in class. Only residents of Arizona and WICHE-certified residents of Alaska, Montana, or Wyoming are considered for admission. Admissions decisions are based on the MCAT, GPA, letters of recommendation, personal interview, character, and motivation. *Correspondence to:* Admissions Office.

MINORITY STUDENTS: Comprise 4% of the first-year class. Various types of financial assistance are available, as is a Summer Prematriculation Program. *For additional information:* Associate Dean for Student Affairs. Application for aid may be made after acceptance.

---

*member AMCAS

University of Arkansas*
College of Medicine
4301 West Markham Street
Little Rock, AR 72205
Tel: (501) 686-5354
E-mail: southtomg@uams.edu
www.uams.edu

MCAT: required

GPA: 3.7

FOUNDED: 1879; *publicly controlled.*

ENROLLMENT: 100 men, 55 women (first-year).

TUITION & FEES: Resident, $16,430; Nonresident, $31,962.

APPLICATIONS: Should be submitted between July 1 and November 1; the application fee is $100. Notification begins December 15; response must be received within two weeks; no deposit required to hold place in class. Preference is given to state residents. Admission factors counted most heavily include GPA, MCAT, premedical advisory committee and faculty evaluation, and medical faculty interview. *Correspondence to:* Office of Student Admissions, Slot 551.

MINORITY STUDENTS: Comprise 3% of the first-year class. *For additional information:* Associate Dean for Minority Affairs. Application for aid should be made after acceptance and prior to matriculation.

---

*member AMCAS

University of Buffalo School of Medicine and Biomedical Sciences*

131 Biomedical Education Building
3435 Main Street
Buffalo, NY 14214
Tel: (716) 829-3466
E-mail: jjrosso@buffalo.edu
www.smbs.buffalo.edu

MCAT: required

GPA: 3.67

FOUNDED: 1846 (acquired by state system in 1962); *publicly controlled.*

ENROLLMENT: 60 men, 75 women (first-year).

TUITION & FEES: Resident, $18,800; Nonresident, $36,000.

APPLICATIONS: Should be submitted between June 1 and November 15; the application fee is $65. Notification begins October 15, response must be received within two weeks; a deposit is needed to hold place in class. Strong preference given to state residents. Admission factors weighted most heavily include GPA, MCAT, letters of recommendation, and the personal interview. Candidates should also demonstrate such personal qualifications as a habit of critical analysis, a spirit of inquiry, and a sense of understanding and sympathy for those who suffer. While admission decisions are based on merit, the percentage of women enrolled has traditionally been greater than the percentage of women in the applicant pool. *Correspondence to:* Office of Medical Admissions.

MINORITY STUDENTS: Comprise 5% of the first-year class. The School of Medicine sponsors a special summer program for minority and disadvantaged students. Remedial sessions are provided for all students during the academic year. *For additional information:* Director, Minority Affairs. Applications for aid are provided upon acceptance.

----

*member AMCAS

University of California—Davis*

School of Medicine
4610 X Street
Sacramento, CA 95817
Tel: (916) 734-4800
E-mail: medadmisinfo@ucdavis.edu
www.som.ucdavis.edu

MCAT: required

GPA: 3.7

FOUNDED: 1963, admitted first class in 1968; *publicly controlled.*

ENROLLMENT: 43 men, 62 women (first-year).

TUITION & FEES: Resident, not available; Nonresident, $36,544.

APPLICATIONS: Should be submitted between June 1 and October 1; the application fee is $60. Notification begins October 15; response must be received within two weeks; no deposit required to secure place in class. Preference is given to state residents. Admission factors include academic record, MCAT results, and motivation and personal qualifications as judged from letters of recommendation and personal interview. *Correspondence to:* Admissions Office.

MINORITY STUDENTS: Comprise 3% of the first-year class. The application fee may be waived. The School of Medicine sponsors special recruitment and orientation programs for students of disadvantaged social and educational backgrounds. *For additional information:* Assistant Dean for Minority Affairs. Applications for aid may be made after acceptance.

---

*member AMCAS

University of California—Irvine*
School of Medicine
Medical Education Bldg. 802
Irvine, CA 92697-4089
Tel: (949) 824-5388
E-mail: medadmit@uci-edu
www.ucrhs.uci.edu/com

MCAT: required

GPA: 3.7

FOUNDED: 1965; *publicly supported.*

ENROLLMENT: 58 men, 51 women (first-year).

TUITION & FEES: Resident, $21,823; Nonresident, $34,068.

APPLICATIONS: Should be submitted between June 1 and November 1; the application fee is $60. Notification begins November 15; response must be received within two weeks; no deposit needed to hold place in class. Preference given to state residents. Admission factors include GPA, MCAT, letters of recommendation, and a personal interview. *Correspondence to:* Office of Admissions.

MINORITY STUDENTS: Comprise 3% of first-year students. Tutorial assistance and counseling are available to students. The college provides financial aid in the form of scholarships, grants, and loans. The application fee may be waived. *For additional information:* Assistant Dean, Outreach Student Affairs. Application for aid should be made after acceptance.

---

*member AMCAS

University of California—Los Angeles*
David Geffen School of Medicine
P.O. Box 95703
Los Angeles, CA 90095
Tel: (310) 825-6081
E-mail: somadmiss@mednet.ucla.edu
www.dgsem.healthsciences.ucla.edu/ms-resources

MCAT: required

GPA: 3.8

FOUNDED: 1951; *publicly supported.*

ENROLLMENT: 94 men, 75 women (first-year).

TUITION & FEES: Resident, $22,551; Nonresident, $34,596.

APPLICATIONS: Should be submitted between June 1 and November 1; application fee is $60. Notification begins January 15; response must be received within two weeks; no deposit needed to secure place in class. Admission criteria include GPA, MCAT results, evaluation of accomplishments and character in letters of recommendation, and the personal interview. *Correspondence to:* Office of Student Affairs.

MINORITY STUDENTS: Comprise 9% of the first-year class; most of these students receive aid. The application fee may be waived. A subcommittee of the Admissions Committee, which includes minority faculty and students, is responsible for the evaluation of all applications from minority and disadvantaged students. *For additional information:* Director, Office of Student Support Services. Applications for aid are forwarded to entering freshmen prior to May.

---

*member AMCAS

University of California—San Diego*
School of Medicine
9500 Gilman Drive
La Jolla, CA 92093
Tel: (858) 534-3880
E-mail: somadmissions@ucsd.edu
meded-portal.ucsd.edu

MCAT: required

GPA: 3.8

FOUNDED: 1968; *publicly controlled.*

ENROLLMENT: 66 men, 68 women (first-year).

TUITION & FEES: Resident, $21,465; Nonresident, $33,710.

APPLICATIONS: Should be submitted between June 1 and November 1; the application fee is $60. Notification begins October 15; response must be received within two weeks; no deposit required to hold place in class. Preference given to state residents. Admission factors most heavily weighted include GPA, MCAT, letters of recommendation, personal interviews, and the nature of scholarly and extracurricular activities. *Correspondence to:* Office of Admissions, Medical Teaching Facility.

MINORITY STUDENTS: Comprise 1% of the first-year class; most of these students receive aid. The application fee may be waived. *For additional information:* Associate Dean. Application for aid may be filed only upon acceptance.

----

*member AMCAS

University of California—San Francisco*
School of Medicine
San Francisco, CA 94143
Tel: (415) 476-4044
E-mail: admissions@medsch.ucsf.edu
www.medschool.ucsf.edu

MCAT: required.

GPA: 3.8

FOUNDED: 1864; *publicly controlled.*

ENROLLMENT: 67 men, 96 women (first-year).

TUITION & FEES: Resident, $21,218; Nonresident, $33,463.

APPLICATIONS: Should be submitted between June 1 and October 15; the application fee is $60. Notification begins November 15; response must be received within two weeks; no deposit needed to secure place in class. Preference is given to state residents. Admission factors include academic record, MCAT scores, evidence of motivation toward medicine, and personal qualifications. *Correspondence to:* School of Medicine, Admissions, C-200, Box 0408.

MINORITY STUDENTS: Comprise 13% of the first-year class; most of these students receive aid. The Health Sciences Minority Program provides admission assistance, financial aid, a comprehensive orientation program, and other services for socioeconomically disadvantaged students. *For additional information:* Admissions Office. Application for aid should be made after acceptance.

----
*member AMCAS

University of Central Florida*
College of Medicine
2201 Research Parkway
P.O. Box 60116
Orlando, FL 32816
Tel: (407) 823-4244
E-mail: mdadmissions@mail.ucf.edu
www.med.ucf.edu

MCAT: required

GPA: no data available.

FOUNDED: 2009; *publicly controlled.*

ENROLLMENT: no data available.

TUITION & FEES: Resident, $22,500; Nonresident, $42,500.

APPLICATIONS: Should be submitted between June 1 and December 1; there is an application fee. Admission criteria include academic background, letters of recommendation, and personal qualifications as judged by an interview and the admissions committee.

MINORITY STUDENTS: no data available.

---

*member AMCAS

University of Chicago*
Pritzker School of Medicine
924 East 57th Street, BLSC 104
Chicago, IL 60637
Tel: (773) 702-1937
E-mail: pritzkeradmissions@bsd.uchicago.edu
www.pritzker.bsd.uchicago.edu

MCAT: required

GPA: 3.8

FOUNDED: 1927; *private.*

ENROLLMENT: 53 men, 59 women (first-year).

TUITION & FEES: Resident, $35,985; Nonresident, $35,985.

APPLICATIONS: Should be submitted between June 1 and October 15; the application fee is $75. Notification begins October 15; response must be received within four weeks; a deposit is needed to hold place in class. Early Decision plan is available. No preference given to state residents, though approximately 40% of recent entering classes have been from Illinois. Selection factors include scholastic record, MCAT results, personal qualifications, and extracurricular activities. *Correspondence to:* Office of Dean of Students.

MINORITY STUDENTS: Comprise 12% of the first-year class; most of these students receive aid. *For additional information:* Director of Student Programs. Applications for aid may be submitted upon acceptance.

---

*member AMCAS

University of Cincinnati*
College of Medicine
P.O. Box 670552
Cincinnati, OH 45267-0552
Tel: (513) 558-7314
E-mail: com.admis@ucmail.uc.edu
med.uc.edu

MCAT: required

GPA: 3.6

FOUNDED: 1819; *publicly controlled.*

ENROLLMENT: 107 men, 52 women (first-year).

TUITION & FEES: Resident, $27,987; Nonresident, $42,987.

APPLICATIONS: Should be submitted between June 1 and November 15; the application fee is $25. Notification begins October 15; response must be received by school within two weeks; no deposit needed to hold place in class. Early Decision plan is available. Preference is given to state residents. *Correspondence to:* Office of Student Affairs/ Admissions.

MINORITY STUDENTS: Comprise 9% the first-year class; most of these students receive aid. The College of Medicine maintains prematriculation and tutorial programs for students of disadvantaged backgrounds. *For additional information:* Assistant Dean for Admissions. Applications for aid should be made by May 31.

----
*member AMCAS

University of Colorado*
School of Medicine
4200 East Ninth Avenue
Denver, CO 80045
Tel: (303) 724-8025
E-mail: somaolmin@uchsc.edu
www.uchsc.edu/sm/sm/mddegree.htm

MCAT: required

GPA: 3.8

FOUNDED: 1883; *publicly controlled.*

ENROLLMENT: 83 men, 74 women (first-year).

TUITION & FEES: Resident, $24,828; Nonresident, $25,891.

APPLICATIONS: Should be submitted between June 1 and November 1; the application fee is $100. Notification begins October 15; response must be received within two weeks; a deposit is needed to hold place in class. Early Decision plan available. Preference is given first to Colorado residents and then to residents of western states without medical schools—Wyoming, Montana, and Alaska. Admission factors counted most heavily include GPA, MCAT, the interview, and references. *Correspondence to:* Medical School Admissions.

MINORITY STUDENTS: Comprise 3% of the first-year class; most of these students receive aid. The application fee may be waived. *For additional information:* Center for Multicultural Enrichment.

---
*member AMCAS

University of Connecticut*

School of Medicine
263 Farmington Avenue
Farmington, CT 06030-1905
Tel: (860) 679-3874
E-mail: sanford@nso1.uchc.edu
www.uchc.edu

MCAT: required

GPA: 3.6

FOUNDED: 1968; *publicly controlled.*

ENROLLMENT: 40 men, 45 women (first-year).

TUITION & FEES: Resident, $24,142; Nonresident, $46,678.

APPLICATIONS: Should be submitted between June 1 and December 15; the application fee is $95. Notification begins October 15; response must be received within two weeks; a deposit is required to hold a place in class. Early Decision plan is available. Preference given to state residents. Admission factors include GPA, MCAT scores, undergraduate curriculum, extracurricular activities, and letters of recommendation. *Correspondence to:* Office of Admissions and Student Affairs.

MINORITY STUDENTS: Comprise 15% of the first-year class; most of these students receive aid. *For additional information:* Associate Dean, Minority Student Affairs.

----
*member AMCAS

University of Florida*
College of Medicine
Gainesville, FL 32610
Tel: (352) 392-4569
E-mail: robyn@dean.medufl.edu
www.med.ufl.edu

MCAT: required

GPA: 3.73

FOUNDED: 1956; *publicly controlled.*

ENROLLMENT: 70 men, 65 women (first-year).

TUITION & FEES: Resident, $23,930; Nonresident, $51,777.

APPLICATIONS: Should be submitted between June 1 and December 1; there is a $30 application fee. Notification begins October 15; response must be received within two weeks; no deposit needed to hold place in class. Preference is given to Florida residents. Admissions decisions are based on the MCAT, GPA, personal interview, and character. *Correspondence to:* Chair, Medical Selection Committee, Box 100216.

MINORITY STUDENTS: Comprise 16% of first-year students. Many types of financial assistance are available; students should apply upon enrollment. *For additional information:* Assistant Dean for Minority Relations.

---

*member AMCAS

University of Hawaii*
John A. Burns School of Medicine
651 Ilalo Street
Honolulu, HI 96813
Tel: (808) 692-1000
E-mail: mnishik@hawaii.edu
www.hawaiimed.hawaii.edu/

MCAT: required

GPA: 3.65

FOUNDED: 1961 as a two-year institution, introduced four-year program in 1973; *publicly controlled.*

ENROLLMENT: 28 men, 34 women (first-year).

TUITION & FEES: Resident, $22,632; Nonresident, $45,624.

APPLICATIONS: Should be submitted between June 1 and November 1; the application fee is $50. Notification begins October 15; response must be received within two weeks; no deposit required to hold place in class. Early Decision plan is available for residents of Hawaii. Preference given to state residents. Admission factors weighted most heavily include GPA, MCAT, interview, and letters of recommendation. *Correspondence to:* Office of Admissions.

MINORITY STUDENTS: Diverse ethnic backgrounds are represented in the faculty and student body. The School of Medicine sponsors 2 programs for students unable to enter directly into the normal medical program: a remedial program in the premedical sciences and a decelerated program permitting the student three years, with tutorial assistance, to complete the work normally completed in two years. These programs are designed primarily for, but are not limited to, persons of Hawaiian, part Hawaiian, Filipino, Samoan, and Micronesian ancestry. There is no application fee. *For additional information:* Student Affairs. Application for aid may be made upon acceptance.

---

*member AMCAS

University of Illinois at Chicago*
College of Medicine
808 South Wood Street m/c 783
Chicago, IL 60612
Tel: (312) 996-5635
E-mail: medadmit@uic.edu
www.medicine.uic.edu

MCAT: required

GPA: 3.7

FOUNDED: 1881; *publicly controlled.* College of Medicine programs are offered in four cities: Chicago, Urbana-Champaign, Peoria, and Rockford.

ENROLLMENT: 170 men, 137 women (first-year).

TUITION & FEES: Resident, $27,828; Nonresident, $56,724.

APPLICATIONS: Should be submitted between June 1 and November 15; the application fee is $70. Notification begins November 1; response must be received within two weeks; a deposit is required to reserve place in class. Early Decision plan is available for residents of Illinois. Strong preference is given to state residents. Admission factors counted most heavily include GPA, MCAT, letters of academic recommendation, and the personal statement in the AMCAS application. *Correspondence to:* Office of Admissions.

MINORITY STUDENTS: Comprise 11% of the first-year class; most of these students receive aid. Preadmissions counseling is provided and tutorial assistants are available to those students requiring additional instruction during the academic year. The application fee may be waived. *For additional information:* Associate Dean and Director of Urban Health Program. Application for aid should be made upon acceptance.

----

*member AMCAS

University of Iowa*
Ray J. and Lucille A. Carver College of Medicine
100 Medicine Administration Building
Iowa City, IA 52242-1101
Tel: (319) 335-8052
E-mail: medical-admission@uiowa.edu
www.medicine.uiowa.edu/osac

MCAT: required

GPA: 3.73

FOUNDED: 1850; *publicly controlled.*

ENROLLMENT: 77 men, 71 women (first-year).

TUITION & FEES: Resident, $26,113; Nonresident, $41,927.

APPLICATIONS: Should be submitted between June 1 and November 1; the application fee is $60. Notification begins October 15; response must be received within two weeks; a deposit is needed to hold place in class. Early Decision plan is available. Preference is given to state residents. Admission factors include GPA (science and overall), MCAT scores, and personal qualifications as judged from recommendations. *Correspondence to:* Office of Admissions.

MINORITY STUDENTS: Comprise 24% of the first-year class; most of these students receive aid. The application fee may be waived. The College of Medicine sponsors the Educational Opportunity Program, which provides financial and academic assistance for minority and disadvantaged students. A summer program is offered for entering students. *For additional information:* Program Associate for Equal Opportunity Programs.

---

*member AMCAS

University of Kansas*
School of Medicine
3901 Rainbow Boulevard
Kansas City, KS 66160-7301
Tel: (913) 588-5245
E-mail: premedinfo@kumc.edu
www.kumc.edu/som

MCAT: required

GPA: 3.7

FOUNDED: 1899 as a one-year institution, introduced four-year program in 1906; *publicly controlled.*

ENROLLMENT: 83 men, 93 women (first-year).

TUITION & FEES: Resident, $22,976; Nonresident, $40,367.

APPLICATIONS: Should be submitted between June 1 and October 15; the application fee is $50 for nonresidents. Notification begins February 1; response must be received within two weeks; a deposit is needed to reserve place in class. Early Decision plan is available. Preference is given to state residents; the class is first filled with Kansas residents, after which a few highly qualified nonresidents are accepted. Admission factors weighted most heavily include GPA, MCAT, premedical adviser's evaluation, interview, performance in required premedical courses, and trends in academic performance. *Correspondence to:* Office of Admissions.

MINORITY STUDENTS: Comprise 8% of the first-year class. The School of Medicine sponsors a prematriculation Summer Enrichment Program and an ongoing recruitment program, in addition to its tutorial and counseling programs for matriculated minority students. *For additional information:* Associate Dean for Minority Affairs. Applications for aid should be made upon acceptance.

---

*member AMCAS

University of Kentucky*
College of Medicine
800 Rose Street
Lexington, KY 40506-0084
Tel: (859) 323-6161
E-mail: kymedap@uky.edu
www.mc.uky.edu/medicine

MCAT: required

GPA: 3.6

FOUNDED: 1956; *publicly controlled.*

ENROLLMENT: 67 men, 46 women (first-year).

TUITION & FEES: Resident, $26,600; Nonresident, $49,670.

APPLICATIONS: Should be submitted between June 1 and November 1, the application fee is $50. Notification is rolling; response must be received within two weeks; a deposit is needed to hold place in class. Early Decision plan is available. Preference given to state residents. Admission factors weighted most heavily include GPA, MCAT scores, premedical letters of recommendation, extracurricular activities, exposure to medicine, and the personal interview. *Correspondence to:* Admissions, Room MN-102.

MINORITY STUDENTS: Comprise 6% of the first-year class: most of these students receive aid. The College of Medicine sponsors a prematriculation program—Med Prep—in which selected students participate in a 1-year academic and work experience in preparation for entering medical school. The Office of Special Student Programs maintains recruitment programs for minorities and women. Tutorial assistance is available during the academic year. *For additional information:* Assistant Dean for Education. Application for aid should be made in April (prior to matriculation).

---

*member AMCAS

University of Louisville*
School of Medicine
Health Sciences Center
Louisville, KY 40202
Tel: (502) 852-5193
E-mail: medadm@louisville.edu
www.louisville.edu/medschool

MCAT: required

GPA: 3.6

FOUNDED: 1833, acquired by state in 1970; *publicly controlled.*

ENROLLMENT: 87 men, 68 women (first-year).

TUITION & FEES: Resident, $27,330; Nonresident, $46,652.

APPLICATIONS: Should be submitted between June 1 and October 15; the application fee is $75. Notification begins October 1; response must be received within two weeks; a deposit is needed to hold place in class. Early Decision plan is available. Preference given to state residents. Admission factors counted most heavily include GPA, MCAT, motivation and personality as evaluated by interview, and extracurricular activities. *Correspondence to:* Office of Admissions.

MINORITY STUDENTS: Comprise 9% of the first-year class; most of these students receive aid. Tutorial assistance is arranged through the Office of Student Affairs for students of disadvantaged backgrounds and who express an interest in securing such help. The application fee may be waived. *For additional information:* Director of Special Programs. Application for aid should be made upon student's acceptance of offer of admission.

---

*member AMCAS

University of Maryland*
School of Medicine
655 West Baltimore Street, Suite 190
Baltimore, MD 21201-1559
Tel: (410) 706-7478
E-mail: mfoxwell@som.umaryland.edu
www.medschool.umaryland.edu

MCAT: required

GPA: 3.7

FOUNDED: 1808; *publicly controlled.*

ENROLLMENT: 67 men, 93 women (first-year).

TUITION & FEES: Resident, $21,988; Nonresident, $40,233.

APPLICATIONS: Should be submitted between June 1 and November 1; the application fee is $70. Notification begins October 15; response must be received within three weeks; no deposit needed to hold place in class. Early Decision plan is available. Preference given to state residents. Admission criteria weighted most heavily include GPA, MCAT, letters of recommendation, and interview. *Correspondence to:* Committee on Admissions, Room 1-005.

MINORITY STUDENTS: Comprise 19% of the first-year class. The application fee may be waived. *For additional information:* Assistant Dean of Student Affairs. Applications for aid are provided upon acceptance.

*member AMCAS

University of Massachusetts*
Medical School
55 Lake Avenue, North
Worcester, MA 01655
Tel: (508) 856-2323
E-mail: admissions@umassmed.edu
www.umassmed.edu

MCAT: required

GPA: 3.7 science

FOUNDED: 1962, admitted first class in 1970; *publicly controlled.*

ENROLLMENT: 46 men, 57 women (first-year).

TUITION & FEES: Resident, $13,414; Nonresident, not applicable.

APPLICATIONS: Should be submitted between June 1 and November 1; application fee is $75. Notification begins October 15; response must be received within two weeks; a deposit is needed to hold place in class. Early Decision plan is available. Currently, only residents of Massachusetts are considered for admission. Admissions decisions are based on the MCAT, GPA, letters of recommendation, character, maturity, and motivation. *Correspondence to:* Associate Dean of Admissions.

MINORITY STUDENTS: Comprise 10% of first-year students. Financial assistance is available; approximately 95% of all students receive aid. *For additional information:* Office of Minority and Community Academic Programs. Application for aid should be made after acceptance.

---

*member AMCAS

University of Miami*
Miller School of Medicine
P.O. Box 016159
Miami, FL 33101
Tel: (305) 243-6791
E-mail: med.admissions@miami.edu
www.miami.edu/medical-admissions

MCAT: required

GPA: 3.8

FOUNDED: 1952; *private*. A special program enables a person with a PhD degree in science or mathematics to earn an MD degree in two years.

ENROLLMENT: 101 men, 75 women (first-year).

TUITION & FEES: Resident, $30,048; Nonresident, $39,254.

APPLICATIONS: Should be submitted between June 1 and December 1; the application fee is $65. Notification begins October 15; response must be received within three weeks; a deposit is required to hold place in class. Preference is given to state residents. Admission factors counted most heavily include GPA, MCAT, faculty evaluations, motivation, and the personal interview. *Correspondence to:* Office of Admissions.

MINORITY STUDENTS: Comprise 6% of the first-year students; a majority of these students receive aid. A Committee on Minority Affairs is involved in recruitment and assistance to minority students. Tutorial programs are available. *For additional information:* Associate Dean for Minority Affairs.

----
*member AMCAS

University of Michigan*
Medical School
1301 East Catherine Street
Ann Arbor, MI 48109
Tel: (734) 764-6317
E-mail: umichmedadmiss@umich.edu
www.med.umich.edu/medschool

MCAT: required

GPA: 3.8

FOUNDED: 1850; *publicly controlled*. Combined eight-year program leading to the baccalaureate and MD degrees offered.

ENROLLMENT: 77 men, 93 women (first-year).

TUITION & FEES: Resident, $24,755; Nonresident, $39,119.

APPLICATIONS: Should be submitted between June 1 and November 15; the application fee is $85. Notification begins December 1; response deadline is flexible; a deposit is needed to hold place in class. Early Decision plan is available. Preference is given to state residents. Selection factors include academic achievement, MCAT scores, and personal qualifications as judged from the personal interview, letters of recommendation, and extracurricular activities. *Correspondence to:* Admissions Committee.

MINORITY STUDENTS: Comprise 7% of the first-year class; most of these students receive aid. A prematriculation summer program is available. *For additional information:* Assistant Dean for Student and Minority Affairs. Applications for aid should be made upon acceptance.

---
*member AMCAS

University of Minnesota
Medical School—Duluth Campus*

10 University Drive
Duluth, MN 55812
Tel: (218) 726-8511
E-mail: medadmis@d.umn.edu
www.semd.d.umn.edu

MCAT: required

GPA: 3.7

FOUNDED: 1972; *publicly controlled* two-year basic medical and clinical sciences school. Upon completion of the two-year program at Duluth, students transfer to the degree-granting program at the University of Minnesota at Minneapolis.

ENROLLMENT: 26 men, 33 women (first-year).

TUITION & FEES: Resident, $29,073; Nonresident, $36,606.

APPLICATIONS: Should be submitted between June 1 and November 15. Application fee is $75. Notification begins October 15; response must be received within two weeks; no deposit is needed to hold place in class. Early Decision plan is available. Strong preference is given to residents of Minnesota. Residents of Manitoba, Canada, and certain northern counties of Wisconsin may also be considered. Admission factors counted most heavily include GPA, MCAT, and potential to practice primary care in rural areas or small towns. *Correspondence to:* Office of Admissions, Room 107.

MINORITY STUDENTS: Comprise 12% of the first-year class. Resident tuition may be granted to minority nonresidents. The school sponsors a special program that offers preparation for health professions to American Indians. *For additional information:* Director, Center of American Indian and Minority Health. Application deadline for aid varies according to specific program applied to.

----

*member AMCAS

University of Minnesota*

Medical School—Minneapolis
420 Delaware Street, SE
Minneapolis, MN 55455-0310
Tel: (612) 625-7977
E-mail: meded@umn.edu
www.med.umn.edu

MCAT: required

GPA: 3.71

FOUNDED: 1888; *publicly supported.* The flexible program permits completion
of the four-year curriculum in three years.

ENROLLMENT: 92 men, 78 women (first-year).

TUITION & FEES: Resident, $29,975; Nonresident, $37,508.

APPLICATIONS: Should be submitted between June 1 and November 15; the
application fee is $75. Notification begins November 15; response must
be received within two weeks; no deposit is required to reserve place in
class. Early Decision plan is available. Preference is given to state residents.
Admissions decisions are based on the MCAT, GPA, and personal interview
as well as the honesty, dedication, and motivation of the applicant.
Correspondence to: Office of Admissions and Student Affairs.

MINORITY STUDENTS: Comprise 24% of first-year students. Financial aid is
available; resident tuition may be granted to minority nonresidents. *For
additional information:* Assistant to the Dean for Student Affairs. Application for aid should be made after notification of acceptance.

----
*member AMCAS

University of Mississippi*
School of Medicine
2500 North State Street
Jackson, MS 39216-4505
Tel: (601) 984-5010
E-mail: AdmitMD@som.umsmed.edu
www.som.umc.edu

MCAT: required

GPA: 3.64

FOUNDED: 1903 as a two-year school, introduced four-year program in 1955; *publicly controlled.*

ENROLLMENT: 55 men, 55 women (first-year).

TUITION & FEES: Resident, $11,649; Nonresident, $27,142.

APPLICATIONS: Should be submitted between June 1 and October 15. Application fee is $50. Notification begins October 15; response must be received within 15 days; a deposit is needed to hold place in class. Early Decision plan is available for Mississippi residents only. Preference given to state residents. Admission factors weighted most heavily include GPA, MCAT, motivation, and the personal interview. *Correspondence to:* Chairman, Admissions Committee.

MINORITY STUDENTS: Comprise 17% of the first-year class. The Office of Minority Student Affairs assists with recruitment. *For additional information:* Director of Minority Affairs. There is no deadline for financial aid applications.

---

*member AMCAS

University of Missouri—Columbia*
School of Medicine
One Hospital Drive
Columbia, MO 65212
Tel: (573) 882-9219
E-mail: mizzoumed@missouri.edu
www.muhealth.org~medicine

MCAT: required

GPA: 3.8

FOUNDED: 1841 as a two-year school, introduced four-year program in 1956; *publicly controlled.*

ENROLLMENT: 52 men, 44 women (first-year).

TUITION & FEES: Resident, $23,846; Nonresident, $46,432.

APPLICATIONS: Should be submitted between June 1 and November 1; application fee is $75. Notification begins December 15; response must be received within two weeks; a deposit is needed to reserve place in class. Early Decision plan is available. Preference is given to state residents. Admission criteria include academic performance, MCAT results, and personal qualifications as evaluated from letters of recommendation, the personal interview, and the formal application. *Correspondence to:* Office of Admissions, MA202 Medical Sciences Building.

MINORITY STUDENTS: Most of these students receive aid. The School of Medicine sponsors flexible curriculum alternatives and summer enrichment programs for students of disadvantaged backgrounds. *For additional information:* Assistant Dean for Minority Affairs.

University of Missouri—Kansas City
School of Medicine
2411 Holmes
Kansas City, MO 64108
Tel: (816) 235-1870
E-mail: umkcmedweb@umkc.edu
www.umkc.edu/medicine

MCAT: not required   **ACT:** required

GPA: not available

FOUNDED: 1971; *publicly controlled.* The School of Medicine sponsors only a combined six-year program, in cooperation with the College of Arts and Sciences, leading to the baccalaureate and MD degrees.

ENROLLMENT: 38 men, 56 women (first-year).

TUITION & FEES: Resident, $28,228; Nonresident, $55,161.

APPLICATIONS: Should be submitted between August 1 and November 15. Notification begins April 1; response must be received by May 1; a deposit is needed to hold place in class. Residency in Missouri is of prime consideration. Admissions requirements include demonstrated ability to perform on a college level based on a combination of high school rank and scores on a standardized college aptitude test. Personal qualities such as leadership, stamina, reliability, motivation for medicine, and range of interests are also considered. *Correspondence to:* Admissions Office.

MINORITY STUDENTS: Aid is available to medical students. *For additional information:* Director, Office of Minority Affairs. Application for aid should be made by March 15.

University of Nebraska*
Medical Center
85517 Nebraska Medical Center
Omaha, NE 68198-6585
Tel: (402) 559-2259
E-mail: johara@unmc.edu
www.unmc.edu/uncom

MCAT: required

GPA: 3.7

FOUNDED: 1902; *publicly controlled.*

ENROLLMENT: 51 men, 73 women (first-year).

TUITION & FEES: Resident, $23,307; Nonresident, $54,653.

APPLICATIONS: Should be submitted between June 1 and November 1; the application fee is $45. Notification begins January 3; response must be received within two weeks; a deposit is needed to hold place in class. Strong preference is given to state residents. Admission criteria include scholastic record, MCAT scores, letters of recommendation, and the personal interview. *Correspondence to:* Office of the Dean—Admissions, Room 5021, Wittson Hall.

MINORITY STUDENTS: Comprise 4% of first-year students; a majority of these students receive aid. Academic assistance is made available to students who require such help. *For additional information:* Director Multicultural Affairs.

----

*member AMCAS

University of Nevada*
School of Medicine
Mail Stop 357
Reno, NV 89557-0046
Tel: (775) 784-6063
E-mail: asa@med.unr.edu
www.medicine.nevada.edu

MCAT: required

GPA: 3.6

FOUNDED: 1969 as two-year basic science school; in 1977 expanded to a four-year program granting the MD degree; *publicly controlled.*

ENROLLMENT: 29 men, 33 women (first-year).

TUITION & FEES: Resident, $13,520; Nonresident, $31,885.

APPLICATIONS: Should be submitted between June 1 and November l; the application fee is $45. Notification begins January 15; response must be received within four weeks; no deposit needed to hold place in class. Early Decision plan is available. Strong preference is given to state residents. The remaining places are filled with first preference to residents of WICHE[1] states without medical schools (Alaska, Montana, and Wyoming), followed by candidates from other WICHE states. Admission factors include GPA, MCAT scores, college attended, letters of recommendation, and health care experience. *Correspondence to:* Office of Admissions.

MINORITY STUDENTS: Comprise 7% of the first-year class. The application fee may be waived. *For additional information:* Director of Recruitment. Application for aid should be made after acceptance, prior to May 1.

----

*member AMCAS
[1]WICHE = Western Interstate Commission for Higher Education

University of New Mexico*
School of Medicine
Albuquerque, NM 87173-5166
Tel: (505) 272-4766
E-mail: somadmissions@salud.unm.edu
hsc.unm.edu/som/admissions

MCAT: required

GPA: 3.6

FOUNDED: 1961; *publicly controlled.*

ENROLLMENT: 33 men, 42 women (first-year).

TUITION & FEES: Resident, $14,671; Nonresident, $42,043.

APPLICATIONS: Should be submitted between July 1 and November 15; the application fee is $50. Notification begins March 15; response must be received within four weeks; no deposit needed to secure position in class. Early Decision plan is available; nonresidents must apply through EDP. Preference is given to state residents and residents of western states without medical schools (Alaska, Montana, and Wyoming). Admission factors include academic performance, MCAT scores, letters of recommendation, and the personal interview. *Correspondence to:* Office of Admissions, Room 107, Basic Medical Sciences Building.

MINORITY STUDENTS: Comprise 40% of first-year students; most of these students receive aid. The School of Medicine sponsors a special Summer Basic Science Course for minority students of disadvantaged backgrounds, in addition to its recruitment program for such students. *For additional information:* Office of Cultural and Ethnic Programs.

----

*member AMCAS

University of North Carolina*
Chapel Hill School of Medicine
CB 9500 121 McNider Building
Chapel Hill, NC 27599-7000
E-mail: randee_alston@med.unc.edu
www.med.unc.edu

MCAT: required

GPA: 3.8

FOUNDED: 1879, became four-year school 1952; *publicly controlled.*

ENROLLMENT: 79 men, 82 women (first-year).

TUITION & FEES: Resident, $11,964; Nonresident, $35,630.

APPLICATIONS: Should be submitted between June 1 and November 15; the application fee is $65. Notification begins October 15; response must be received by school within three weeks; a deposit is needed to hold place in class. Early Decision plan is available. Preference is given to state residents. The percentage of women enrolled usually reflects trends in the distribution of the applicant pool. Selection factors include academic achievement, personal qualifications, and potential for medicine. *Correspondence to:* Admissions Office, CB9500 121 McNider Building.

MINORITY STUDENTS: Comprise 12% of the first-year class; most of these students receive aid. The School of Medicine sponsors an elective Summer Medical Sciences Program for minority and disadvantaged students. The Admissions Committee includes both minority students and faculty. *For additional information:* Dr. Marion Phillips, Associate Dean.

----

*member AMCAS

University of North Dakota
School of Medicine and Health Sciences
501 North Columbia Road, Box 9037
Grand Forks, ND 58202-9037
Tel: (701) 777-4221
E-mail: jdheit@med.nodak.edu
www.med.und.nodak.edu

MCAT: required

GPA: 3.7

FOUNDED: 1905 as a two-year basic science school; 1981 introduced a full four-year program; *publicly controlled.*

ENROLLMENT: 26 men, 36 women (first-year).

TUITION & FEES: Resident, $22,515; Nonresident, $41,675.

APPLICATIONS: Should be submitted between July 1 and November 1; the application fee is $50. Notification begins December 15; response should be received by school within four weeks; a deposit is needed to hold place in class. Strong preference given to state residents; any remaining places will be filled with preference to residents of neighboring western states without medical schools (Alaska, Montana, and Wyoming). Admission criteria include academic record, MCAT results, letters of recommendation, and the personal interview. *Correspondence to:* Secretary, Committee on Admissions.

MINORITY STUDENTS: Comprise 13% of the first year class; 95% of these students receive aid. The School of Medicine sponsors a special recruitment program, INMED, to encourage applications from Native Americans; approximately 5 places in the entering class are reserved for students accepted under this program. *For additional information:* Director, INMED Program. Application for aid should be made upon acceptance.

University of Oklahoma*
College of Medicine
P.O. Box 26901
Oklahoma City, OK 73162
Tel: (405) 271-2331
E-mail: adminmed@uohsc.edu
www.medicine.uohsc.edu/admissions

MCAT: required

GPA: 3.8

FOUNDED: 1910; *publicly controlled.*

ENROLLMENT: 102 men, 64 women (first-year).

TUITION & FEES: Resident, $17,945; Nonresident, $42,063.

APPLICATIONS: Should be submitted between June 1 and October 15; the application fee is $65. Notification begins December 1; response must be received by school within two weeks; a deposit is needed to hold place in class. Preference is given to state residents. Admissions decisions based on the MCAT, GPA, recommendations, and personal interview. *Correspondence to:* Admissions.

MINORITY STUDENTS: Comprise 21% of first-year students. A majority of these students receive aid. Students may apply upon acceptance. *For additional information:* Office of Recruitment and Multicultural Affairs.

---

*member AMCAS

University of Pennsylvania*
School of Medicine
Suite 100, Stemmler Hall
3450 Hamilton Walk
Philadelphia, PA 19104
Tel: (215) 898-8001
E-mail: admiss@mail.med.upenn.edu
www.med.upenn.edu

MCAT: required

GPA: 3.8

FOUNDED: 1765; *private.*

ENROLLMENT: 74 men, 79 women (first-year).

TUITION & FEES: Resident, $42,873; Nonresident, $42,873.

APPLICATIONS: Should be submitted between June 1 and October 15; the application fee is $80. Notification begins in February; response must be received by school within two weeks; a deposit is needed to hold place in class. Admission criteria include performance in academic courses, record of extracurricular activities and community service, MCAT scores, and character as judged by the Committee on Admissions. *Correspondence to:* Director of Admissions, Suite 100, Medical Education Building.

MINORITY STUDENTS: Comprise 10% of the first-year class; most of these students receive aid. *For additional information:* Director, Minority Affairs. Application for aid may be submitted upon acceptance.

---

*member AMCAS

University of Pittsburgh*
School of Medicine
Pittsburgh, PA 15261
Tel: (412) 648-9891
E-mail: admissions@medschool.pitt.edu
www.medschool.pitt.edu

MCAT: required

GPA: 3.7

FOUNDED: 1886; *state-related.*

ENROLLMENT: 88 men, 59 women (first-year).

TUITION & FEES: Resident, $36,752; Nonresident, $40,772.

APPLICATIONS: Should be submitted between June 1 and November 1; the application fee is $25. Notification begins October 15; response must be received within two weeks; a deposit is needed to hold place in class. Early Decision plan is available. Selection factors include scholastic achievement, MCAT results, letters of recommendation, extracurricular activities, and the personal interview. *Correspondence to:* Office of Admissions, Scaife Hall.

MINORITY STUDENTS: Comprise about 16% of first-year students. Most of these students receive aid. *For additional information:* Director, Minority Programs. Applications for aid may be submitted by accepted students.

---

*member AMCAS

University of Puerto Rico*
School of Medicine
P.O. Box 365067
San Juan, PR 00963-5067
Tel: (787) 743-3038
www.md.rcm.upr.edu

MCAT: required

GPA: not available.

FOUNDED: 1949; *publicly controlled.*

ENROLLMENT: 60 men, 60 women (first-year).

TUITION & FEES: Resident, $18,770; Nonresident, $34,801.

APPLICATIONS: Should be submitted between June 1 and December 15; the application fee is $75. Notification begins December 15; response must be received by school within 15 days; a deposit is needed to hold place in class. Preference is given to residents. Admission criteria counted most heavily include GPA, MCAT, recommendations, personal interview, and extracurricular activities. Application for aid may be made with application for admission or after acceptance. *Correspondence to:* Central Admissions Office.

---

*member AMCAS

University of Rochester*
School of Medicine
601 Elmwood Avenue
Rochester, NY 14642-8601
Tel: (585) 275-4539
E-mail: mdadmish@urmc.rochester.edu
www.urmc.rochester.edu/smd

MCAT: required

GPA: 3.7

FOUNDED: 1920; *private.*

ENROLLMENT: 50 men, 54 women (first-year).

TUITION & FEES: Resident, $38,700; Nonresident, $38,700.

APPLICATIONS: Should be submitted between June 1 and October 15; the application fee is $75. Notification begins December 15; the response must be received within two weeks; no deposit needed to hold place in class. Admission factors weighted most heavily include GPA, with specific emphasis on performance in the natural sciences. Candidates are also expected to provide evidence of a varied background, intellectual curiosity, and demonstrated commitment. *Correspondence to:* Director of Admissions.

MINORITY STUDENTS: Comprise 19% of the first-year class; most of these students receive aid. Tutorial assistance and remedial work are provided for all students who exhibit special academic needs. *For additional information:* Associate Dean for Ethnic and Multicultural Affairs. Application for aid can be made either at the time of application or upon acceptance.

----

*member AMCAS

University of South Alabama*
College of Medicine
Mobile, AL 36688-0002
Tel: (251) 460-7176
www.southalabama.edu/com

MCAT: required

GPA: 3.7

FOUNDED: 1969, accepted first class in 1973; *publicly controlled.*

ENROLLMENT: 42 men, 32 women (first-year).

TUITION & FEES: Resident, $16,082; Nonresident, $29,562.

APPLICATIONS: Should be submitted between June 1 and November 15; the application fee is $75. Notification begins October 15; response must be received within two weeks; a deposit is needed to hold place in class. Early Decision plan is available for Alabama residents only. Preference given to state residents. Admission factors counted most heavily include GPA, MCAT, premedical advisory committee recommendations, and personal interview. *Correspondence to:* Office of Admissions.

MINORITY STUDENTS: Comprise 7% of first-year students. The application fee may be waived. *For additional information:* Assistant Dean for Special Programs. Application for aid should be made upon acceptance.

---

*member AMCAS

University of South Carolina*
School of Medicine
Columbia, SC 29208
Tel: (803) 733-3325
E-mail: jeanette@gw.med.sc.edu
www.med.sc.edu

MCAT: required

GPA: 3.5

FOUNDED: 1974, first class admitted 1977; *publicly controlled.*

ENROLLMENT: 43 men, 43 women (first-year).

TUITION & FEES: Resident, $24,776; Nonresident, $60,458.

APPLICATIONS: Should be submitted between June 1 and January 15; the application fee is $75. Notification begins October 15; response must be received within two weeks; a deposit is needed to hold place in class. Early Decision plan is available. Preference is given to state residents. Selection factors include academic and personal qualifications. *Correspondence to:* Associate Dean for Student Programs.

MINORITY STUDENTS: Comprise 5% of the first-year class. *For additional information:* Associate Dean for Student Programs.

----
*member AMCAS

University of South Dakota*
Sanford School of Medicine
414 East Clark Street
Vermillion, SD 57069
Tel: (605) 677-5233
E-mail: sdadmissions@usd.edu
www.usd.edu/med/md

MCAT: required

GPA: 3.8

FOUNDED: 1907 as two-year school, became four-year school in 1974; *publicly controlled.*

ENROLLMENT: 29 men, 25 women (first-year).

TUITION & FEES: Resident, $15,281; Nonresident, $36,603.

APPLICATIONS: Should be submitted between June 1 and November 15; the application fee is $35. Notification begins December 23; response must be received by school within two weeks; a deposit is needed to hold place in class. Strong preference is given to state residents. Applicants are selected on the basis of academic achievement as indicated on all scholastic records, MCAT, curiosity, study habits, learning ability, and fitness for the study of medicine as perceived by their instructors and estimates of character, motivation, and intellect as observed during the personal interview. Application for aid is made after fall classes begin. *Correspondence to:* Office of Student Affairs, Room 105.

MINORITY STUDENTS: Comprise 1% of the first-year class. *For additional information:* Minority Affairs Officer.

---

*member AMCAS

University of South Florida*
College of Medicine
12901 Bruce B. Downs Boulevard
Tampa, FL 33612-4799
Tel: (813) 974-2229
E-mail: md-admissions@health.usf.edu
www.hsc.usf.edu

MCAT: required

GPA: 3.7

FOUNDED: 1965, accepted first class in 1971; *publicly controlled.*

ENROLLMENT: 57 men, 63 women (first-year).

TUITION & FEES: Resident, $21,000; Nonresident, $53,000.

APPLICATIONS: Should be submitted between July 6 and December 1; the application fee is $30. Notifications begin October 15; response must be received within two weeks; no deposit is necessary to hold a place in class. Early Decision plan is available for Florida residents only. Strong preference given to state residents. Admissions criteria include the MCAT, GPA, letters of recommendation, personal interviews, character, and motivation. *Correspondence to:* Admissions Office, Box 3.

MINORITY STUDENTS: Comprise 13% of the first-year class; some financial assistance is available. *For additional information:* Coordinator for Minority Affairs.

---

*member AMCAS

University of Tennessee, Health Science Center*

College of Medicine
910 Madison Avenue
Memphis, TN 38163
Tel: (901) 448-5559
E-mail: nstroter@utmem.edu
www.utmem.edu/medicine

MCAT: required

GPA: 3.6

FOUNDED: 1851; merged with University of Tennessee in 1911; *publicly controlled.*

ENROLLMENT: 88 men, 62 women (first-year).

TUITION & FEES: Resident, $19,385; Nonresident, $37,297.

APPLICATIONS: Should be submitted between June 1 and November 15; the application fee is $50. Notification begins October 15; response must be received within two weeks; a deposit is needed to hold place in class. Strong preference is given to state residents. Admission factors counted most heavily include GPA, MCAT, course load and content, extracurricular activities, work experience, personal interview, recommendations, and evaluations. *Correspondence to:* Director of Admissions.

MINORITY STUDENTS: Comprise 13% of the first-year class. *For additional information:* Assistant Dean for Student Affairs. Application for aid should be submitted after acceptance.

---

*member AMCAS

University of Texas
Southwestern Medical School at Dallas
5323 Harry Hines Boulevard
Dallas, TX 75390
Tel: (214) 648-5617
E-mail: admissions@utsouthwestern.edu
www.utsouthwestern.edu

MCAT: required

GPA: 3.81

FOUNDED: 1943, acquired by state 1949; *publicly controlled.*

ENROLLMENT: 109 men, 111 women (first-year).

TUITION & FEES: Resident, $12,100; Nonresident, $25,200.

APPLICATIONS: Should be submitted between May 1 and October 15; the application fee is $65. Notification begins January 15; response must be received within two weeks; no deposit needed to hold place in class. Preference is given to state residents. Admission factors weighted most heavily include GPA, MCAT, the personal interview, and preprofessional advisory committee recommendations. All applications are processed by the University of Texas System Medical and Dental Application Center, Suite 620, 702 Colorado, Austin, TX 78701. *Correspondence to:* Office of the Registrar.

MINORITY STUDENTS: Comprise 49% of the first-year class. Tutorial assistants are available for those who require additional academic help. *For additional information:* Assistant Dean for Minority Student Affairs.

University of Texas
Medical Branch at Galveston
301 University Boulevard
Galveston, TX 77555
Tel: (409) 772-3517
E-mail: tsilva@utmb.edu
www.som.utmb.edu

MCAT: required

GPA: 3.8

FOUNDED: 1891; *publicly controlled.* The School of Medicine offers a three-year program leading to the MD degree in addition to the four-year curriculum.

ENROLLMENT: 122 men, 125 women (first-year).

TUITION & FEES: Resident, $6,550; Nonresident, $19,650.

APPLICATIONS: Should be submitted between May 1 and October 1; there is no application fee. Notification begins January 15; response must be received by school within two weeks; no deposit needed to hold place in class. Preference is given to state residents. Admission factors counted most heavily include GPA, MCAT, letters of recommendation, and the personal interview. All applications are processed by the University of Texas System Medical and Dental Application Center, Suite 620, 702 Colorado, Austin, TX 78701. *Correspondence to:* Office of Admissions, Ashbel Smith Building, G-210.

MINORITY STUDENTS: Comprise 23% of the first-year class; most of these students receive aid. The School of Medicine sponsors a Summer Orientation program and an ongoing tutorial program for minority and disadvantaged students. A Minority Student Office provides special training and counseling programs. *For additional information:* Associate Dean for Student Affairs. Application for aid should be made after acceptance.

University of Texas
Medical School at Houston
P.O. Box 20708
Houston, TX 77030
Tel: (713) 500-5116
E-mail: msadmissions@uth.tmc.edu
www.med.uth.tmc.edu

MCAT: required

GPA: 3.7

FOUNDED: 1972; *publicly controlled.*

ENROLLMENT: 137 men, 93 women (first-year).

TUITION & FEES: Resident, $9,775; Nonresident, $22,875.

APPLICATIONS: Should be submitted between May 1 and October 1; the application fee is $55. Notification begins January 15; response must be received by school within two weeks, no deposit needed to hold place in class. Preference is given to state residents. Selection factors include GPA, MCAT results, premedical advisory committee recommendations, personal interviews, as well as evidence of leadership and potential for medicine. All applications are processed by the University of Texas System Medical and Dental Application Center, Suite 620, 702 Colorado, Austin, TX 78701. *Correspondence to:* Office of Admissions, Room G-024.

MINORITY STUDENTS: Comprise 21% of the first-year class. *For additional information:* Associate Dean for Educational Programs.

University of Texas
Medical School at San Antonio
7703 Floyd Curl Drive
San Antonio, TX 78229
Tel: (210) 567-6080
E-mail: medadmissions@uthscsa.edu
www.som.uthscsa.edu

MCAT: required

GPA: 3.5

FOUNDED: 1959, first class matriculated in 1966; *publicly controlled.*

ENROLLMENT: 111 men, 110 women (first-year).

TUITION & FEES: Resident, $11,970; Nonresident, $27,157.

APPLICATIONS: Should be submitted between May 1 and October 1; there is a $55 application fee. Notification begins January 15; response should be received within two weeks; no deposit needed to hold place in class. Preference is given to state residents. Admission criteria include academic background, MCAT scores, recommendations from premedical adviser, achievements in areas other than academics, maturity, and motivation. All applications are processed by the University of Texas System Medical and Dental Application Center, Suite 620, 702 Colorado, Austin, TX 78701. *Correspondence to:* Registrar.

MINORITY STUDENTS: Comprise 23% of first-year students; most of these students receive aid. There are affirmative action programs for the women and minority applicants, students, and staff of the Health Science Center. *For additional information:* Associate Dean for Student Affairs.

University of Toledo
College of Medicine*

3045 Arlington Avenue
Toledo, OH 43614
Tel: (419) 383-4229
E-mail: medadmissions@utuet.utoledo.edu
www.usc.utoledo.edu

MCAT: required

GPA: 3.6

FOUNDED: 1964; *publicly controlled.*

ENROLLMENT: 98 men, 78 women (first-year).

TUITION & FEES: Resident, $24,072; Nonresident, $51,508.

APPLICATIONS: Should be submitted between June 15 and November 1; the application fee is $80. Notification begins October 15; response must be received by school within two weeks; no deposit needed to hold place in class. Early Decision plan is available to Ohio residents only. Preference is given to state residents. *Correspondence to:* Admissions Office.

MINORITY STUDENTS: Comprise 5% of the first-year class. *For additional information:* Associate Dean of Minority Affairs.

*member AMCAS

University of Utah*
School of Medicine
30 North 1900 East, Room 1C029
Salt Lake City, UT 84132
Tel: (801) 581-7498
E-mail: deans.admissions@hsc.utah.edu
www.uuhsc.utah.edu/som

MCAT: required

GPA: 3.7

FOUNDED: 1905 as a two-year school, introduced four-year program in 1943; *publicly controlled.*

ENROLLMENT: 70 men, 32 women (first-year).

TUITION & FEES: Resident, $20,692; Nonresident, $38,528.

APPLICATIONS: Should be submitted between June 1 and November 1; the application fee is $100. Notification begins November 1; response must be received within two weeks; a deposit is needed to hold place in class. Early Decision plan is available; nonresidents must apply through EDP. Preference is given to state residents. Approximately one half of the out-of-state students are residents of western states without medical schools (Alaska, Montana, and Wyoming). Applicants are considered on the basis of scholarship, evaluation by premedical instructors, MCAT scores, personality, and motivation. *Correspondence to:* Director, Medical School Admissions.

MINORITY STUDENTS: The Admissions Committee has an active subcommittee on minority admissions recruiting qualified minority students. *For additional information:* Coordinator, Minority Affairs. The school notifies incoming freshmen when it is time to submit applications for aid.

---

*member AMCAS

University of Vermont*
College of Medicine
89 Beaumont Avenue
Burlington, VT 05405-0068
Tel: (802) 656-2154
E-mail: medadmissions@uvm.edu
www.med.uvm.edu

MCAT: required

GPA: 3.7

FOUNDED: 1822; *publicly controlled.*

ENROLLMENT: 56 men, 58 women (first-year).

TUITION & FEES: Resident, $26,280; Nonresident, $46,700.

APPLICATIONS: Should be received between June 1 and November 1; the application fee is $85. Notification begins in December; response must be received within two weeks; a deposit is required to hold place in class. Preference is given to residents of Vermont and Maine. Admission criteria include GPA, MCAT, the personal interview, and letters of evaluation from faculty. *Correspondence to:* Admissions Office, C-225, Given Building.

MINORITY STUDENTS: Comprise 11% of the first-year class. *For additional information:* Associate Dean for Admissions. Application for aid should be made after acceptance.

---

*member AMCAS

University of Virginia*
School of Medicine
P.O. Box 800725
Charlottesville, VA 22908
Tel: (434) 924-5571
E-mail: bab7g@virginia.edu
www.med.virginia.edu/home.html

MCAT: required

GPA: 3.73

FOUNDED: 1824; *publicly controlled.*

ENROLLMENT: 76 men, 66 women (first-year).

TUITION & FEES: Resident, $32,650; Nonresident, $42,650.

APPLICATIONS: Must be received between June 1 and November 1; the application fee is $75. Notification begins October 15; response must be received within three weeks; no deposit required to hold place in class. Preference is given to state residents. Admission factors weighted most heavily include the MCAT, GPA, recommendations, interview, and personal qualities. *Correspondence to:* Director of Admissions.

MINORITY STUDENTS: Comprise 27% of the first-year class. There are various scholarships and loans available to students. The application fee may be waived. *For additional information:* Associate Dean.

---

*member AMCAS

University of Washington*
School of Medicine
Seattle, WA 98195-6340
Tel: (206) 543-7212
E-mail: askuwsom@u.washington.edu
www.uw.medicine.org/education/mdprogram

MCAT: required

GPA: 3.7

FOUNDED: 1945; *publicly controlled.* In 1971 the School of Medicine introduced the WAMI program, a decentralized curriculum in which students may take part of their elective phase (third and fourth years) at community clinical units away from the University.

ENROLLMENT: 89 men, 102 women (first-year).

TUITION & FEES: Resident, $17,425; Nonresident, $41,429.

APPLICATIONS: Should be submitted between June 1 and November 3; the application fee is $35. Notification begins November 1; response must be received within two weeks; a deposit is needed to hold place in class. Preference is given to residents of Washington and western states without medical schools (particularly Alaska, Montana, and Idaho). Candidates are considered comparatively on the basis of academic performance, medical aptitude, motivation, maturity, and demonstrated humanitarian qualities. *Correspondence to:* Admissions Office, Health Sciences Center A-300.

MINORITY STUDENTS: Comprise 1% of the first-year class. *For additional information:* Director, Minority Affairs Program. Applications for aid should be made after acceptance.

*member AMCAS

University of Wisconsin*
Madison School of Medicine and Public Health
750 Highland Avenue
Madison, WI 53705
Tel: (608) 263-4925
E-mail: jyshepard@wisc.edu
www.med.wisc.edu

MCAT: required

GPA: 3.7

FOUNDED: 1907 as a two-year school, introduced four-year program in 1924; *publicly controlled.*

ENROLLMENT: 76 men, 87 women (first-year).

TUITION & FEES: Resident, $23,060; Nonresident, $34,190.

APPLICATIONS: Should be submitted between June 1 and November 1; the application fee is $56. Notification begins November 1; response must be received within two weeks; no deposit needed to hold place in class. Early Decision plan is available for Wisconsin residents only. Preference is given to state residents. Admission factors include academic performance, MCAT results, and personal qualifications as judged from interviews and letters of recommendation. *Correspondence to:* Admissions Committee, Medical Sciences Center.

MINORITY STUDENTS: Comprise 11% of first-year students; most of these students receive aid. *For additional information:* Assistant Dean, Minority Affairs. Applications for aid should be made upon acceptance.

---

*member AMCAS

Vanderbilt University*

School of Medicine

21st Avenue South at Garland Avenue
Nashville, TN 37232
Tel: (615) 322-2145
E-mail: pat.sageh@vanderbilt.edu
www.mc.vanderbilt.edu/medschool

MCAT: required

GPA: 3.78

FOUNDED: 1873; *private.*

ENROLLMENT: 54 men, 51 women (first-year).

TUITION & FEES: Resident, $38,400; Nonresident, $38,400.

APPLICATIONS: Should be submitted between June 1 and November 15; the application fee is $50. Notification begins October 15; response must be received by school within two weeks; no deposit needed to hold place in class. Early Decision plan is available. Admission factors weighted most heavily include GPA, MCAT, recommendations, and evidence of motivation. *Correspondence to:* Office of Admissions, 109 Light Hall.

MINORITY STUDENTS: Comprise 19% of the first-year class. The application fee may be waived. The School of Medicine seeks to enroll a diversified entering class and encourages application from women and members of ethnic minority groups currently underrepresented in medicine. *For additional information:* Director, Office of Minority Student Affairs. Application for aid should be made by June 1.

----

*member AMCAS

Virginia Commonwealth University*

School of Medicine
P.O. Box 980565
Richmond, VA 23298-0565
Tel: (804) 828-9629
E-mail: somadm@hsc.vcu.edu
www.medschool.vcu.edu

MCAT: required

GPA: 3.6

FOUNDED: 1838; *publicly controlled.* The School of Medicine offers the option to earn the MD degree in three years.

ENROLLMENT: 104 men, 88 women (first-year).

TUITION & FEES: Resident, $25,644; Nonresident, $39,281.

APPLICATIONS: Should be submitted between June 1 and October 15; the application fee is $80. Notification begins October 15; response must be received within two weeks; a deposit is needed to hold place in class. Early Decision plan is available. Preference given to state residents. Admission factors counted most heavily include GPA, MCAT, personal characteristics, premedical evaluations, and interviews. *Correspondence to:* Admissions.

MINORITY STUDENTS: Comprise 6% of the first-year class; most of these students receive aid. *For additional information:* Medical School Admissions. Application for aid should be made upon acceptance.

----

*member AMCAS

Virginia Tech*
Carilion School of Medicine and Research Institute
2 Riverside Circle, Suite M140
Roanoke, VA 24016
Tel: (540) 526-2500
E-mail: jrlemons@carilionclinic.org
www.vtc.vt.edu

MCAT: required

GPA: 3.5

FOUNDED: 2009; *publicly controlled.*

ENROLLMENT: 30 men, 12 women (first-year).

TUITION & FEES: Resident, $42,600; Nonresident, $42,600.

APPLICATIONS: Should be submitted between June 1 and December 1. Admission criteria include MCAT scores, GPA, general academic background, letters of recommendation, and personal qualifications as judged by the admissions committee.

MINORITY STUDENTS: The school has an active minority recruitment program.

----

*member AMCAS

Wake Forest University*
School of Medicine
Winston-Salem, NC 27157-1090
Tel: (336) 716-4264
E-mail: medadmit@wfubmc.edu
www.wfubmc.edu

MCAT: required

GPA: 3.7

FOUNDED: 1902 as two-year school, became four-year school in 1941; *private*. A Parallel Curriculum is problem- rather than discipline-based and emphasizes critical thinking and clinical reasoning; not all students participate.

ENROLLMENT: 75 men, 47 women (first-year).

TUITION & FEES: Resident, $38,248; Nonresident, $38,248.

APPLICATIONS: Should be submitted between June 1 and November 1; the application fee is $55. Notification begins November 1; response must be received by school within two weeks; a deposit is needed to hold place in class. Admissions decisions are based on the MCAT, GPA, letters of recommendation, interview, and personal characteristics. *Correspondence to:* Office of Medical School Admissions.

MINORITY STUDENTS: Comprise 11% of first-year students. A summer program is available to entering minority students. *For additional information:* Director of Minority Affairs.

----

*member AMCAS

The Warren Albert Medical School of Brown University*

97 Waterman Street, Box GA213
Providence, RI 02912-9706
Tel: (401) 863-2149
E-mail: medschool_admissions@brown.edu
www.bms.brown.edu

MCAT: required only for Brown-Dartmouth Medical Program

GPA: 3.8

FOUNDED: 1975; *private*. Eight-year combined BA–MD program; certain students also accepted to four-year degree-granting program, entering in the fourth year of the eight-year program.

ENROLLMENT: 42 men, 53 women (first-year).

TUITION & FEES: Resident, $38,672; Nonresident, $38,672.

APPLICATIONS: Should be submitted between June 1 and November 1; the application fee is $95. Notification begins March 15; response must be received within three weeks; no deposit is required to hold place in class. Admission factors weighted most heavily include GPA, letters of recommendation, personal qualities, and the interview. *Correspondence to:* Office of Admissions and Financial Aid.

MINORITY STUDENTS: Comprise approximately 7% of the first-year class. *For additional information:* Associate Dean. Application for aid should be made upon acceptance.

----

*member AMCAS

Washington University*

School of Medicine
660 South Euclid Avenue
St. Louis, MO 63110
Tel: (314) 362-6858
E-mail: wumscoa@wustl.edu
www.medschool.wustl.edu

MCAT: required

GPA: 3.87

FOUNDED: 1899; *private.*

ENROLLMENT: 63 men, 49 women (first-year).

TUITION & FEES: Resident, $45,550; Nonresident, $45,550.

APPLICATIONS: Should be submitted between June 15 and November 30; the application fee is $50. Notifications begins October 15; response must be received within two weeks; a deposit is needed to hold place in class. Admissions decisions are based on the MCAT, GPA, extracurricular activities, personal interview, motivation, character, and attitude. *Correspondence to:* Committee on Admissions.

MINORITY STUDENTS: Comprise 11% of first-year students. *For additional information:* Minority Admissions. Application for aid may be filed upon acceptance.

----

*member AMCAS

Wayne State University*
School of Medicine
540 East Canfield Avenue
Detroit, MI 48201
Tel: (313) 577-1466
E-mail: admissions@med.wayne.edu
www.med.wayne.edu

MCAT: required

GPA: 3.7

FOUNDED: 1868; *publicly controlled.*

ENROLLMENT: 181 men, 121 women (first-year).

TUITION & FEES: Resident, $28,660; Nonresident, $56,656.

APPLICATIONS: Should be submitted between June 1 and December 15; the application fee is $50. Notification begins October 15; response must be received within three weeks; a deposit is required to hold place in class. Early Decision plan is available. Wayne State gives preference to state residents. Admission criteria include academic record, MCAT scores, interview, recommendations, and personal character. *Correspondence to:* Director of Admissions.

MINORITY STUDENTS: Comprise 8% of first-year students; most of these students receive aid. *For additional information:* Student Affairs. Application for aid should be made after acceptance.

Weill Medical College of Cornell University*

445 East 69th Street
New York, NY 10021
Tel: (212) 746-1067
E-mail: wcumc-admissions@med.cornell.edu
www.med.cornell.edu

MCAT: required

GPA: 3.8

FOUNDED: 1898; *private.*

ENROLLMENT: 48 men, 53 women (first-year).

TUITION & FEES: Resident, $40,890; Nonresident, $40,890.

APPLICATIONS: Should be submitted between June 1 and October 15; the application fee is $75. Notification begins October 15; response must be received within two weeks; a deposit is needed to reserve place in class. Early Decision plan is available. Admission factors include academic records, letters of evaluation, personal qualifications, extracurricular activities, and the personal interview. *Correspondence to:* Office of Admissions

MINORITY STUDENTS: Comprise 18% of the first-year class. The application fee may be waived. The Medical College sponsors a summer fellowship program for about 20 minority-group premedical students who have completed their junior year. *For additional information:* Associate Dean, Equal Opportunity Programs. Application for aid should be made upon acceptance.

---

*member AMCAS

West Virginia University*
School of Medicine
P.O. Box 9111
Morgantown, WV 26506-9815
Tel: (304) 293-2408
E-mail: medadmissions@hsc.wvu.edu
www.hsc.wvu.edu/som

MCAT: required

GPA: 3.8

FOUNDED: 1902 as a two-year school, introduced four-year program in 1961; *publicly controlled.*

ENROLLMENT: 55 men, 53 women (first-year).

TUITION & FEES: Resident, $19,204; Nonresident, $41,866.

APPLICATIONS: Should be submitted between June 1 and November 1; the application fee is $100. Notification begins October 15; response must be received within two weeks; a deposit is needed to hold place in class. Early Decision plan is available for West Virginia residents only. Preference is given to state residents. Admission factors counted most heavily include GPA, MCAT, and personal qualifications exhibited through the interview and recommendations. *Correspondence to:* Assistant Director of Admissions and Records.

MINORITY STUDENTS: Comprise 3% of the first-year class. *For additional information:* Associate Dean for Student Affairs.

----

*member AMCAS

Wright State University*
Boonshaft School of Medicine
P.O. Box 1751
Dayton, OH 45401
Tel: (937) 775-2934
E-mail: somssq@wright.edu
www.med.wright.edu

MCAT: required

GPA: 3.58

FOUNDED: 1973; *publicly controlled.*

ENROLLMENT: 52 men, 48 women (first-year).

TUITION & FEES: Resident, $25,190; Nonresident, $35,660.

APPLICATIONS: Should be submitted between June 1 and October 15; the application fee is $45. Notification begins October 15; response must be received within three weeks; no deposit needed to hold place in class. Early Decision plan is available. Preference is given to Ohio residents. *Correspondence to:* Office of Student Affairs/Admissions.

MINORITY STUDENTS: Comprise 20% of the first-year class. Financial aid is available. *For additional information:* Director of Recruitment.

---

*member AMCAS

Yale University
School of Medicine
367 Cedar Street
New Haven, CT 06510
Tel: (203) 785-2696
E-mail: medical.admissions@yale.edu
www.info.med.Yale.edu

MCAT: required

GPA: 3.8

FOUNDED: 1810; *private.*

ENROLLMENT: 53 men, 47 women (first-year).

TUITION & FEES: Resident, $35,865; Nonresident, $35,865.

APPLICATIONS: Should be submitted between June 1 and October 15; the application fee is $85. Notification begins March 15; response must be received within three weeks; a deposit is necessary to hold place in class. Early Decision plan is available. Admission decisions are based on the MCAT, GPA, recommendations of instructors, integrity, common sense, scientific skill, stability, and dedication. *Correspondence to:* Office of Admissions.

MINORITY STUDENTS: Comprise 13% of the first-year class. Numerous fellowships, scholarships, and loans are obtainable. *For additional information:* Assistant Dean for Multicultural Affairs. Application for aid should be made upon acceptance.

Directory of U.S. Schools of Osteopathic Medicine

T his index provides a listing of Osteopathic Schools of Medicine in the United States. It is set up similarly to the directory in Appendix III.

For the most current information on each school, you should contact the school directly.

A.T. Still University
Kirksville College of Osteopathic Medicine
800 West Jefferson
Kirksville, MO 63501
Tel: (866) 626-2878
E-mail: admissions@atsu.edu
www.atsu.edu

MCAT: required

GPA: not available

FOUNDED: 1892

ENROLLMENT: 102 men, 72 women (first-year).

TUITION & FEES: Resident, $38,980; Nonresident, $38,980.

APPLICATIONS: Should be submitted between June 1 and February 1; the application fee is $60. Admission factors include letters of recommendation and interviews.

MINORITY STUDENTS: Comprise about 5%.

A.T. Still University
School of Osteopathic Medicine in Arizona
5850 E Still Circle
Mesa, AZ 85206
Tel: (480) 219-6000
www.atsu.edu

MCAT: required

GPA: not available

FOUNDED: 2007

ENROLLMENT: 107 students (first-year).

TUITION & FEES: no data available.

APPLICATIONS: Should be submitted after June 1.

MINORITY STUDENTS: no data available.

Arizona College of Osteopathic Medicine of Midwestern University

19555 North 59th Avenue
Glendale, AZ 85308
Tel: (632) 572-3215
E-mail: admissaz@midwestern.edu
www.midwestern.edu

MCAT: required

GPA: not available

FOUNDED: 1995

ENROLLMENT: 155 men, 95 women (first-year).

TUITION & FEES: Resident, $41,242; Nonresident, $41,242.

APPLICATIONS: Should be submitted between June 1 and January 1; the application fee is $50. Admission factors include letters of recommendation.

MINORITY STUDENTS: Comprise about 10%.

Chicago College of Osteopathic Medicine of Midwestern University

555 31st Street
Downers Grove, IL 60515
Tel: (630) 515-7200
E-mail: admiss@midwestern.edu
www.midwestern.edu

MCAT: required

GPA: not available

FOUNDED: 1900

ENROLLMENT: 93 men, 80 women (first-year).

TUITION & FEES: Resident, $40,122; Nonresident, $44,643.

APPLICATIONS: Should be submitted between June 15 and March 2; the application fee is $40. Admission factors include letters of recommendation and interviews.

MINORITY STUDENTS: Comprise about 30%.

Des Moines University
College of Osteopathic Medicine
3200 Grand Avenue
Des Moines, IA 50312
Tel: (515) 271-1499
E-mail: doaadmit@dmu.edu
www.dmu.edu

MCAT: required

GPA: not available

FOUNDED: 1898

ENROLLMENT: 106 men, 115 women (first-year).

TUITION & FEES: Resident, $34,100; Nonresident, $34,100.

APPLICATIONS: Should be submitted between June 1 and February 1; the application fee is $50. Admission factors include letters of reccomendation, interviews, and AACOMAS and supplemental applications.

MINORITY STUDENTS: Comprise about 15%.

Edward Via College of Osteopathic Medicine—Carolinas Campus
364 Magnolia Street
Spartanburg, SC 29301
www.vcom.vt.edu

MCAT: required

GPA: not available

FOUNDED: 2010

ENROLLMENT: 94 men, 95 women (first-year).

TUITION & FEES: no data available.

APPLICATIONS: Should be submitted after June 1.

MINORITY STUDENTS: Comprise about 25%.

Edward Via Virginia College of Osteopathic Medicine

2265 Kraft Drive
Blacksburg, VA 24060
Tel: (541) 231-6138
E-mail: admissions@vcom.vt.com
www.vcom.vt.edu

MCAT: required

GPA: not available

FOUNDED: date not available

ENROLLMENT: 91 men, 97 women (first-year).

TUITION & FEES: Resident, $32,900; Nonresident, $32,900.

APPLICATIONS: Should be submitted between May 1 and February 1; the application fee is $85. Admission factors include letters of recommendation, academic achievement and potential, as well as candidate's sense of compassion and commitment to primary patient care in a rural setting.

MINORITY STUDENTS: Comprise about 20%.

Georgia Campus— Philadelphia College of Osteopathic Medicine

625 Old Peachtree Road NW
Suwanee, GA 30024
Tel: (867) 225-7500
E-mail: admissions@pcom.edu
www.pcom.edu

MCAT: required

GPA: not available

FOUNDED: This school is a branch of the same-named institution in Philadelphia, Pennsylavania.

ENROLLMENT: 47 men, 39 women (first-year).

TUITION & FEES: Resident, $36,984; Nonresident, $36,984.

APPLICATIONS: Should be submitted between May 1 and February 1; the application fee is $50. Admission factors include letters of recommendation and interviews.

MINORITY STUDENTS: Comprise about 35%.

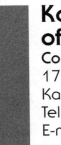

Kansas City University of Medicine and Biosciences

College of Osteopathic Medicine
1750 Independence Ave.
Kansas City, MO 64106
Tel: (818) 283-2352
E-mail: admissions@kcumb.edu
www.kcumb.edu

MCAT: required

GPA: not available

FOUNDED: 1916

ENROLLMENT: 146 men, 120 women (first-year).

TUITION & FEES: not available.

APPLICATIONS: Should be submitted between June 1 and February 1; the application fee is $50. Admission factors include letters of recommendation and interviews.

MINORITY STUDENTS: Comprise about 5%.

Lake Erie College of Osteopathic Medicine—Bradenton Campus

5000 Lakewood Branch Boulevard
Bradenton, FL 34211
Tel: (941) 756-0690
E-mail: Bradenton@lecom.edu
www.lecom.edu

MCAT: required

GPA: not available

FOUNDED: 2009

ENROLLMENT: no data available.

TUITION & FEES: Resident, $25,000; Nonresident, $26,000.

APPLICATIONS: Should be submitted between June 1 and March 1; the application fee is $50.

MINORITY STUDENTS: no data available.

Lake Erie College of Osteopathic Medicine

LECOM at Seton Hill
One Seton Hill Drive
Greensburg, PA 15601
Tel: (724) 261-2020
E-mail: admissions@lecom.edu
www.lecom.edu

MCAT: required

GPA: not available

FOUNDED: 1992

ENROLLMENT: 234 men, 202 women (first-year).

TUITION & FEES: Resident, $25,900; Nonresident, $27,250.

APPLICATIONS: Should be submitted between June 1 and March 1; the application fee is $50. Admission factors include letters of recommendation and interviews.

MINORITY STUDENTS: Comprise about 80%.

Lincoln Memorial University
DeBusk College of Osteopathic Medicine
6965 Cumberland Gap Parkway
Harrogate, TN 37752
Tel: (800) 325-0900
E-mail: jonathan.leo@lmunet.edu
www.lmunet.edu

MCAT: required

GPA: not available

FOUNDED: 2007

ENROLLMENT: 84 men, 76 women (first-year).

TUITION & FEES: Resident, $31,500; Nonresident, $31,500.

APPLICATIONS: Should be submitted between June 1 and February 15; the application fee is $50.

MINORITY STUDENTS: Comprise about 7%.

Michigan State University
College of Osteopathic Medicine
A136 East Fee Hall
East Lansing, MI 48824
Tel: (517) 353-7740
E-mail: comadm@com.msu.edu
www.com.msu.edu

MCAT: required

GPA: not available

FOUNDED: 1892

ENROLLMENT: 112 men, 119 women (first-year).

TUITION & FEES: Resident, $28,011; Nonresident, $60,891.

APPLICATIONS: Should be submitted between June 1 and December 1; the application fee is $75. Admission factors include letters of recommendation and interviews.

MINORITY STUDENTS: Comprise about 2%.

New York College of Osteopathic Medicine of New York Institute of Technology

Old Westbury, NY 11568
Tel: (516) 686-3747
E-mail: comader@nyit.edu
www.nyit.edu

MCAT: required

GPA: not available

FOUNDED: 1977

ENROLLMENT: 154 men, 144 women (first-year).

TUITION & FEES: Resident, $39,895; Nonresident, $39,895.

APPLICATIONS: Should be submitted between April 15 and February 1; the application fee is $60. Admission factors include letters of recommendation.

MINORITY STUDENTS: Comprise about 10%.

Nova Southeastern University

College of Osteopathic Medicine
3301 College Avenue
P.O. Box 299000
Fort Lauderdale, FL 33329
Tel: (954) 262-1101
E-mail: com@nsu.nova.edu
www.medicinenova.edu

MCAT: required

GPA: not available

FOUNDED: 1964

ENROLLMENT: 125 men, 105 women (first-year).

TUITION & FEES: Resident, $29,030; Nonresident, $35,545.

APPLICATIONS: Should be submitted between June 1 and March 1; the application fee is $50. Admission factors include letters of recommendation and interviews.

MINORITY STUDENTS: Comprise about 40%.

Ohio University College of Osteopathic Medicine

102 Grosvernor Hall
Athens, OH 45701
Tel: (740) 593-4313
E-mail: admissions@exchange.oucom.ohiou.edu
www.oucom.ohiou.edu

MCAT: required

GPA: not available

FOUNDED: 1975

ENROLLMENT: 51 men, 65 women (first-year).

TUITION & FEES: Resident, $24,111; Nonresident, $35,031.

APPLICATIONS: Should be submitted between June 1 and January 2; the application fee is $30.

MINORITY STUDENTS: Comprise about 25%.

Oklahoma State University
College of Osteopathic Medicine
111 West 17th St.
Tulsa, OK 74107
Tel: (800) 677-1972 or (918) 561-8421
E-mail: lindsay.kirkpatrick@chs.okstate.edu
www.healthsciences.okstate.edu

MCAT: required

GPA: not available

FOUNDED: 1972

ENROLLMENT: 42 men, 46 women (first-year).

TUITION & FEES: Resident, $18,545; Nonresident, $36,467.

APPLICATIONS: Should be submitted between June 1 and February 1; the application fee is $40. Admission factors include supplemental applications, letters of recommendation, and interviews.

MINORITY STUDENTS: Comprise about 35%.

Pacific Northwest University of Health Sciences

College of Osteopathic Medicine
111 South 3rd Street
Yakima, WA 98901
Tel: (509) 452-5101
E-mail: admissions@pnwu.edu
www.pnwu.org

MCAT: required

GPA: not available

FOUNDED: 2005

ENROLLMENT: 49 men, 51 women (first-year).

TUITION & FEES: no data available.

APPLICATIONS: Should be submitted between June 1 and April 1.

MINORITY STUDENTS: no data available.

Philadelphia College of Osteopathic Medicine

4170 City Avenue
Philadelphia, PA 19131
Tel: (215) 871-6700
E-mail: admissions@pcom.edu
www.pcom.edu

MCAT: required

GPA: not available

FOUNDED: 1899

ENROLLMENT: 137 men, 130 women (first-year).

TUITION & FEES: Resident, $36,984; Nonresident, $36,984.

APPLICATIONS: Should be submitted between June 1 and February 1; the application fee is $50. Admission factors include letters of recommendation and interviews.

MINORITY STUDENTS: Comprise about 20%.

Pikeville College
School of Osteopathic Medicine
214 Sycamore Street
Pikeville, KY 41501
Tel: (606) 218-5408
E-mail: pcsem@pc.ledu
www.pc.edu

MCAT: required

GPA: not available

FOUNDED: date not available

ENROLLMENT: 49 men, 34 women (first-year).

TUITION & FEES: Resident, $32,800; Nonresident, $32,800.

APPLICATIONS: Should be submitted between June 1 and February 1; the application fee is $75.

MINORITY STUDENTS: Comprise about 8%.

Rocky Vista University
College of Osteopathic Medicine
8401 Chambers Road
Parker, CO 80134
Tel: (303) 373-2008
E-mail: admissions@rockyvistauniversity.org
www.rockyvistauniversity.org

MCAT: required

GPA: not available

FOUNDED: 2008

ENROLLMENT: 80 men, 80 women (first-year).

TUITION & FEES: Resident, $34,200; Nonresident, $38,000.

APPLICATIONS: Should be submitted between May 1 and March 15.

MINORITY STUDENTS: Comprise about 10%.

Touro College, New York

School of Osteopathic Medicine
230 West 125th Street
New York, NY 10027
Tel: (646) 981-4556
E-mail: obedf@touro.edu
www.touro.edu/med

MCAT: required

GPA: not available

FOUNDED: 2007

ENROLLMENT: 68 men, 67 women (first-year).

TUITION & FEES: Resident, $32,625; Nonresident, $32,625.

APPLICATIONS: Should be submitted between June 1 and January 2.

MINORITY STUDENTS: Comprise about 45%.

Touro University
California College of Osteopathic Medicine
Vallejo, CA 94592
Tel: (888) 880-7336 or (707) 638-5227
E-mail: admit@touro.edu
www.tu.edu

MCAT: required

GPA: not available

FOUNDED: date not available

ENROLLMENT: 70 men, 45 women (first-year).

TUITION & FEES: Resident, $35,000; Nonresident, $35,000.

APPLICATIONS: Should be submitted between June 1 and March 15; the application fee is $100.

MINORITY STUDENTS: Comprise about 30%.

Touro University
Nevada College of Osteopathic Medicine
874 American Pacific Drive
Henderson, NV 89014
Tel: (702) 777-1751
E-mail: rcorbman@touro.edu
www.tu.edu

MCAT: required

GPA: not available

FOUNDED: date not available

ENROLLMENT: not available.

TUITION & FEES: Resident, $36,786; Nonresident, $36,786.

APPLICATIONS: Should be submitted between June 1 and May 15; the application fee is $100. Admission factors include letters of recommendation and interviews.

MINORITY STUDENTS: Comprise about 1%.

University of Medicine and Dentistry of New Jersey
School of Osteopathic Medicine
1 Medical Center Drive
Stratford, NJ 08084
Tel: (856) 566-7050
E-mail: somadm@umduj.edu
www.som.umduj.edu

MCAT: required

GPA: not available

FOUNDED: 1976

ENROLLMENT: 59 men, 51 women (first-year).

TUITION & FEES: Resident, $25,218; Nonresident, $39,461.

APPLICATIONS: Should be submitted between May 1 and February 1; the application fee is $90. Admission factors include letters of recommendation and interviews.

MINORITY STUDENTS: Comprise about 50%.

University of New England
College of Osteopathic Medicine
11 Hills Beach Road
Biddeford, ME 04005
Tel: (207) 602-2329
E-mail: unecomadmissions@une.edu
www.une.edu/com/admissions

MCAT: required

GPA: not available

FOUNDED: 1979

ENROLLMENT: 61 men, 72 women (first-year).

TUITION & FEES: Resident, $41,260; Nonresident, $41,260.

APPLICATIONS: Should be submitted between February 1 and March 15; the application fee is $55. Admission factors include letters of recommendation and interviews.

MINORITY STUDENTS: Comprise about 9%.

University of North Texas
Texas College of Osteopathic Medicine
3500 Camp Bowie Boulevard
Fort Worth, TX 76107
Tel: (817) 735-2204
E-mail: tcomadmissions@hsc.unt.edu
www.hsc.unt.edu

MCAT: required

GPA: not available

FOUNDED: 1970

ENROLLMENT: 92 men, 83 women (first-year).

TUITION & FEES: Resident, $18,598; Nonresident, $29,348.

APPLICATIONS: Should be submitted between June 1 and November 1; the application fee is $55.

MINORITY STUDENTS: Comprise about 11%.

Western University of Health Sciences
College of Osteopathic Medicine of the Pacific
309 East Second Street
Pomona, CA 91766
Tel: (909) 469-5335
E-mail: admissions@westernu.edu
www.westernu.edu

MCAT: required

GPA: not available

FOUNDED: 1977

ENROLLMENT: 123 men, 88 women (first-year).

TUITION & FEES: Resident, $41,350; Nonresident, $41,350.

APPLICATIONS: Should be submitted between February 15 and April 15; the application fee is $60.

MINORITY STUDENTS: Comprise about 45%.

West Virginia School of Osteopathic Medicine

400 North Lee Street
Lewisburg, WV 24901
Tel: (304) 647-6373
E-mail: admissions@wvsom.edu
www.wvsom.edu

MCAT: required

GPA: not available

FOUNDED: 1974

ENROLLMENT: 119 men, 92 women (first-year).

TUITION & FEES: Resident, $20,426; Nonresident, $50,546.

APPLICATIONS: Should be submitted between June 1 and February 15; the application fee is $50. Admission factors include letters of recommendation and interviews.

MINORITY STUDENTS: Comprise about 25%.

William Carey University
College of Osteopathic Medicine
498 Tuscan Avenue
Hattiesburg, MS 39401
Tel: (601) 318-6235
E-mail: ebennett@wmcarey.edu
www.wmcarey.edu

MCAT: required

GPA: not available

FOUNDED: 2009

ENROLLMENT: no data available.

TUITION & FEES: Resident, $38,000; Nonresident, $38,000.

APPLICATIONS: Should be submitted after June 1.

MINORITY STUDENTS: no data available.

APPENDIX V

Survival Bibliography

In my second book, *You Can Get into Medical School: Letters from Premeds,* I ended with a bibliography of books, periodicals, and articles that I found indispensable. They covered such major topics as statistics on applicants, medical school admission policies, undergraduate preparation for medicine, the MCAT, minority admissions, older applicants, and financial aid, as well as some less common areas, such as the premed syndrome, the student with disabilities, and the approaching physician glut. I implored students to keep a file of relevant premedical literature, having collected over 70 magazine, journal, and newspaper articles myself.

I remember how I obtained my information: through frequenting bookstores and libraries. Because I live in the country, articles had to be ordered through the library's interloan service and took one to two months to arrive. Books only took a week or two. If I had specific questions, I had either to write letters or try to track people down by telephone. The process was extremely laborious.

How things have changed over the years! I did all my research for this revision at home on my PC through the Internet. What follows is a listing of Web sites that are useful jumping-off places for you in amassing information. If you know of other home pages with health professions links, clue me in!

ChronoNet

The best predmedical Web site that I have ever found no longer exists. In fact, it was so good that when its creator, Greg Chronowski, who was then a third-year medical student at Jefferson Medical College in Philadelphia, couldn't afford the costs of keeping it in cyberspace, I offered to help. The site was a treasure trove of information including a personal statement by now Dr. Chronowski. I include it here as a prequel to other Internet sites for premeds because the soundness of his advice still rings true for me:

"In the fall of 1993 I had just completed two years of a postbaccalaureate premedical program at Columbia University in New York City with the hope of getting into medical school. I sat down with my adviser in order to evaluate my record and to determine what schools I should apply to. She perused my credentials, placed them on the desk, and calmly said, 'I don't think that this is going to happen for you. My advice is that you choose another career and get on with your life.'

"It is now 1996, I am presently a third-year medical student at Jefferson Medical College in Philadelphia, I'm doing well academically, and, ironically, I served as an admissions coordinator for the Admissions Committee here at Jefferson. I offer the above anecdote as an example of how cheap advice really is and how easy it is to doubt yourself and be led astray through the maze that is the medical school admissions process. With that said, it's still my opinion that most advice should be taken with a grain of salt, including mine.

"The admissions process for medical applicants has become increasingly competitive within the last few years. Contrary to what many believe, I feel that this is probably due to the perception of many college students that medicine is a sure thing in an increasingly bleak job market, and probably not a result of a miraculous upwelling of altruism in the youth of today. Nevertheless, medicine is a calling and you will be *very* unhappy as a physician, especially in the present uncertain climate, unless you have a fundamental love of what the profession entails.

"With regard to the mechanics of applying, unfortunately grades and MCATs do matter. A very rough estimate is 10s on the MCAT with a science GPA of around 3.4. (Medical school has been more competitive in recent years. According to the 2010–2011 Medical School Admission Requirements (MSAR) published by the AAMC, the national median for the MCAT is 32Q

(10V, 11B, 11P). GPA averages are also much higher. Of course, out-of-country schools such as the University of Puerto Rico have significantly lower matriculant medians, with a 23M for the MCAT.) I realize that many readers are groaning already, 'Does that mean it's hopeless if I don't make that cut?' The answer is probably no, but here's my opinion of what you need to consider if you decide to continue.

"First of all, it's imperative that you take a long, hard look at yourself and assess whether or not you feel that you're capable of making it through the academic and emotional rigors of medical school. In reality, if you've never liked school or studying you're not going to miraculously become a scholar once accepted. If after some hard reflection you decide you're both capable and motivated, you should begin the application process. However, keep the following in mind.

"You need to *prove* that you can maintain at least around a 3.4 GPA in the sciences; however to be fair, 3.4 is the low end of the cutoff. However, don't despair. Bottom line, medical school admissions is not just about numbers—it's about your ability to make a good physician, and that concept transcends grades. However, this may mean going back to school and taking some core upper-level science courses such as physiology, biochemistry, and histology. A structured postbaccalaureate program may not be necessary, but extra work is mandatory. There is nothing more self-defeating than reapplying year after year without showing the admissions committee that you can maintain a minimum level of scholarship. Let's be frank—you won't get in by just wishing it so. With that in mind, I earned a C in one of my physics courses during my postbac. This isn't a fatal grade; however, a 2.7 GPA is unfortunately not competitive in the present climate.

"I would also not recommend applying until you feel that you've improved your academic record significantly. Sending out an uncompetitive application can cost a lot of money, time, and heartache. It may be advisable to wait for a year or two; it's better to send one strong application than to potentially compromise your record by sending a mediocre application. In addition, it often helps to put some distance between a lackluster undergraduate record and your present one.

"My biggest piece of advice, and one I did not live by, is *to have a contingency plan for if you don't get in.* Medical applicants are unique in that for some odd reason, many of us tie our whole sense of self-worth to whether or not we become physicians. This is unhealthy and potentially devastating. I certainly don't want to discourage anyone from trying, but there *are* worse things in life than not becoming a doctor (I know—that's easy for me to say). Professions such as physical therapist and physician's assistant can be very rewarding and provide just as much patient contact as medicine. In addition, the lifestyle of these professions is excellent, although the monetary compensation may not be as high. However, if you factor in the high cost of loans for medical education, this becomes far less of an issue.

"OK. Let's assume that you've gone back to school, gotten decent grades (3.4 and above), and done well on the MCATs (10s and 11s). Basically, you're in the running, but frankly, literally thousands of applicants just like you are out there. Now it's time to do something that will distinguish you from the pack. Winning a Nobel Prize in biochemistry isn't necessary, but research and volunteer work can help. The ultimate goal in research is to coauthor an abstract or paper that is published or presented at a national meeting. I realize that it sounds trivial, but for some dubious reason, many medical schools look more favorably at an applicant who has his or her name on a mediocre abstract far more than someone who just worked in a lab. Volunteer work can also make a difference, but it should be something you believe in rather than just something to put on your application. Furthermore, shadowing a physician is a good way to learn more about what being a physician entails, however, most medical schools do not rate the experience nearly as highly as meaningful volunteer work. I often recommend hospice as a very high-yield experience. It provides valuable insight into the psychosocial aspects of medicine as well as allows students to speak to dying patients one-on-one.

"Another unsavory fact of life in medical school admissions is that connections are extremely valuable. Thus, it's time to get your own PR machine rolling. Try to get letters of recommendation from physicians you know who are somehow connected to the schools to which you are applying. If you don't have these connections, try hard to develop them. This is very difficult. I know that I felt pretty pushy asking to meet with people I didn't really know to ask for a letter, but students need to be proactive in this regard. Prepare a packet consisting of your resume and perhaps some essays regarding medically relevant topics. Even if the individual is unfamiliar with you, this shows that you're serious, and it also provides substance for the letter.

"Next, you need to sell yourself. Stay in touch with the admissions offices of the schools you are applying to. Be polite and sincere with the office staff. Trust me—if you're rude and terse, it can hurt you. As a physician, you will be interacting with many different individuals, and it's imperative that you always behave with respect toward everyone from the lab techs to your attending. Write letters to the dean or the committee telling them what you've been up to (you *have* been doing things, right?). I have yet to hear of someone who was rejected because they stayed in touch with a school by calling and writing frequently. I know that many schools track such interest calls; they can only help. If you're in that area, stop by the admissions office and introduce yourself. Always make sure that your application is complete. The burden to do so is on you, *not* the admissions office. If something has been misplaced or lost, don't get mad—overnight mail the document ASAP.

"On the same note, a key factor is gaining acceptance to a medical school is to distinguish yourself as a person as opposed to just a file. That means that you need to speak with or actually visit with someone directly involved with making a decision on your application. This takes finesse in order not to seem pushy or make a nuisance or yourself. However, if done right, it can make the difference between acceptance or rejection; I know that it did in my case. Sell yourself—what do you have to lose?

"Moreover, take some time with your personal statement. At all costs, avoid taking the why-I-want-to-be-a-doctor approach. Committees read thousand of letters of that type. Rather, think of an interesting anecdote or quotation to start your essay with and base your essay around that theme. If you choose a good one, it makes your essay memorable, which is what counts. Without saying, syntax and spelling must be flawless. And of course, get your application in *at the very earliest time possible,* even if your MCATs or transcripts aren't ready yet. This is crucial, as it can take up to six weeks for the American Medical College Application Service to process the primary application. Thus, a late primary application would entail a late secondary application and, ultimately, late interviews. This is probably one of the most important things you can do to assure your acceptance to medical school. It's also probably one of the most common mistakes made by unsuccessful applicants.

"The interview. Be prepared! Some schools have an easygoing style whereas other have interviewers who grill applicants. Read up on managed care, know what HMOs and PPOs are, and know what *capitation* means. Be prepared with explanations (not excuses) regarding the weak points in your application. Come up with questions that *you* have regarding the school. Don't hem and haw if you don't know the answer to a question; simply tell your interviewer 'I don't know.' This is often a trick played on you by interviewers. What's important is how you handle the question, not your answer. Wear a suit and leave flashy accessories and jewelry behind. At many schools, the student interview is the most important part of the application. If you have a student interview, don't trivialize it by slipping into a colloquial or casual tone. Don't appear uptight, but students are often tougher on applicants than attendings are. Always send a thank-you letter to your interviewer. Again it might not help, but it can't hurt.

"Now, once you've been through this whole mind-numbing process, it may happen that you don't get in your first time around (I didn't). If so, it's time for another round of reevaluation and soul-searching regarding reapplication. Did you get interviews and were wait-listed? If so, these are the schools that you need to target when you reapply. Strongly consider applying Early Decision to the school you feel you were most competitive at. Call the schools that rejected or wait-listed you. They may have valuable feedback regarding your weak points (have you noticed the stay-in-touch theme?). Some schools may even cut a deal with you such as promising you admission if you fulfill certain criteria, i.e., A's in your next two science courses. Whatever you do, don't reapply unless you have in some way improved your application. In closing, I recommend reapplication; however, there comes a point when things may become futile. A rough estimate is that if after three years of unsuccessful application you're still not in, it may in fact be time to move on (God, I *hate* that term).

"Let me close with two quotations. The first is by Norman Cousins and pertains to the doctor-patient relationship. However, I think that it has relevance to medical school admissions as well.

" 'The human body experiences a powerful gravitational pull in the direction of hope. That is why the patient's hopes are the physician's secret weapon. They are the hidden ingredients in any prescription.'

"The second quote is from my late grandfather. It accurately sums up my opinion of medical school admissions.

" 'If they don't let you through the door, climb in through the window!' "

Stephen Georges Health Professions Page
www.amherst.edu/~sageorge/health.html

This is Amherst College's page, with links to information sources for premedical students, personal accounts of students' experiences, questions and advice, summer opportunities, MCAT preparation services, information about health professions careers other than medicine, med school application info, postbac programs, and listings of premedical student organizations. This is an excellent place to start your search.

☐ The Interactive Medical Student Lounge
www.studentdoctor.net/

A top Web site, this home page includes links to medical student blogs, medical school interview feedback, a chat room, a forum, information about essay writing and student loans, and a big guide to medical school. There are some awesome links to MCAT study pearls as well.

☐ The American Association of Medical Colleges (AAMC)
www.aamc.org

The *first* place to start surfing the net, the AAMC controls medical education in this country. As an organization, the AAMC is involved in the accreditation of MD-granting medical schools in the United States and Canada. It also administers the MCAT and processes applications via the American Medical College Application Service (or AMCAS). For students looking to take the MCAT, the AAMC Web site is the place to prepare, reserve a seat, and check scores. There is a free MCAT available for practice, as well as seven others available for purchase. For students looking to apply, the AMCAS section includes the online application, frequently asked questions, the AMCAS letter service, and a comprehensive instruction book on how to apply. Students can also find information on financial aid and minority programs on this site.

☐ National Association of Advisors for the Health Professions (NAAHP)
www.naahp.org

This site has listings of publications the association has for sale to premeds and hyperlinks to many worthwhile health professions sites, including ones for allopathic medicine, osteopathy, nursing, physical therapy, and physician assistant programs.

☐ Stanley Kaplan MCAT page
www.Kaplan.com

Although Kaplan is a commercial operation and is trying to sell you their course and study materials, there is some useful information here about the structure and scoring of the MCAT with test dates and registration information. There is also a message board and student links that are quite good.

Princeton Review
www.princetonreview.com

Another proprietary service, Princeton Review's Web site offers useful information about medical schools that do not accept out-of-state residents, the few medical schools that do not participate in AMCAS, and those that do not require the MCAT. The MCAT information is rudimentary, but there is a free MCAT available for downloading.

American Medical Student Association
www.amsa.org

This site has a section for premeds but requires that you become a member. The fees are $30 for one year, $50 for two years, $60 for three years or $70 for four years. A premed I know used it extensively in determining which schools he wanted to apply to. Members get access to a password-protected section of the site that has the results of medical student surveys regarding their satisfaction with their education institution. Besides medical school student reviews, there are sections on what you need to know to get into medical school and writing the personal statement. Member benefits also include receiving *The New Physician* magazine.

The following is a useful listing of other health professions Web sites:

American Association of Colleges of Osteopathic Medicine
   (AACOM)
www.aacom.org

American Dental Education Association
www.adea.org

American Association of Naturopathic Physicians (AANP)
www.naturopathic.org/

American Medical Association (AMA)
www.ama-assn.org

American Podiatric Medical Association (APMA)
www.apma.org/

US Nursing Network
www.usnursingnetwork.com/

The Premed Network
www.premednetwork.com/

This is another great networking site for premedical students. The well-organized forum contains various discussion threads, with topics such as research and clinical experiences, internships, volunteer opportunities, the MCAT, and the application process.

Future Doctor
www.futuredoctor.net/

This site is a comprehensive guide geared toward premedical students. For the students beginning their undergraduate careers, it contains advice on how to choose a major and field of study, how to improve grades, and suggested non-academic activities. In addition, for the readers that are looking to apply to medical school, the Web site provides a comprehensive guide on the application process, covering topics such as MCAT advice and help, personal statements, letters of recommendation, and interview preparation. The Web site also includes a "Personal Statement of the Month" section, where it critiques student-submitted essays, pointing out weak and strong areas. Overall, this is a great resource for aspiring medical students.

Alex's Illicit Guide to Medical School Admissions
www.bestpremed.com/

This is another Web site with a comprehensive guide to getting into medical school. Written by a former medical student, this site informs readers about the process of medical school admissions. In addition, it addresses three targeted audiences (premedical students, high school students, and "nontraditional" applicants) and gives advice to each of the three. The guide includes sections on premedical requirements, the MCAT, the application process, interviews, personal statements, statistics, GPA, links, and more. Overall, it is a fantastic site with great advice.

☐ Premed Guide
www.premedguide.com/

This web site offers a comprehensive guide for students looking to work in the medical field, including advice on medical, nursing, dental, and physician assistant schools. For the premedical student, it offers lists of top medical schools, scholarships, admissions advice, and more. In addition, it offers a statistics calculator, which matches a list of medical schools appropriate to the student's GPA and MCAT scores.

☐ Studentdoc
www.studentdoc.com/

Like the other Web sites, this site also offers a lot of advice on the application process, MCAT preparation, personal statements, interviewing skills, and more. However, it also includes information on medical careers, physician salaries, and alternative careers in medicine. By browsing through this site, the prospective medical student can learn more about the lifestyle of a physician and see if it would meet his or her expectations.

☐ A Premed Guide from the University of Alaska Anchorage
www.uaa.alaska.edu/ours/hpa/preparation/guide.cfm/

This Web site offers a helpful timeline for undergraduates seeking to enter medical school immediately following the completion of the traditional four-year undergraduate work. Premedical students at any point in these four years will find this timeline useful as a checklist of activities to do.

Recommended Books:

☐ Essays That Will Get You Into Medical School
www.amazon.com/gp/product/0764142275

For the premedical student who fears the personal statement on the application. Contains many great example essays.

WITHDRAWAL

Med School Confidential: A Complete Guide to the Medical School Experience: By Students, for Students
www.amazon.com/gp/product/0312330081

A book covering the entire medical school journey, including medical school and residency.

How to Become a Straight-A Student
www.amazon.com/gp/product/0767922719

A useful book that describes the process of being a great student while simultaneously enjoying a great college life.

Any of the search engines on the Internet are great places to start looking for premedical links. In fact, that's where I found most of mine. Many individual college premed programs and services will come up there as well as more general sources. Spend the time surfin' the Net and you'll be surprised how much data you will find.

I do not mean to imply that there is no useful knowledge other than that gleaned from cyberspace. To the contrary, your premedical library should include the current AAMC *Medical School Admissions Requirements*, the *MCAT Student Manual*, and the eight MCAT Practice Tests, also put out by the AAMC. Barron's also publishes *How to Prepare for MCAT—Medical College Admission Test* and *Guide to Medical & Dental Schools*. James L. Flower's book, *A Complete Preparation for the New MCAT*, published by Betz, is helpful, as are the quarterly issues of *The Advisor* and *Between the Issues*, put out by the NAAHP, and, of course, my other book, *You Can Get into Medical School: Letters from Premeds*.

Write to the AAMC at 2450 N Street NW, Washington, DC, 20037, the NAAHP at P.O. Box 5017, Station A, Champaign, IL 61820. My book is available for $9.95 postpaid c/o the Mendocino Foundation, P.O. Box 1377, Mendocino, CA 95460.

Good luck in your quest to become a physician!

Index to U.S. Medical Schools

Albany Medical College, NY, 190
Albert Einstein College of Medicine of Yeshiva University, NY, 191
Baylor College of Medicine, TX, 192
Boston University, MA, 193
Brody School of Medicine at East Carolina Univeristy, 194
Case Western Reserve University, OH, 195
Chicago Medical School, IL, 196
Columbia University, NY, 197
Commonwealth Medical College, The, 198
Creighton University, NE, 199
Dartmouth Medical School, NH, 200
Drexel University, PA, 201
Duke University, NC, 202
East Tennessee State University, TN, 203
Eastern Virginia Medical School, VA, 204
Emory University, GA, 205
Florida International University, FL, 206
Florida State University, The, FL, 207
Georgetown University, D.C., 208
George Washington University, The, D.C., 209
Harvard Medical School, MA, 210
Hofstra North Shore—LIJ, NY, 211
Howard University, D.C., 212
Indiana University, IN, 213
Jefferson Medical College of Thomas Jefferson University, PA, 214
Johns Hopkins University, The, MD, 215
Keck School of Medicine, CA, 216
Loma Linda University, CA, 217
Louisiana State University (School of Medicine in New Orleans), LA, 218
Louisiana State University (School of Medicine in Shreveport), LA, 219
Loyola University of Chicago, IL, 220
Marshall University, WV, 221

Mayo Clinic College of Medicine, MN, 222
Medical College of Georgia, GA, 223
Medical College of Wisconsin, WI, 224
Medical University of South Carolina, SC, 225
Meharry Medical College, TN, 226
Mercer University, GA, 227
Michigan State University, MI, 228
Morehouse School of Medicine, GA, 229
Mount Sinai School of Medicine of New York University, NY, 230
New Jersey Medical School, NJ, 231
New York Medical College, NY, 232
New York University, NY, 233
Northeastern Ohio Universities, OH, 234
Northwestern University, IL, 235
Oakland University, MI, 236
Ohio State University, OH, 237
Oregon Health and Science University, OR, 238
Paul L. Foster School of Medicine at Texas Tech University, TX, 239
Pennsylvania State University, PA, 240
Ponce School of Medicine, PR, 241
Robert Wood Johnson Medical School, NJ, 242
Rush Medical College of Rush University, IL, 243
Saint Louis University, MO, 244
San Juan Bautista School of Medicine, PR, 245
Southern Illinois University, IL, 246
Stanford University, CA, 247
State University of New York (Downstate Medical Center), NY, 248
State University of New York (Upstate Medical University), NY, 249
Stony Brook University School of Medicine, NY, 250
Temple University, PA, 251
Texas A&M University, TX, 252
Texas Tech University, TX, 253
Tufts University, MA, 254
Tulane University, LA, 255
Uniformed Services University of the Health Sciences, MD, 256
Universidad Central del Caribe, PR, 257
University of Alabama, AL, 258
University of Arizona, AZ, 259

University of Arkansas, AR, 260
University of Buffalo School of Medicine and Biomedical Sciences,
   NY, 261
University of California—Davis, CA, 262
University of California—Irvine, CA, 263
University of California—Los Angeles, CA, 264
University of California—San Diego, CA, 265
University of California—San Francisco, CA, 266
University of Central Florida, FL, 267
University of Chicago, IL, 268
University of Cincinnati, OH, 269
University of Colorado, CO, 270
University of Connecticut, CT, 271
University of Florida, FL, 272
University of Hawaii, HI, 273
University of Illinois at Chicago, IL, 274
University of Iowa, IA, 275
University of Kansas, KS, 276
University of Kentucky, KY, 277
University of Louisville, KY, 278
University of Maryland, MD, 279
University of Massachusetts, MA, 280
University of Miami, FL, 281
University of Michigan, MI, 282
University of Minnesota—Duluth Campus, MN, 283
University of Minnesota Medical School, MN, 284
University of Mississippi, MS, 285
University of Missouri—Columbia, MO, 286
University of Missouri—Kansas City, MO, 287
University of Nebraska, NE, 288
University of Nevada, NV, 289
University of New Mexico, NM, 290
University of North Carolina, NC, 291
University of North Dakota, ND, 292
University of Oklahoma, OK, 293
University of Pennsylvania, PA, 294
University of Pittsburgh, PA, 295
University of Puerto Rico, PR, 296

University of Rochester, NY, 297
University of South Alabama, AL, 298
University of South Carolina, SC, 299
University of South Dakota, SD, 300
University of South Florida, FL, 301
University of Tennessee, Health Science Center, TN, 302
University of Texas (Southwestern Medical Center at Dallas), TX, 303
University of Texas (Medical School at Galveston), TX, 304
University of Texas (Medical School at Houston), TX, 305
University of Texas (Medical School at San Antonio), TX, 306
University of Toledo College of Medicine, OH, 307
University of Utah, UT, 308
University of Vermont, VT, 309
University of Virginia, VA, 310
University of Washington, WA, 311
University of Wisconsin, WI, 312
Vanderbilt University, TN, 313
Virginia Commonwealth University, VA, 314
Virginia Tech, VA, 315
Wake Forest University, NC, 316
Warren Albert Medical School of Brown University, The, RI, 317
Washington University, MO, 318
Wayne State University, MI, 319
Weill Medical College of Cornell University, NY, 320
West Virginia University, WV, 321
Wright State University, OH, 322
Yale University, CT, 323

Index to U.S.
Osteopathic Schools

A.T. Still University, MO, 325

A.T. Still University, AZ, 326

Arizona College of Osteopathic Medicine, AZ, 327

Chicago College of Osteopathic Medicine, IL, 328

Des Moines University, IA, 329

Edward Via College of Osteopathic Medicine, SC, 330

Edward Via Virginia College of Osteopathic Medicine, VA, 331

Georgia Campus—Philadelphia College of Osteopathic Medicine, GA, 332

Kansas City University of Medicine and Biosciences, MO, 333

Lake Erie College of Osteopathic Medicine, FL, 334

Lake Erie College of Osteopathic Medicine, PA, 335

Lincoln Memorial University, TN, 336

Michigan State University, MI, 337

New York College of Osteopathic Medicine, NY, 338

Nova Southeastern University, FL, 339

Ohio University College of Osteopathic Medicine, OH, 340

Oklahoma State University, OK, 341

Pacific Northwest University of Health Sciences, WA, 342

Philadelphia College of Osteopathic Medicine, PA, 343

Pikeville College, KY, 344

Rocky Vista University, CO, 345

Touro College, New York, NY, 346

Touro University, CA, 347

Touro University, NV, 348

University of Medicine and Dentistry of New Jersey, NJ, 349

University of New England, ME, 350

University of North Texas, TX, 351

Western University of Health Sciences, CA, 352

West Virginia School of Osteopathic Medicine, WV, 353

William Carey University, MS, 354